CULTURE AND CAPITALISM IN CONTEMPORARY IRELAND

For Tim,
Margaret, Helen, Irene and Valerie and in
memory of John.

Culture and Capitalism in Contemporary Ireland

PAUL KEATING

DERRY DESMOND

Avebury

Aldershot · Brookfield USA · Hong Kong · Singapore · Sydney

Published by
Avebury
Ashgate Publishing Limited
Gower House
Croft Road
Aldershot
Hants GU11 3HR
England

Ashgate Publishing Company
Old Post Road
Brookfield
Vermont 05036
USA

British Library Cataloguing in Publication Data

Keating, Paul
    Culture and Capitalism in Contemporary Ireland
    I. Title   II. Desmond, Derry
    306.09415

ISBN 1 85628 362 3

Printed and Bound in Great Britain by
Athenaeum Press Ltd, Newcastle upon Tyne.

Contents

CHAPTER 8: ENTREPRENEURSHIP AND THE IRISH CULTURE COMPLEX

Acknowledgements

We would like to thank the Universities of Exeter and Salford for grants made in connection with this study. Rene Spenser-Woods is also due special thanks; her help in the preparation of the work for publication cost her much time and effort and was valuable beyond price.

1 The problem and its setting

Introduction

Although it is concerned with economic behaviour this study is not another economist's analysis of Ireland and its economic problems. Far from it. Being concerned, as its title suggests, with analysing the impact of culture on entrepreneurial conduct, the book belongs to sociology, more especially to those tendencies in sociology which take account of so called subjective factors, i.e. actors' subjective meanings and motives, the latter being treated as complexes of meanings in which the springs of action have their sources. Our interest in the entrepreneurial problem stems from the conviction that it is of some importance to Ireland. Irish society is a liberal-capitalist society, the leading elements of which, supported by and large by public opinion, are committed to the achievement of economic development via the private enterprise, free market route. By the common consent of both government and governed, therefore, state activity in the sphere of the economy is circumscribed; it is limited to the provision of an infrastructure, grants and tax incentives to private enterprise and to the production of those goods and services which are seen to be essential to the economy but beyond the present provisioning capacities of the private sector.

Given these restraints on state activity, the economic development to which the Irish aspire must depend largely on the private sector for its achievement. Unless the country is to rely entirely on foreign direct investment - and this is nowadays often difficult to attract - there is no escaping the conclusion that Ireland's economy will only develop if its entrepreneurs conduct their economic lives in ways that are appropriate to

1

development-achievement. It is for this reason that an inquiry into the economic conduct of Irish entrepreneurs, and into the determinants of that conduct, assumes importance, especially when it reveals the existence of behaviour patterns that are not well suited to the achievement of development. And this is the point: The evidence we have suggests that Irish entrepreneurs have low propensities to engage in development-appropriate economic action; it shows them to be 'poor' opportunity takers and thus suggests that Ireland's failure to achieve economic development is due in some measure to the 'inadequacies' of its entrepreneurial establishment.

In using words like 'poor' and 'inadequacies' we are, of course, entering a judgement against the Irish entrepreneurial community. As we shall try to show in Chapter 2, however, this judgement is a 'technical' and not at all a moral judgement. It is no part of our business here to take morally evaluative stances towards the behaviour we are describing and analysing; we are social scientists, not moral entrepreneurs; we claim no prescriptive rights to set social objectives which are framed in the light of our values and to hand down judgements about peoples' behaviour which derive from those values and objectives. Our concerns lie, rather, with the values and objectives which people carry and set for themselves, and with the analysis, in the present case, of manifest disjunctions between their self-proclaimed goals and their behaviour. The only rights we claim to exercise here, therefore, are the rights of science: namely, the right to describe, and, if we can, to try to explain what it is we have described. Simply put, we note that the Irish establishment has proclaimed economic development as a goal that is desirable and that many members of that establishment conduct their economic lives in ways that do nothing to enhance - and indeed sometimes positively hinder - the prospects of their society achieving that goal. All we want to do is to find out, if we can, why they behave as they do and not in some other way that might be more conducive to the promotion of the economic growth which development requires. In undertaking this study we had no other objectives in view. We have developed no other objectives in the courses of its completion and presentation.

We make these preliminary points because some Irish people may find parts of this book painful to read; they may come to the conclusion that the picture it paints is an unflattering one that is biased, morally judgemental and hostile to Ireland and to Irish culture. For this reason it is necessary to say immediately that nothing could be further from the truth; the book's concerns are descriptive and analytical; it is the result of social scientific curiosity, stimulated by 'the smell' of an interesting research problem which is pertinent to any adequate appreciation of the economic and social conditions prevailing in modern Ireland. To repeat, therefore, nothing in its pages should be taken as enshrining either positive or negative value judgements about Irish society, its entrepreneurs or its cultural values; the study which the book describes was driven by curiosity, not animosity; both authors are, in any case, Irish and have no desire whatever to hurt the feelings of those who share their nationality.

Discerning readers will probably infer from the nature of the foregoing disclaimers that we are about to present material that many Irish readers -

and others who are sympathetic towards Ireland - may find embarrassing and/or offensive. The reason for this is easily demonstrated by reference to a study of Irish entrepreneurs which Professor Michael Fogarty conducted in the nineteen-seventies. In the course of his study Fogarty interviewed a number of Irish entrepreneurs. According to his own report (Fogarty, 1973, pp. 96-7),

> one of the most disturbing features of these interviews was how often informants came back to the thesis that what families, schools, the Church, the social system and the business system itself have failed to produce in Ireland is people with the basic virtues of honesty, integrity and hard and purposeful work.

Few peoples, we may guess, would be happy to see themselves described as lacking in 'the basic virtues of honesty, integrity and hard and purposeful work'. Suggesting as they do that the Irish are somewhat wanting in terms of their industry and morals, the remarks could easily be taken as a racist insult, and would, in all probably, be so taken had they been spoken by foreigners. The remarks were not, however, spoken by ill-disposed foreigners, but by Irish entrepreneurs who had wide experience of the behaviour of those in membership of the Irish business community. To speak as they did implies - and, as we shall see, the weight of the evidence will support the implication - that Irish entrepreneurial conduct is characterised by low levels of commitment to economic activity and by low levels of ethical, and therefore prudential, regulation of business behaviour. Entrepreneurial conduct that is distinguished by these tendencies is likely to be problematic in the development context for two reasons: Firstly, entrepreneurs who exhibit low levels of commitment, and thus motivation, are not the kind of people who will drive the production threshold beyond the limits of what was traditionally regarded as necessary and desirable in their communities - something the achievement of development seems to require as a first priority. Secondly, ethically unregulated business behaviour tends to be commercially imprudent; it can alienate customers, suppliers and other salient persons; it can damage a nation's commercial reputation; it can react adversely on the viability of other productive units in an economy, and can even damage the national state. Entrepreneurial behaviour which does not exhibit the virtues of 'honesty, integrity and hard and purposeful work' is, in consequence, unlikely to assist in achieving economic development; at best its impact on the process will be neutral, while, at worst, it may actually work destructive effects.

In Chapters 2,3 and 4 we will look at Irish entrepreneurs in action. The material presented in these chapters will force us to conclude that Irish entrepreneurial behaviour is indeed distinguished by low levels of commitment to regular productive activity and by weak patterns of ethical/prudential regulation. As a result Irish entrepreneurs will be shown to be poor opportunity-takers who have not contributed optimally to the economic development of the country in which they have their beings and make their profits. All this, of course, suggests that the 'blame' for Ireland's failure to achieve economic development must be laid, partly, at the door of its own entrepreneurial community, and thus lies, to some extent, in subjective factors, i.e. in the motives, dispositions and preferences of Irish economic actors. If this is the case, and it is one that we shall have to substantiate, then the obvious question becomes: Why do Irish entrepreneurs behave as they do and not in some other way or ways that might be more conducive to the achievement of economic development?

As is the case with many good questions this one is easier to ask than to answer. Likewise our hypothetical answer to it is rather more easily formulated than demonstrated. Briefly stated our answer will suggest that Irish entrepreneurs behave as they do by reason of the cultural values to which they relate, and thus give meaning to, their economic and other life activities. A proposition of this kind is likely to be controversial and will require some detailed supporting argumentation in the process of its demonstration. We will begin this process by asking whether and to what extent the behaviour which we are analysing, and the underdevelopment which results from it, can be explained by reference to objective factors. Objective factors in this connection pertain to conditions which appear to both actors and observers as sources of external constraint on action; they advert to states of affairs which can structure and condition action by imposing restrictions on the options available to actors. Limitations in the natural resource base, shortages of capital and appropriate expertise, and, not least, restricted access to exploitable opportunities (markets) through entry barriers are examples of objective factors which can constrain entrepreneurial behaviour and thus limit the development possibilities available to particular national economies. Our analysis in Chapter 5 will show that Irish entrepreneurial conduct and economic underdevelopment cannot be fully explained as the outcomes of the operation of objective factors. Establishing this will require a close attention to two issues: Firstly, the resources and opportunities which are, and which historically have been, available to Irish entrepreneurs. Secondly, the degree of effectiveness which is manifest in Irish entrepreneurial exploitation of the available stocks of resources and opportunities. Simply put our analysis will show that Irish entrepreneurs have not been deprived of resources and opportunities on which to work; though Ireland is not as well endowed with resources and opportunities as some countries, she has not suffered, and does not suffer, from shortages which are absolute enough to preclude development-appropriate entrepreneurial conduct and thus a greater degree of economic development than she has attained. The problem does not, therefore, lie in objective factors alone: subjective factors are also crucial in connection with entrepreneurial behaviour which has resulted in the under-utilisation of the available resource-opportunity base.

Having established the need to invoke subjective factors we will move in what remains of the book to an analysis of the impact of cultural values on entrepreneurial orientations. In doing this we shall examine the emergence of the modern Irish culture complex and the institutions through which it was created and sustained. Irish cultural identity will be shown to derive principally from the values of Roman Catholicism and nationalism. As the reference to nationalism suggests, the country's long and sometimes troubled relationship with Great Britain had a crucial

4

impact on the Irish value system, and two broad processes will be shown to be operative in this connection. The first of these was adoptive; a process by which certain institutions and values, principally those having to do with bourgeois property rights and parliamentary democracy were allowed to diffuse into the Irish culture complex. The second was reactive and based on a rejection of certain aspects of British influence which were held to be destructive of an Irish cultural identity which the votaries of the nationalism that emerged in the late nineteenth century wanted to restore. From the Nationalist perspective Irish identity came to be associated with Gaelicism, ruralism and Catholic spirituality, the defence of which required the rejection of all aspects of modernity that touched on urbanism, industrialism, commercialism, materialism, secularism and cosmopolitanism. In consequence the modern Irish culture complex, in terms of its relationship to economic life, represents a curious mix. On the one hand bourgeois property rights are asserted and maintained; there is an 'ethic of possession'. On the other hand those rights are qualified by a value system, which, since it is reticent about crucial aspects of capitalist modernity, does little to promote what might be called an ethic of responsibility towards resources among the property owning fraternity.

The values in which we are interested did not emerge as an ideological reflection of the material interests of any section of the Irish people; the priests, poets, writers and revolutionaries, of whose 'value-entrepreneurship' they are the result, were drawn from all segments of Irish society, not excluding the Anglo-Irish aristocracy and the urban working class. Nevertheless, it is arguable that they took root in Irish society because an elective affinity existed between their ideal content and the life situations of a predominantly rural people, regardless of their locations in the social stratification system. The Catholic-nationalist values could appeal to the materially less well-off because they invested their unprosperous rural lives with the health, dignity and spirituality which were seen to be lacking in the materialistic rat races of the urban industrialised world. They appealed also to the comfortably-off professionals, traders and farmers because they infused the status quo with an aura of sanctity and because adherence to them demanded no changes in the traditional patterns of action and social structure. As such they came to lend an air of dignity to lives of comfortable prosperity, and did so, moreover, without giving rise to the feeling that it had to be paid for by undue exertion and extension of commitment to the development of the economic resources on which that prosperity was based. This, of course, is the crucial point. The canon of identity, into which the Irish are encultured and thus learn to make their lives - including their economic lives - meaningful, came to be located in an ideal of civilisation expressed through values which extolled the subordination of economic activity to non-economic interests. The result is a value-directed limitation of commitment to economic activity, of which the Irish themselves are often well aware. Thus:

> Managerial people in Dublin quite commonly acknowledge that their more relaxed attitude to business activity stems from their religious outlook on life. In the words of one husband: 'I think we Irish are

quite different from the English and Americans: the ones I've met seem to be wrapped up in the almighty pound and dollar. I've dealt with many Englishmen and my impression is that money and what it brings are their God. But we cannot get as concerned as they over business and material things. We are less active in these matters because always in the background of our minds we are concerned with a more fundamental philosophy' (Humphries, 1966, p. 219).

Unless we are to disregard the self-reporting of these economic actors, the remarks just quoted must serve to indicate the importance of subjective factors in which we are interested; they stand as a simple, open acknowledgement, offered without apology, of a value determined world view in which economic life is subordinated to more fundamental concerns which dictate a limitation of commitment to it, and in which the Irish distinguish themselves from other peoples in terms of a comparative limitation of commitment. Enshrined in this view is a meaningful interpretation of economic life as a materialism; it is seen as the pursuit of 'money and what it brings' which the sensible human being will not cultivate with too much avidity because it is dangerous to a higher interest; economic life is given a lowish priority, and is given it, moreover, because of an orientation to cultural values of a religious kind. On the face of things, therefore, we have good grounds for pursuing our enquiry into the impact of values in the Irish case; they do, indeed, seem to be operatively influential in determining a relaxed, anti-materialist approach to economic life. The anti-materialism implied in the views of the Dublin managers must not, however, be taken at face value. As we shall see, and as the comments about the absence of honesty and integrity suggest, there is a robust materialism evident in Irish economic life which expresses itself in bouts of ethically irregular economic activity. It is with the analysis of this combination of low prioritisation and weak ethical regulation that this book will be principally concerned - these are the terms in which the absence of an ethic of responsibility towards resources is most distinctly manifested. As the study develops we shall try to show that it - and the economic underdevelopment which results from it - are to a significant extent a 'product' of the cultural values to which the Irish relate their economic activity.

The background to the study

The background to this study is the persistent failure of the Irish to develop and modernise their economy and society in line with the levels of development achieved by other European countries. In 1913 Ireland ranked tenth in the list of twenty-three European countries in terms of its gross product *per capita*; It was behind, in order of their ranking, Britain, Switzerland, Denmark, Belgium, West Germany, Netherlands, Sweden, Austria and France, but ahead of, again in the order of their ranking, Norway, Finland, Czechoslovakia, Italy, Spain, Poland, Hungary, Rumania, Soviet Union, Greece, Portugal, Yugoslavia and Bulgaria. By 1985 Ireland had dropped to seventeenth place in the rankings, being overtaken by Norway, Finland, Czechoslovakia, Italy, Spain, Hungary and the Soviet Union and thus remained ahead of only six of the nations on the list in 1913: namely, Poland, Rumania, Greece, Portugal, Yugoslavia and Bulgaria. Ireland's 'failure' can be illustrated graphically if we measure the increases in gross product achieved by different states in the period between 1913 and 1985. Using index numbers (UK = 100) the data shows the Irish performance in a very bad light, with figures of 61 for 1913 and only 62 for 1985. For those countries that were behind Ireland in 1913, but which had overtaken her by 1985, the situation is often dramatically different. Thus Norway increased its gross product from 57 to 128 over the period; Finland raised hers from 49 to 105; Czechoslovakia from 47 to 86; Italy from 43 to 99; Hungary from 35 to 67; and the Soviet Union from 32 to 72. Even those countries which remained behind Ireland in 1985 managed to achieve higher average annual growth rates of *per capita* gross product than Ireland, which, in growing its economy at an average annual rate of only 1.6 per cent between 1913 and 1985, came second from the bottom of the twenty-three European countries under consideration (see Kennedy, Giblin and McHugh, 1988, pp. 14,18).

These figures relate to the Irish Republic, that part of Ireland which gained its independence from the United Kingdom in 1921, and the part of Ireland with which this book is concerned. On the whole the figures indicate that the economic 'career' of independent Ireland has tended to be a comparatively undynamic one. Between 1926 and 1938 the economy of what was then the Irish Free State grew at an annual average rate of only 1.3 per cent, while in the years following down to 1950 it fared even worse, growing at an annual rate of only 1.1 per cent (Kennedy, Giblin and McHugh, 1988, p. 60). Alongside this relative economic stagnation the population declined through emigration; the decade 1926-36 saw a net migration rate of -5.1 per thousand of the population and this worsened to a rate of -5.4 per cent in the decade following, before soaring to -8.2 per thousand between 1946 and 1951 (Brunt, 1988, p. 63). By the nineteen-fifties a deep gloom had descended over Ireland and her people; economic performance did not improve and in the seven years between 1951 and 1958 the population decline was nearly twice as great as in the whole of the preceding period since independence (Kennedy, Giblin and McHugh, 1988, p. 60). This, however, is the point at which we shall take up the story in Chapter 2.

The decline in population which Ireland experienced after independence was, in fact, a continuation of a trend which was firmly established with the great famine occasioned by the failures of the potato crop between 1845 and 1849. The scale of this tragedy can easily be gathered from the fact that the population of the island fell by some two million between 1845 and 1851, when about one million people perished from starvation and disease and another million saved themselves by leaving the country (Cullen, 1987, p. 132). Prior to the famine the population of Ireland had increased in line with increases in other European countries, facilitated, in Ireland's case, by, among other things, ease of marriage and high fertility rates. These were associated with ease of access to a plot of land, which was, in turn, the result of the stimulus to labour intensive cultivation imparted by rising corn prices, which doubled between 1760 and 1810; many of the tenant farmers lacked the working capital to pay wages, so they remunerated those who worked for them by letting small plots on which the cottiers and labourers - the classes who suffered most from the famine and subsequent developments in rural Ireland - could grow the potatoes which were their staple diet. After the Napoleonic wars agricultural prices slumped and landlords began the process of consolidating holdings and turning them over to pasture. Thus began a tendency for Irish agriculture to move away from labour intensive cultivation and towards pasture farming, a tendency that was consolidated after the famine as cattle prices rose massively in relation to the prices obtainable for the products of arable cultivation. As might be expected the move from intensive to extensive patterns of agriculture lead to a decline in the demand for rural labour; the number of rural labourers fell from 700,000 in 1845 to 310,000 in 1910, while over the same period the number of cottiers with less than five acres, and the number of farmers with between five and fifteen acres fell from 300,000 to 62,000 and from 310,000 to 154,000 respectively (Kennedy, Giblin and McHugh, 1988, p. 6).

An industrialising Irish economy might have been able to absorb the surplus labour created by these developments. However, if we except North-east Ulster - now located in that part of Ireland which remained in the United Kingdom after the rest of the island gained independence - Ireland never experienced an industrial revolution and so could not absorb the displaced rural population in newly created industrial employment. The result was economic and social stagnation coupled with emigration and a continuing pattern of population decline which was arrested only in the nineteen-sixties.

Historically speaking Irish nationalist opinion has attributed Ireland's failure to industrialise, and thus the generality of its economic and social ills, to the country's subordination to, and exploitation by, Britain - a proposition on which, as we shall see, modern scholarship casts considerable doubt. For all that, however, no account of Ireland's social and economic development could ignore its relationship with its larger and more developed neighbour; Ireland was Britain's - initially England's - first colony, and was an integral part of the United Kingdom of Britain and Ireland between 1801 and 1921, in which latter year the people of what is now the Republic of Ireland achieved their independence. In doing so they created what one Irish historian (Curtis, 1942, p. 1) has characterised as 'the only Celtic nation state left in the world'.

A note on the longer-term historical background

The heritage out of which this Celtic consciousness was fashioned was itself the result of a conquest of Ireland; the ancient *Book of Invasions* tells how, in the time of Alexander the Great, the three sons of Mileadh of Spain, Heremon, Heber and Ir, led the Celtic intrusion into Ireland. The Celtic victories were due to the superiority of their iron weapons over those of the bronze using aboriginal peoples, and, if Curtis (1942, p. 2) is to be believed, to 'their warlike, aristocratic and masterful temper'. The religion of the Celts was Druidism, though we may presume that it was blended to some extent with the beliefs and traditions of the earlier inhabitants. In any case the keepers of the Celtic tradition were a powerful and much respected group of intellectuals; these preserved the Celtic laws, genealogies and sagas, and thus, in effect, developed the history of the race. Like the other inhabitants of the island the intellectuals adapted to Christianity from the fifth century, and, together with monkish scholars and ecclesiastics, contributed to a situation in which:

> By A.D. 800 Ireland has become a unity of civilisation and law, and no languages save the Gaelic of the ruling classes and the Latin of the Church were spoken. The Gaels had subjected and absorbed the former peoples and created a race-consciousness [among the Irish] which has never been lost (Curtis, 1942, p. 19).

The social structure of Gaelic society was hierarchical and formed around three basic groupings: the *Clann*, the *Sept* and the *Fine*. The *Clann* unit was roughly equivalent to the Roman tribe and consisted of an aggregation of *Septs* which were, in turn, subdivided into the *Fina*, the basic family units. Territory occupied by the *Clanna* was regarded as a collective possession and was subdivided among the *Septs,* which groups, in turn, allocated land to the *Fine*. In its fully developed form the *Fine* consisted of seventeen men divided into four groups ranked in order of their importance and in terms of the share of the collective property to which they were entitled; the head of the family *(Flaith)* and his four closest kinsmen constituted the true family, and were, together with their dependents and slaves, constituted as a basic productive unit, above the three other ranks, based again on groupings of four kinsmen. The common affairs of the *Sept* were managed through a council of family heads, one of whose number was appointed as chief. The *Septs* proved to be strong and enduring centres of social solidarity and were the last of Gaelic institutions to perish in the face of enforced Anglicisation. Traditional Irish law reflected the collectivistic tendencies; a person's identity was derived from membership of the solidary groupings; only the intellectual classes passed freely around the country, for the rest no legal personality existed outside of the collectivities. Being the property of the collective, land was not individually alienable.

Jackson (1973, p. 29) is, perhaps, not far from the truth when he describes the political structure of Gaelic society as 'a transitional form in between a kinship society and a territorial state'. The basic unit was the *Tuath*, being a grouping of neighbouring *clanna* under a local *Ri* (King). These petty states were further aggregated into provincial clusters under a second, and higher, tier of Kingship, the whole being under the formal jurisdiction of a High Kingship. There was an elective element in the Kingship system, and the right to depose a King was jealously guarded. In any case the authority of the higher Kings was limited, and often contested; their functions seem to have been largely ceremonial.

For all that Gaelic society developed a unified culture and a race

9

consciousness, therefore, it did not evolve into a unified territorial state. Cattle raiding and warfare, based on shifting alliances between the petty kingdoms, were recurring features of Gaelic society and weakened any tendencies towards effective political and military centralisation. The Celtic economy was based largely on pasture, with some crop growing and handicrafts, with much of the menial work being undertaken by slaves. Production was for consumption rather than exchange; such surpluses as were generated were consumed conspicuously by the ruling strata.

The two centuries or so after the year 800 were turbulent years in Irish history as the country became subject to the predatory attentions of Scandinavian raiders. Considerable havoc ensued and this resulted in some degree of social reorganisation; some *Clanna* were displaced and their dispersed *Septs* were forced to reconsolidate into larger groupings, unrelated by kinship, under *Ri Mor* (Great Kings). As a result more powerful defensive alliances emerged which were eventually consolidated sufficiently, under a national High King, to enable the Irish to finally defeat the Scandinavians in 1014. If the predatory Norsemen wreaked some destruction in Ireland, they also, it has to be said, made a constructive contribution to the country's development; they were traders as well as pirates and some settled and founded the main seaports and trading centres, the first urban developments of any significance in Ireland.

If the defeat of the Scandinavians provided an object lesson in the benefits of unity, it was a lesson which the Irish did not learn; disputes continued to rage and one of them, a minor affair concerned with wife-stealing over which one MacMurrogh was expelled from the Kingship of Leinster, helped to bring about the Norman invasion in 1169. MacMurrogh fled to England and asked Henry II, to whom he promised allegiance, for help in regaining his rights. Henry, prompted no doubt by the prospect of finding suitable 'employment' for such of his vassals who had time on their hands and by the fact that the papacy - in the interests of promoting the unity of Christendom - had granted him the Lordship of Ireland some twenty years earlier, felt able to oblige. Thus began the English conquest of Ireland.

The conquest, to begin with, was a partial and equivocal affair, and was to remain so until the sixteenth century when it began to be pursued with a greater seriousness of purpose. After some initial successes - the Irish formally submitted to Henry in 1171 - the enterprise simply ran out of steam; the Normans lacked the power to extend and consolidate their hold on large areas of the country; settlers from Britain did not arrive in anything like the numbers anticipated; and the Crown was often not in a position to become over-actively involved in helping to push the process forward through policies of direct intervention. From the perspective of the Crown, therefore, the conquest of Ireland was a conquest by proxy, and the proxies simply lacked the power, the drive and the support needed to carry it through. As a result the Normans began to function as magnates interested mainly in promoting their localised interests; they took to squabbling among themselves, and, of course, with the Irish; they also formed alliances with the Irish, in many cases intermarrying with them and adopting Irish customs and speech to the point at which they began to be regarded as *Hiberniores ipsos Hibernos* (more Irish than the Irish themselves), and thus as traitors to the English interests and jurisdiction which never had more than the most precarious of holds over large tracts of the island. Outside of the immediate environs of the towns, therefore, feudalism did not take root, meaning that the socio-economic impact of the conquest was as patchy as were its political effects. There was, however, some cross-fertilisation between the feudal and the Gaelic systems; as the feudal Normans became Gaelicised, so the Gaelic chiefs became, to some extent, feudalised; chiefdom became hereditary and the clan chiefs began to exercise more power over the clansmen than had hitherto been the case.

Ireland's economy exhibited no spontaneous tendency to develop in line with the economies of Western and Central Europe; it remained in the pastoral-tribal state described earlier, and was, by West-central European standards, underdeveloped and lacking in any signs of the drift towards the emergence of bourgeois capitalism that was, by the age of the Renaissance and Reformation, becoming quite marked elsewhere. For one thing property lacked a secure basis in law and the social recognition of individual's rights to it; the basis to title was the sword. For another, capital intensive crop growing on the West-central European pattern was little developed in Ireland; climatic conditions were not entirely suitable, favouring pastoralism in conditions which, in any case, because mild winters greatly reduced the need for winter fodder, provided no incentive to crop growing on any substantial scale. As an Irish economic historian describes it, therefore,

> The Irish economy in the sixteenth century was an undeveloped one. Its exports revealed its character. Fish and hides were the main items in shipments outwards from its ports, evidence of the unsophisticated nature of the island's production. Fish were the harvest of its rivers and of the rich fishing grounds off its coasts. Skins and hides came from the wild animal life of the forests as well as from the domesticated herds of cattle and flocks of sheep. In all probability, the population at the outset of the century was scarcely a million. It was, it seems, not much larger a century later, some probable rise in numbers in the first half of the century being more or less offset by a reduction in population through war losses and more substantially through plague or famine during the military campaigns of the closing two decades of the century. It was a primitive country, thinly settled, the people themselves underemployed. Woodlands occupied perhaps an eighth of the country around 1600. Woodland growth was strongest below the 500-foot line, hence woodlands covered rich ground and alluvial valleys that could be turned to pasture or arable use. The wolf, extinct in England by 1500, was still present in Ireland, a further testimony to the relatively lightly settled nature of the country (Cullen, 1987, p. 7).

As Cullen's reference to military campaigns, perhaps, suggests, the sixteenth century saw a quickening of England's interest in the colonisation of Ireland. Unlike Ireland, England's economy and society had, by the sixteenth century, been subjected to some degree of transformation in a broadly capitalistic direction; in reducing population the black death had raised living standards and given a fillip to capital formation, thus stimulating demand and development through further capital formation and a growing interest in production for the market and profit among the landed element, and not least among the rising bourgeoisie. Later developments saw the consolidation of power at the centre in the guise of Tudor absolutism, the spread of the profit motive and the increasing importance of the burgher class, the progression of whose economic interests required the moral acceptance of individualistic profit seeking, and both social recognition of, and legal protection for, their personal and property rights. These were not, of course, secured without a struggle; the old order resisted and it took a civil war and a 'glorious revolution' to make it come to terms with the votaries of new capitalistic dispensation, whose victories had, by the end of the seventeenth century, made England a land fit for capitalists to live in.

Two broad reasons can be adduced to account for England's increased determination to consolidate its hold on Ireland. The first of these was strategic and arose from the increasing maritime power of England's continental rivals; a foothold in Ireland would have permitted all or any of these to attack England from the West as well as from across the channel, something no government could contemplate with equanimity - as an old Tudor saying had it: 'He who would England win, let him in Ireland first begin'. The second lay in the simple search for profit opportunities associated with land; land in England was scarce and so enterprising Englishmen turned towards Ireland as a useful potential source of profit opportunities. The struggle that ensued was a protracted and often bloody affair that lasted through the Tudor, Stuart, Commonwealth and Restoration periods and ended only with the Williamite victories in 1690. Intensified by religious issues - the Irish remained steadfast in their refusal to embrace Protestantism - and by the willingness of the Catholic Irish to become involved in the struggles taking place in England - they supported King Charles against parliament and King James against William - the struggle ended in defeat for the Irish, the effective elimination of the old Gaelic ruling class, and with them the last remnants of the Gaelic social and economic order. The old native ruling class was replaced by a Protestant ascendancy to which the native, Catholic Irish were to be subordinated in the economic, political, social and civic senses of that term.

Subordination was achieved restricting Catholics' access to economic resources and through the enactment of a legal code which deprived them of their civil and political rights. Catholic land was confiscated on a vast scale - the Catholics' share of Irish land declined from fifty-nine per cent in 1641 to fourteen per cent in 1703 - and handed over to loyal Protestant settlers who thus came to constitute a new Protestant landlord ascendancy. Ideally that ascendancy would have liked to populate its estates with loyal, Protestant settler tenants from England and Scotland, though it was only in the North-east of the country that any large scale Protestant plantation was successfully accomplished. In the rest of the country Catholics had to be retained to work the ascendancy estates as tenants, and made up, as they do today, the overwhelming majority of the population. In order to maintain its power and position the ascendancy enacted a code of legislation which deprived the Catholic majority of their economic, civil and political rights:

> No Catholic was suffered to buy land, or inherit or receive it as a gift from Protestants, or to hold life annuities, or mortgages on land, or leases of more than thirty-one years, or any lease on such terms as the profits of the land exceeded one third of the rent. If a Catholic leaseholder, by his skill or industry, so increased his profits that they exceeded this proportion, and did not immediately make a corresponding increase in his rent, his farms passed to the first Protestant who made the discovery (Lecky, 1916, p. 146).

In addition Catholics in trade were precluded from keeping more than two apprentices, though given the small size of many businesses this restriction was probably nothing like so harmful to the prospects of Catholic accumulation as the law on leases to which we have just made reference (Wall. 1958, p. 95). In the wider civic and political spheres Catholics were harshly discriminated against; they could neither vote nor stand for parliament; they were excluded from membership of municipal corporations and the guilds; they could not, medicine excepted, enter the professions; they were ineligible for commissions in the armed forces and the civil service; they were not allowed to own a horse worth more than five pounds; they were prohibited from keeping schools - any Protestant who discovered a Catholic schoolmaster could claim a reward of ten pounds - and from publishing books and newspapers; they were not forbidden their religious observances, though priests were required to register with the authorities, severe restrictions were placed on their numbers and Catholics were allowed no provision for the education of their priesthood - there was even a proposal to brand and castrate registered priests, which the English House of Lords evidently thought too extreme in the circumstances.

The fact that laws like these were not always rigorously or systematically enforced in no way detracts from the purposes of those who legislated them into existence; they were designed to secure a Protestant ascendancy over Ireland through processes of economic, social, religious and political repression, intended, in the words of Inglis ((1987, p. 99), 'to demean and demoralize'. Deprived of their lands, hindered in their economic activities, denied access to education and, often, the ministry, moral teaching and example of Christianity, the Roman Catholic Irish were thought unlikely to be able to raise themselves to challenge the ascendancy effectively.

Those who pushed forward the colonisation process which resulted in the developments just described were avowedly capitalist in orientation; the subsistence-oriented tribal pastoralism of traditional Gaelic society was thus replaced by individualistic capitalism, the votaries of which saw land and economic resources, not as means to the end of subsistence, but as means to the end of making profits. The result was some rapid and effective economic development:

> The appropriation of the clan lands as private property, following the Elizabethan conquest ... opened for the first time the possibility of deriving profit, as distinct from a livelihood, from Irish land. That profit was to be made by shipping livestock to England .... Ireland, which had previously exported little except hunted, gathered and crude pastoral products, developed under the early Stuarts an export trade in cattle and sheep that almost certainly exceeded any similar trade in the world at that time. Given that the trade only commenced after the Elizabethan conquest which was completed by the battle of Kinsale in 1601; and given that England's population at the time was about one-tenth its present size with average real incomes about one-tenth the present level, annual exports of around 45,000 cattle and a similar number of sheep around 1640 were a remarkable testimony to the efficacy of capitalist colonialism in mobilising resources for profit (Crotty, 1986, p. 40).

Development of this kind took place against the background of war which, though it disrupted it, clearly did not destroy economic life in Ireland. The colonisation of the Americas opened up further markets for the products of Irish agriculture both as exports and as provisions for ships' crews. Although there were setbacks the general tendency in the seventeenth century seems to have been one of progress and rising living standards down to the sixteen-eighties (Cullen, 1987, p. 23). Such progress is reflected in the volume of wool and linen exports; the exports of woollen frieze rose from 444.361 yards in 1665 to 1,129,716 yards in 1687, while the quantity of linen cloth exported grew from 14,570 yards 131,568 yards over the same period (Cullen, 1987, pp. 23-24).

English interests, however, reacted adversely to imports into their market of cattle and wool from Ireland. As a result legislation was passed in the English parliament which inhibited the imports of Irish cattle and wool (the Cattle Acts and the Woollen Act of 1699). Promoted by vested interests in England, these Acts were, in fact, passed against the wishes of the English government, which, while it was not overly hostile to the development of Irish economic interests, did, nevertheless, seek to regulate them so as to prevent them from running counter to English interests. With this end the Navigation Acts were applied to Ireland; these restricted Ireland's capacity to trade directly with third countries in certain commodities and thus arguably prevented the growth of an entrepot trade in tobacco and colonial products which some Irish ports, notably Cork on the South coast, were well placed to develop. England also placed higher tariffs on Irish goods than Ireland did on English goods, prevented Ireland from importing hops, except from Britain (in 1710) and banned the export of glass from Ireland (in 1746).

Eighteenth century Irish opinion grew increasingly resentful of these restrictions, seeing them as harmful to the growth and prosperity of the Irish economy. Modern scholarship, however, suggests that Irish opinion, at best, overstated its case; the Woollen Act, for example, affected only the finer cloths in which Ireland enjoyed cost advantages that were due to the rate of exchange between the Irish and English currencies. While the Navigation Acts may have been a nuisance, they were qualified and even conferred certain advantages on Irish interests; direct trade was permitted in provisions, horses and servants; linen goods could be shipped directly; Irish ships and seafarers were treated as English and were allowed to engage in the English coastal trade and in trade between England and the colonies. In all, therefore, English legislation did not prevent the growth in trade between Ireland and Britain and the colonies. After about 1730, in fact, Irish exports began a period of rapid and sustained growth; butter and beef performed well and grain began to figure in outward trade from the seventeen-eighties onwards. Linen was, however, the 'star performer':

> Exports of linen were less than 500,000 yards in 1698; in the 1790s they were above 40,000,000 yards. The Irish linen industry was perhaps the most remarkable instance in Europe of an export-led advance in the eighteenth century. England's major export, woollen cloth, increased by only 136 per cent between 1700 and 1796 (Cullen, 1987, p. 53).

Although it later concentrated on Ulster, the linen industry was, in fact, widespread throughout Ireland in the eighteenth century; it was encouraged by the Irish Parliament, which established a Linen Board, and, being organised on a domestic basis, provided a great deal of employment in agricultural districts without which there would have been a great deal of underemployment, and thus poverty, among the smaller farmers. Ireland's woollen industry also expanded in the eighteenth century, which also saw growth in brewing, distilling, sugar refining, flour milling and glass making.

Inland trade also experienced an upsurge in line with export growth. Linen, wool and worsted, butter and cattle were the principal commodities involved in the inland trade which was serviced by an extension of the road network from the seventeen-thirties onwards. Irish roads were constructed by turnpike trusts, but local authorities were empowered to levy a cess for the construction and maintenance of roads, and after 1760 most of the construction was undertaken by the County Grand Juries (the forerunners of the modern County Councils). Attention was also given to the development of inland navigation, not least by the Irish Parliament, which, in 1730, set aside the proceeds of certain duties to finance canal building. In 1752 these were entrusted to a national corporation, The Corporation for Promoting and Carrying on an Inland Navigation in Ireland. This undertook construction work itself and made grants to private operators, and its work was supplemented, from 1787, by Navigation Commissioners who were given responsibility for affecting improvements on individual rivers. Canal construction and improvements to river navigations carried out under the auspices of these bodies ensured that Ireland's transport infrastructure developed in line with, if not indeed ahead of, the needs of its commerce.

Capital investment in Irish industry often came from landlords, though

English capital was also invested and the Irish Parliament was very active in the business of industrial promotion. With this end in view Parliament made funds available to aid development in agriculture, mining, industry and communications. Most Irish enterprises were small and served local markets, though some increases in scale were evident especially in brewing, glass making and flour milling. Power technology, both steam and water, was in use and labour was cheaper, if less skilled and less well managed than in Britain.

Notwithstanding the Penal laws, Roman Catholics played a substantial part in the commercial life of Ireland in the eighteenth century. Protestant resentment at the level of their involvement, and their success, is evident from a succession of petitions to Parliament and the outbursts of publicists on behalf of the Protestant interest. Typical of the latter are the outpourings of Alexander the Coppersmith, a Cork pamphleteer who complains in 1737 about increasing Catholic domination over that city's lucrative provisions trade. Altogether notwithstanding the Navigation Acts it seems:

> the French in galleys of four or five hundred ton come hither themselves, always consigned to a popish factor, whose relations and correspondence abroad and union at home; whose diligence being more, and luxury being less than protestants, will at last swallow up the trade and suck the marrow of this city; and like the ivy will grow to be an oak, and prove absolute in their power over the commerce of those on whom they should be dependent for bread (quoted in Wall, 1958, p. 100).

As Wall (1958, 1969) has shown, protests of this kind came in 'thick and fast' in the eighteenth century from the corporate towns in Ireland. In 1762, for example, the Corporation of Galway pointed out that Protestants in that city were:

> Discouraged from following trade or business, papists in general declining to deal with them; and the wealth of the town, or by much the greater part of it, being in their hands, they thereby acquired considerable influence and power over the indigent protestant tradesman (quoted in Wall, 1958, p. 102).

Protestant to the core, the Irish Parliament, nevertheless, ignored the pleas and petitions demanding restraint on Catholics in trade; it did not want to put the revenues generated by Catholic activities at hazard, and so, provided they 'kept their heads down', Catholics were allowed to continue their commercial operations in spite of the Protestant protests. The protests do, however, indicate that the Catholics were quite capable of exercising the virtues that came to be associated with the Protestant ethic, cultivating them, if Alexander the Coppersmith is to be believed, more assiduously than Protestants themselves. Religion, however, was not the inspiration behind the eighteenth century Irish Catholics' 'inner-worldly asceticism'. Excluded, as they were, from land-owning and the professions they had few options available when it came to the business of making a living; the penal code channelled their enterprise into commerce. And so it was with their frugality. As Wall (1958, p. 102) explains:

> Their opportunities for lavish spending and luxurious living were circumscribed. They did not belong to the guilds nor attend city jamborees; and, shut out as they were from any part in the borough representation in parliament, elections cost them nothing. They could not buy land, and the attractions of the turf were not for them since under a statute of King William they could not possess a horse valued for more than five pounds. There was little outward display in their lives, nor did the law permit them to build schools or churches or endow charities of a purely Catholic nature.

That the stimulus to Catholic commercial activity was indeed provided by the Penal Code is demonstrated by what happened once the provisions of that Code began to be relaxed, as they were between 1778 and 1793 when the prohibitions on land ownership and entry into the professions were removed. Again Wall (1969, pp. 47-8) tells us what changes took place in 'the patterns of investment and the ways of life of ... wealthy Catholics':

> Hitherto they had led lives in which ostentation could play little part and their opportunities for lavish spending were circumscribed. The desire, so long suppressed, to cut a figure in society, was now given opportunities for satisfaction, and Catholic merchants and manufacturers tended to divert more money than perhaps they should, from their commercial interests, while in many instances their sons turned to the professions instead of entering the family business. It was unfortunate, perhaps, that in this way money and talents were withdrawn from commercial enterprise at the time of the union, when Ireland had, for the first time, met the great challenge of free trade.

Union between Great Britain and Ireland came about in 1801; it was precipitated by the old British fear that an alliance between Irish radicals and a continental enemy - an alliance which Irish radicals had forged and were trying to develop - might provide that enemy, in this case Napoleon, with a platform from which to attack Britain from the West. The Act of Union was a bitterly contested piece of legislation, though the debates surrounding it were concerned with political rather than economic questions. Ireland's economy was doing well out of the Napoleonic wars, and there was a general air of optimism about the future in which the union with Great Britain, and the free trade which was to follow it, was not seen as problematic. Agricultural prices, however, fell sharply at the war's end, and the recessions in 1819-20 and 1825-26 hit Irish industry hard. Although both recessions were short-lived, more fundamental tendencies were at work in Ireland's economy and society. These, as we have seen, involved a long-term, price-driven move from tillage to pasture and a failure to industrialise to an extent sufficient to absorb the numbers

17

displaced in the extensivisation of Irish agriculture.

After the eighteen-twenties cotton and woollen textiles maintained only a precarious foothold in the Irish economy. Linen textiles developed well, but were increasingly concentrated in the North-east of the country. Textile developments were also built around the application of powered processes in factories, a tendency which led to the decline of domestic textiles and which, in conjunction with the rising population in the years before the famine, made Ireland 'more rural, more agricultural than it had been' (Cullen, 1987, p. 121). Outside of the textile sectors other industries seem to have held their own; paper and glass survived; shipbuilding and ironworking continued in many areas. Shipbuilding was carried on in several centres, with the yards in Cork and Waterford being among the most progressive; steam locomotives were manufactured in Dublin, Cork and Belfast. With significant exceptions, however, Irish industry remained small in scale and oriented to limited local markets; and, in general, nothing remotely resembling industrialisation on the British pattern could be discerned outside of the North-east. Other developments of note were the spread of banking - in 1845 the banks had 172 branches in eighty-nine towns (Cullen, 1987, p. 126) and continuing improvements to the transport infrastructure through further canal construction and Ireland's entry into the railway age.

As we saw above the famine brought about a drastic reduction in Ireland's population. Between 1731 and 1841 Ireland's population had risen from about three million to 8.2 million. In 1851 population had declined to 6.5 million and it continued on a downward trend, standing at only 4.4 million at the beginning of the twentieth century. If nothing else these figures suggest that Ireland had one thriving 'export industry': 'people exporting'; 1,163,418 people emigrated in the decade 1851-61; 849,836 left in the decade following and so a trend was established which, as we have seen, ended only after 1960. Those who remained behind in rural Ireland after the famine, however, experienced rising prosperity; bank deposits, a good measure of agricultural incomes, rose from £8 million in 1845 to £33 million in 1876 (Cullen, 1987, p. 138). Rising rural living standards were reflected in the growing importance of towns as commercial centres; the number of retail shops expanded greatly as did the range of products sold; provincial wholesaling developed on a large scale; the banks' branch networks expanded further, reaching 809 in 1910, by which time bank deposits amounted to some £60 million. Expansion of the railway system had a major impact on the commercialisation process, opening up the remote areas to the products and influences of the more developed regions; after a slow start the network grew rapidly in mid-century and by 1914 Ireland had some 3,500 miles of railways, giving it, in relation to its size, one of the most extensive networks in the world.

These progressive trends were interrupted after 1874 by a sharp recession in both industry and agriculture; the world-wide industrial boom ended in 1874 and English manufacturers dumped products into the Irish market. This, combined with a fall in rural incomes and purchasing power, made life difficult for such Irish industry as there was. For all this the truth seems to be that 'the writing was on the wall' for much of this industry before the depression made its effects felt; employment in cotton was declining; paper making suffered a similar fate; glass making, sugar refining, tanning, footwear, soapmaking, ropemaking and milling were also in decline as were many of the local craft trades. Craft producers were crushed by cheaper factory made goods, and many of the smaller Irish factories went under to the competition of larger, more efficient units. The larger Irish companies that survived to see economic upturn which took place after 1890 were large, export-oriented units, with world-wide reputations. In all the achievements of industrial Ireland at the turn of the nineteenth and twentieth centuries were a long way from being unimpressive, with about one-third of the total output of agriculture and industry being accounted for by industry. More, as Cullen (1987, p. 158) tells us:

> The proportion of total industrial output exported was remarkably high. The gross value of industrial output in 1907 was £67 million. The value of manufactured exports was £20.9 million. If processed food and drinks are added - a further £13.5 million - the total of all manufactures comes to £34.4 million, or half the total industrial output itself. This is a remarkably high proportion, well in excess of the corresponding total for Britain or any major country. Outstanding among the export-based industries were linen, shipbuilding, distilling and brewing. In each case a high proportion of output was exported - the bulk of output in linen and shipbuilding, well over half in whiskey and about a fifth in brewing - and the product had an international reputation of the first order.

Impressive though this picture is it does not tell the whole story. Ireland's industrial base was a very narrow one in two crucial respects: First, it was confined to a small number of industries, mainly shipbuilding and engineering, linen, brewing, distilling and mineral waters. Second, it was heavily concentrated in regional terms, with the Belfast area accounting for £19.1 million of Ireland's total non-food manufactured exports of £20.9 million (Cullen, 1987, p. 161). Belfast was absolutely dominant in shipbuilding, engineering and linen, though its preeminence was by no means restricted to these sectors; it accounted for some sixty per cent of the country's whiskey exports, and for all but a small fraction of its substantial exports of tobacco products. Over the remainder of the country industry remained thinly spread. According to Cullen (1987, p. 163) some recovery took place in woollens, tanning and bootmaking, but industry in general remained small in scale and oriented towards local markets - brewing and distilling were among the few significant exceptions to this rule. Outside of the Belfast region, therefore, the Irish economy remained firmly based on agriculture, to the processing of the products of which much of its industrial activity was devoted. The first Census of Production in 1907 indicated just how important the food and drink industries were to the Irish economy. Total output in these activities was nearly twice that of textiles. Ireland produced nearly two-thirds of the butter made in the U.K., over a third of the bacon and a quarter of the spirits (Green, 1969, p. 99). As we shall see, however, the agricultural processing industries were by no means as developed as they might have been, a situation which, for one Irish economic historian, constituted 'the real failure of nineteenth century Ireland' (Green, 1969, p. 99).

The pattern of industrial distribution just described prevailed in 1921 when the people of what was to become the Irish Free State - later the Republic of Ireland - left the United Kingdom and established an independent state. Irish independence was the result of a long and sustained struggle by Irish nationalists which lasted throughout the nineteenth century and continued into the twentieth - indeed, as the tragedy of Northern Ireland shows, it is a struggle that is by no means over. Irish nationalism was, and remains, a complex and variegated phenomenon. Its nineteenth century manifestations arose from a rejection of the Union settlement of 1801 and rested in the perception that Irish grievances and Irish problems were best addressed by Irish people working through Irish institutions, rather than through the United Kingdom Parliament at Westminster. Irish nationalists, therefore, wanted a measure of self-government for Ireland. They did not always agree on how much self-government was appropriate and differed also on the question of how the required measure of independence was to be achieved. In its mainstream Irish nationalism was constitutionalist in orientation; its votaries used the parliamentary process to press their case and, from the eighteen-sixties onwards, nationalist politicians were increasingly successful in making nationalism the dominant tendency in Irish politics and in establishing the Irish Party as the effective voice of the Irish people in the Westminster parliament. The nationalist movement, however, also had its extra-parliamentary activists. For the most part these represented a minority tendency, whose demands, in terms of the degree of separation from Britain, and whose methods, including resorts to insurrectionary violence, were more extreme than those of their constitutional counterparts. Relations between the two wings of the movement were complex and ambiguous; they were often hostile, yet sometimes opportunistically tolerant and even collaborative over some issues, notably land reform, when, for example, parliamentary nationalists found a little extra-constitutional pressure helpful to the cause which they were seeking to advance. Land became a serious issue after the world economic boom petered out in 1874; prior to this agriculture had been prosperous, with prices rising ahead of rents, and the depression changed this exposing farmers to reduced incomes and to threats of eviction. The result was a thorough questioning of the whole basis of Landlordism in its Irish Protestant-Ascendancy manifestation and a prolonged campaign for rent control and later for peasant proprietorship on terms which enabled the tenants to purchase the land from the landlords on reasonable terms. The campaigns were successful; by the first decade of the twentieth century Ireland had become transformed from a nation of tenants into a nation of peasant proprietors. Success in the quest for political devolution or independence, however, was not so marked. Though it achieved a measure of success in persuading elements of the Liberal Party to accept a measure of devolved self-government for Ireland, the Irish Party encountered resolute opposition from the Conservative Party and from Irish Protestants who happened to be heavily concentrated in the North-east region of the country. Those opposed to Home Rule for Ireland were able to use the Conservative majority in the House of Lords to veto any devolution legislation, and did so, until 1911, when the Liberal Government forced through a Parliament Act which reduced the power of the Lords to an ability to delay rather than to veto legislation. A Home Rule Bill passed the Commons in 1912 and was due to become law in 1914. Unionist opposition, however, remained intransigent; unionists in Ulster, supported by the Conservative Party in Britain, imported arms and prepared to defend the status quo by resort to force. As 1914 approached the United Kingdom of Great Britain and Ireland faced a constitutional crisis of the first magnitude.

World War One averted this crisis; the Irish Party agreed to the suspension of Home Rule for the duration of the conflict, and its leaders were generally supportive of the war effort. Less moderate Irish nationalists, however, saw England's difficulty (the war) as Ireland's opportunity and organised an armed insurrection which started on Easter Sunday 1916. Irish public opinion was initially unsympathetic to the rising and within a week of the commencement of hostilities the insurrectionists were forced to surrender. Thereafter, however, their leaders were tried and executed by the British, a move that did much to produce a change in the tenor of Irish public opinion, which moved away from supporting the Irish Party and began to back the more extreme nationalism of Sinn Fein and the armed struggle which resulted in the establishment of an independent Irish jurisdiction over twenty-six of the island's thirty-two counties. Unionist opinion in the North-east was strong enough to ensure that the six counties of what was to become Northern Ireland were allowed to opt out of independence and remain in the United Kingdom, though with a measure of devolved government of its own.

Thanks to the opposition of the Ulster Unionists, therefore, the jurisdiction of the newly independent Irish state did not encompass the whole island of Ireland; six counties in the Northern province of Ulster remained in the United Kingdom, and these included the Belfast region, the district which, to remember, contained Ireland's only significant concentration of heavy industry. As a result the society of the new state was predominantly rural and its economy remained rooted in farming; in 1926 sixty-one per cent of its population lived outside of towns and villages and fifty-three per cent of its economically active population were engaged in agriculture (Brown, 1985, pp. 18-19). No significant private sector developments in either agriculture or industry took place, though the State became involved in electricity, peat, sugar and steel production and in the provision of industrial and agricultural credit and attempted to foster an industrialisation drive in the nineteen-thirties with a view to making Ireland as economically self-sufficient as possible. Some private sector industrialisation took place behind the tariff protection that was provided as part of this drive. Again, however, the operations were small in scale and oriented to local markets and did not provide enough employment opportunities to stem the tide of emigration. In all the population of the twenty-six counties which came under independent Irish jurisdiction in 1921 fell from 3,140,000 to 2,961,000 between 1911 and

1951 and declined further to 2,818,000 in 1961. These national figures mask important regional variations; the population of the Western province of Connaught dropped from 611,000 to 472,000 between 1911 and 1951 and stood at only 419,000 a decade later; Munster, the Southern province, also lost significantly between 1911 and 1951, its population declining from 1,035,000 to 899,000 between these dates before falling by another 50,000 in the decade down to 1961 (Meenan, 1970, pp. 184-6). Behind emigration lurked the spectres of economic stagnation, unemployment and poverty, the triple effects of Ireland's failure to develop her economy to the point at which she could provide a living for all her people. A pervasive consciousness of this failure made the nineteen-fifties,

> a period of great trauma in Irish economic and social life, which at the time inspired titles like *The Vanishing Irish* and to which phrases have been applied subsequently like 'national malaise' and 'symptoms ... resembling the "death wish" of a society'. It is certainly true that economic performance was poor, being characterised by two serious depressions and a decline in population nearly twice as great as in the whole of the preceding period since independence. It is also true, however, that during this period the basis of the development strategy was laid which propelled the economy towards unprecedented growth in the fifteen year period 1958-73 (Kennedy, Giblin and McHugh, 1988, p. 60).

This development strategy emerged under state auspices. To begin with state-sponsored bodies were established to assist the private sector with export marketing (*Coras Trachtalla* - Irish Export Board), to stimulate industrial expansion through the attraction of foreign firms and the encouragement of native units (The Industrial Development Authority) - an earlier foundation which was revivified, to develop tourism (*Bord Failte Eareann* - Irish Tourist Board), to foster expansion in the fishing industry (*Bord Iascaigh Mhara* - Irish Sea Fisheries Board) and to provide an agricultural research and advisory service (*An Foras Taluntis* - The Agricultural Institute). These agencies, and others, were established in conjunction with the provision of generous grant and tax incentives to private sector operators who were willing to establish and/or expand export-oriented operations; grants of up to two-thirds of the costs of sites and buildings were made available - more if the enterprise was established in areas designated as underdeveloped - and profits derived from new or increased manufacturing exports were exempted from taxation. Thus began the State's intensified interest in the active promotion of industrial development in Ireland. Its intentions were serious, and, given the stagnation described here, they had to be. The programme achieved some initial success, giving hope, for a while at least, that a brighter future lay ahead for Ireland and its people. After the downturn in the world economy in the seventies, however, growth slackened once more and the old problems of unemployment, poverty and emigration raised their haunting presence once again. In the end the programme turned out to be an expensive failure. For all that, the measures just described amply confirm that the government's interest was developed in the direction of making Ireland a very hospitable environment for capitalist entrepreneurs to operate in.

Conclusion

In this chapter we have tried to do two things: Firstly, we have tried to say what our problem is and what we intend to try to do about it. Secondly, we have attempted to provide a sketch of the historical background to our problem by reference to a brief review of the economic, social and political development of Ireland. That review was clearly, and inevitably, a limited one, if only because it is impossible to do justice to the history of any country within the confines of a single chapter, let alone a section of a chapter. Since Ireland is no exception to this rule, we could not hope to do more than provide a brief historical overview which concentrated selectively on those issues which are most relevant to our study. We shall have to refer to historical material again later in the book, and we can but hope that the material covered in the all too brief historical section will help to give point to such further references to Ireland's past. Readers who are familiar with Irish history will probably not have found the historical references in the chapter very informative; they will be familiar with the ground it covers and we can only apologise for hauling them over it once again. Nevertheless, the historical coverage was not primarily directed at those who are informed about Ireland and its history. It was designed to provide those who are not familiar with the Irish situation with an outline of the historical context in which the activities we are studying must be situated. If it does that much it will have served its purpose.

From our perspective one feature of the Irish situation has to be seen as dominant: namely, the persistent failure of the Irish economy to develop in line with the capitalist-industrial economies of Great Britain and the other countries of the North-west European geographical area, the area of which Ireland forms a part. Resulting, as it has, in persistent poverty, unemployment and mass emigration, this failure has concentrated the minds of thoughtful Irish people for a century or more. It has also been a major preoccupation of Irish governments, especially since the nineteen-fifties when, as we have seen, radically new policies were introduced with a view to promoting industrial development and economic modernisation. Since these policies were directed to the achievement of development *via* the private enterprise route, they point directly to the heart of this study, which lies, of course, in an examination of the conduct of the entrepreneurs and managers, upon whose commitment, dynamism and acumen the success of the policies was to depend. The crucial question now becomes: Was the necessary entrepreneurial commitment forthcoming? In Chapter 2 we shall begin the task of providing an answer to that question.

2 Irish entrepreneurs do for themselves

Introduction

In this chapter our focus switches from the historical to the modern Irish scene, with special reference, as the title to the chapter suggests, to the practices and performance of the Irish entrepreneurial establishment. To write about the subject of modern Ireland is, of course, to write about the Ireland of our own time, and this is what we intend to do. Our sense of the modern is, however, also conditioned by the historical events outlined in the opening chapter; our choice of boundary date is not, therefore, exclusively determined by an egocentric time consciousness, but rests additionally in the sense which actors and commentators historically located in the nineteen-sixties - our much younger selves included - had that a new kind of Ireland was emerging in that period. For us, therefore, modern Ireland starts at about 1960. It does so precisely because that date - in so far as any single date can - represents what many at the time felt to be a turning point in Irish social and economic history. Mother Ireland it seemed had stirred her dry old bones; she had mended her broken heart; there was new life in her, life that was seen to be driving her forward, confidently and purposefully towards a brighter and more prosperous future.

Looking back at the nineteen-sixties it is easy to understand the euphoria exhibited in much of the economic and social commentary produced in that period. In Ireland the fifties had been a truly traumatic decade, full of gloom and despondency. The year 1958, however, saw the inauguration of a new development strategy which was to drive the economy through fifteen years of unprecedented growth. By the middle of the following decade the strategy had worked enough of an impact to convince commentators that the bad old days were over; a decisive turning point seemed to have been reached, and, what is more, passed successfully. A new Ireland was seen to be emerging, self-confident, ambitious and in total contrast to what had gone before. Traditional Ireland was seen to be dead, and an 'authentically Irish, Catholic Nationalist aspiration to social and economic improvement' has been liberated from its constraining ideologies (Brown, 1985, p. 246). This aspiration found its ultimate expression in the Prime Minister of the day, Sean Lemass, the man who called forth a new breed of entrepreneurs and managers to 'the centre of the Irish stage' with a view to unleashing a new dynamism in Irish social and economic life (Brown, 1985, p. 247). Lemass's call was warranted, indeed necessitated, by Irish economic and social conditions. In driving for development Ireland opted for the free enterprise route. In consequence she could only achieve that goal through the agency of development-appropriate entrepreneurial conduct.

All this, of course, prompts the question: In what do patterns of entrepreneurial conduct that are appropriate to development consist? Joseph Schumpeter (1934) helps to provide the beginnings of an answer to this question, at least in general terms. Schumpeter saw the entrepreneur as playing a vital role in the process of economic development. To his view entrepreneurs were innovators who were decisive precisely because they were the engineers of economic change. Five types of innovation were identified and predicated to the entrepreneur by Schumpeter: the introduction of new products and/or the improvement of existing ones; the introduction of new processes; the opening-up of new markets (not least export markets); the identification of new sources of supply; and the development of more efficient organisation.

Schumpeter's list of entrepreneurial functions does not, however, seem complete. We say this because economic activity carries risks and because enterprises need management. From this it follows that, for our purposes at any rate, entrepreneurship must be considered also in relation to the functions of uncertainty-bearing and management - whether and to what extent these are embodied in the person of the entrepreneur and/or whether the entrepreneur simply coordinates them in others is not germane to our purposes here. What is relevant is the observation that the economic development of countries like Ireland depends on a supply of highly committed innovators, risk-bearers and managers who orient their efforts towards the generation of the self-sustaining economic growth which the achievement of economic development requires.

Applied to the particularities of the Irish situation, the general specifications just outlined provide a standard for the comparison and measurement of the reality of Irish entrepreneurial activity. After all Industrial development *via* the private enterprise, free market route was the principal item on the agenda of those who sought to foster Ireland's new dispensation; existing industry was to be expanded, and new industries, native and foreign, were to be established as the engines that would drive the economy forward to prosperity. Given the emphasis on private enterprise, the new breed of entrepreneurs and managers were clearly going to have to take the leading roles in the modernisation drama;

these were to be the men and women of destiny, upon whose commitment, dynamism and drive, and upon whose willingness to undertake the burdens of leadership, grasp opportunities and accept risks and challenges, the promises of the new dispensation were to depend for their fulfilment. Irish entrepreneurs were not, however, expected to march to their destiny alone; government was to assist them by providing a climate for enterprise, a greatly expanded opportunity structure and a generous package of grant incentives and tax breaks designed to attract foreign direct investment and to help Irish entrepreneurs to face the challenges that would inevitably result from the widening of the opportunity struture through free trade. Free trade was an essential element in the Irish development strategy, and it had to be; the Irish home market was too small to provide a base for industrial expansion in the tariff-walled cocoon that had been around it since the nineteen-thirties. Access to wider markets had to be achieved, and was, in stages, as Ireland first concluded a free trade agreement with Britain and later, in 1971, joined what was then the European Economic Community. In the process a whole new world of opportunities was opened to Irish entrepreneurs; they could now grow their businesses by exporting into the British and European markets aided by an extensive package of grant and tax incentives. With the opportunities, of course, came the challenge; Irish entrepreneurs had to 'get stuck in' to the internationally-traded goods and services sectors; they had to learn to compete in export markets, and, indeed, in their own hitherto protected home markets for traded goods and services which were now open to foreign competition. If members of the Irish entrepreneurial establishment were willing and able to meet these challenges, if, *a la* Schumpeter, they were capable of innovating in the product and organisational fields, of opening up new markets, and, in a wider sense, of exhibiting a willingness to work, to manage effectively and to accept risks, then they would be able to contribute to the development and modernisation of their economy and society. That is clearly what Lemass and the development strategists were calling on them to do. It is now time to see whether and to what extent they were willing to answer the call.

The Challenge of development: the general nature of the entrepreneurial response

There is some evidence to suggest that, by the nineteen-seventies, Ireland had grown a small crop of entrepreneurs who measured up well to the Schumpeterian standards outlined in the introduction to this chapter. These individuals were evidently committed to growing their companies; they were interested in the achievement of industrial development and were proud of the parts they saw themselves as playing in the process of bringing it about. People like these were quite willing to speak about their ideals and about the situation which they saw themselves as confronting, and their comments provide a valuable source of evidence as to the 'quality' of Irsh entrepreneurial behaviour in general. Consider, for example, the following remarks addressed to a researcher in the early nineteen-seventies a decade or so into the so called 'new era':

> In most towns you go to in Ireland, particularly rural Ireland, you
> get a shopkeeping class who are very adept at merchandising ... they
> are very competent people, they are well educated, they have
> financial resources. There is the paradox ... you can go into several
> of these small towns in depressed areas .... Now Ballinrobe is a
> small town, about 2,000 people, and for their size they are said to
> have the largest amount of deposits ... in Ireland, and there are three
> banks there: and yet there is no big industry, and there is no
> development, and there is absolutely no work ... and these funds in
> the town are being used to build offices in Grafton Street [Dublin]
> or perhaps even in Drogheda (quoted in Fogarty, 1973, p. 45).

Thus speaks a dynamic Irish entrepreneur who has an interest in industrial
development. And his frustrated comments hardly suggest that he sees
much new dynamism about in the Ireland of the early seventies. There is
no shortage of capital, education and ability - but as to the new
dynamism? He clearly finds that curiously confined and not much
manifest in the realms of productive industry.

Observations like those of the entrepreneur just quoted are accurate,
though they need qualification to this extent at least: If the shopkeeping
classes did well out of property, a new class of politically-dependent
capitalists did a lot better. This new class was a distinct product of the
new era and its members exhibited much of the dynamism that
commentators hoped would be a feature of that era. Its dynamism was,
however, concentrated almost exclusively on property development and
the construction industry, much of its activity being predicated on the
exploitation of relationships with the *Fianna Fail* party, whose ministers
'were anxious to fix things for their friends' (McDonald, 1985, p. 11).
McDonald (1985, p. 36) describes the situation well, with reference to the
case of one developer, though his remarks apply to many of them:

> [A.B's] close relationship with Fianna Fail politicians was well
> known. Notable among these was Charles J. Haughey [the future
> Prime Minister], who obtained his first cabinet post as Minister for
> Justice in 1961. Haughey had married the daughter of Sean
> Lemass; he was a chartered accountant by profession, in which
> career he had been immensely successful prior to his entry to the
> political field. Along with Harry Boland, who would later become
> secretary of TACA, the notorious Fianna Fail fund raising group, he
> established the firm of Haughey Boland and Company, with offices
> at 61 Amiens Street. Many new companies set up during the Lemass
> boom thought it worthwhile to hire Haughey Boland and Co. as
> their accountants, and throughout the past two decades, the firm has
> looked after the affairs of a staggering number of companies, many
> of them in the property field.

What McDonald calls 'a charmed circle of young men on the make'
(1985, p. 38) emerged and built on their political connections with

successive *Fianna Fail* governments; deals were arranged; planning permission secured - often through the Minister for Local Government overturning Local Authority decisions to refuse planning consent; above all the government itself rented some seventy-five per cent of the new office space developed in Dublin in the twenty years or so after 1961, and thus underwrote the property boom that changed the face of Ireland's capital (McDonald, 1985, p. 36). The government could, of course, have built its own office space. It could, as a more economical expedient, have renovated the buildings it already occupied. It did not need to generate a boom out of which private entrepreneurs, often linked to it by ties of personal and political friendship, would benefit massively at the taxpayers' expense. And boom there was: Between 1962 and 1982 5,969,600 square feet of office space was completed in Dublin alone, and mean rents in the city rose from £1 per square foot in 1966 to £8.25 per square foot in 1982 (Bradley, 1983, pp. 35,39). During the sixties most of the development was undertaken by Irish entrepreneurs, though they were joined in the seventies by U.K. based operators who wished to 'cash in' on the Dublin boom; rental levels were higher than anywhere else except London; there was no capital gains tax; the government was renting the preponderance of the space coming onto the market, taking most of the speculative element out of building; so, in all, there was more than enough for both the natives and the immigrants.

When viewed in the light of the development needs of an economy like Ireland's, office building, while not an entirely useless activity, has one major drawback: Investment in it does not generate the self-sustaining economic growth that would follow from successful investment in the production of internationally-traded goods and services. When it comes to investment in the development of traded goods and services production, however, the Irish entrepreneurial establishment has shown little of the dynamism exhibited in its enthusiastic attack on the opportunities that were available in the property field; when the attractiveness of property speculation waned, many of its members turned their attention to investing in government gilt, and so made money by financing the massively increasing government debt, much of which accrued through the financing of the tax breaks and grants that were used to attract the foreign direct investment on which Ireland, thanks to the failure of its own entrepreneurs, has had to rely for so much of its recent industrial development - at present some eighty per cent of the country's non-food manufacturing exports are accounted for by the activities of foreign-owned enterprises. Elements in the Irish entrepreneurial establishment have thus been enabled to profit massively from the economic development that has taken place since the nineteen-sixties, and to do so, moreover, while undertaking few of the burdens and risks involved.

This may seem a harsh judgement, and no doubt it is a harsh judgement. Nevertheless, a moment or two's reflection on the facts of the situation - and the evidence to be presented below - will do much to bear it out. Irish economic development has been heavily underwritten by government expenditure which has to be financed through taxation and through the high levels of government borrowing. Government expenditure here falls under three broad heads: first, expenditure directed to providing the needs of its own administration, i.e. the office development noted above; second, expenditure on much needed improvements in the country's infrastructure; and finally, expenditure on financing the grants and tax breaks which are designed to encourage private sector investment in industrial production. All this expenditure provided the native entrepreneurial establishment with a rash of profit opportunities, both directly and indirectly. Direct opportunities resulted from the construction and leasing of office blocks, construction work on the infrastructure, the supply of building materials and construction equipment, and associated design and technical services; a pool of potential profits from which property and land speculators, building firms, importers, wholesalers, plant hire operators, building material suppliers (non-traders) and self-employed professionals (architects etc.) could, and did, drink freely. Indirect opportunities resulted from the employment created as a result of this public expenditure and also from the private investment which much of that expenditure was used to subsidise; this created a greatly expanded consumer demand, not least for services and consumer goods many of which were imported, and so gave rise to a second pool from which publicans, eating-house proprietors, importers, wholesalers, retailers, leisure and travel companies, local non-traders, builders, building suppliers, land speculators and self-employed professionals were again able to quench their thirst for profits. There is, of course, a development chain evident here through which wealth and jobs were created, and this much we are not denying; expansion in the private enterprise services sector did create wealth and jobs. The point is, of course, that the demand on which the expansion in services fed resulted from government investment and from government subsidised investment in the secondary sector, dominated by the activities of grant and tax subsidised multinationals, whose activities were responsible for so much of the growth in the economy. Operating as they did in the internationally-traded goods and services sectors the multinationals took most of the risks associated with Irish economic growth, or rather the Irish taxpayers, who had to·finance the grant and tax incentives needed to attract the multinationals, did. In avoiding the traded sectors the Irish entrepreneurial establishment avoided many of the risks and burdens associated with development, but they 'cleaned up' on the basis of the wealth created by those who financed most of the risky activity, namely, the taxpayers, by expanding services and by investing in government gilt to fund, and profit from, the massive borrowing which the state was compelled to engage in. While the Irish entrepreneurial establishment profited massively from development, therefore, they did very little to generate the growth on which the development was based, and from which, of course, their profits were derived, and paid less than their share of the costs involved - as we shall see the Irish, excepting the 'broad masses of the workers' whose earnings are taxed on a pay as you earn basis, are ardent tax avoiders.

If anyone doubts the veracity of this 'unhappy' conclusion, they will have to consider the evidence that bears on the point. It is quite unequivocal:

The major weakness of Irish indigenous industry is its poor ability to compete in internationally traded, high value-added industries. This is seen in the marked (and increasing) degree of concentration of indigenous firms in non-traded industries, low value-added basic processing industries, and in a limited range of trading activities with low barriers to entry which will probably become increasingly liable to low-wage competition from newly industrialising countries. This confinement to such a limited range of activities has constrained the development of indigenous industry quite severely, resulting in no net contribution to employment creation and little contribution to export development (O'Malley, 1985, p. 54).

Written as it was in 1985, this passage describes the situation that prevailed two and half decades after the date at which Ireland was supposed to have entered into its new era under the enlightened and dynamic direction of its 'new breed of entrepreneurs and managers'. These had clearly shown no disposition to take on the challenges of the new era at all, with indigenous industry making no net contribution to either job creation or export development. It is true, of course, that Irish entrepreneurs made money from speculation and from the other activities described above. It is now time to see in more detail how they made their money, and to show, more especially, the 'spirit' that animated their money-making activities.

In factories, offices and places where they work

Given the somewhat negative tenor of the preceding section we need to remember that some Irish entrepreneurs did try to measure up to the challenge of the new era. As we have seen these entrepreneurs were willing to wax critical of the entrepreneurial establishment to which they belonged; the shopkeeping property developers of Ballinrobe, to remember, being the first case in point. Development-oriented entrepreneurs who spoke out, however, did not confine their criticism to shopkeeping property developers; people involved in industry also came under their critical hammer because far too many of them were seen to be happy to make 'a nice, neat little profit ... without much growth' (quoted in Fogarty, 1973, p, 67), or to exhibit the sort of stupid complacency described, and condemned, by the textile manager:

> who explained how efforts to rationalise his branch of the trade, specialise firms' production, and so build up stronger units in the face of growing overseas competition collapsed through firms' reluctance to contract out of even marginally profitable markets, to miss short-term gains, or to accept a sober assessment of the long-term possibilities of their markets as protection disappeared (Fogarty, 1973, p. 55).

The slaughter of native Irish industry that accompanied the dismantling of protection is easy to understand against the background of the

30

complacency and 'short-termism' exhibited in these comments from the 1970s. And the evidence suggests that it was all too typical of the Irish entrepreneurial establishment:

> Another unresolved problem was the comparative failure of indigenous private enterprise to respond to the incentives which proved so successful in attracting foreign enterprise. This failure threatened large job losses once protection of the home market was progressively dismantled. Indeed the figures on industrial job losses were already beginning to mount in the early 70s offsetting much of the gain in employment in new enterprises (Kennedy, Giblin and McHugh, 1988, p. 72).

The comparative failure referred to here is understandable enough when considered against the background of evidence touching on three crucial aspects of the entrepreneurial situation: Firstly, evidence concerning the vital area of investment in research and development. Secondly, evidence which speaks to the topic of commitment levels. Thirdly, evidence relating to what, for want of a better expression, we shall refer to as the moral sphere. It is through examining these issues in some detail that we shall be able to form some impression of the spirit of Irish entrepreneurship.

When measured against international standards and/or the development needs of the economy, Irish industry's research and development record is a poor one. Irish investment under this vital head ranked among the lowest of any OECD country at the beginning of the nineteen-seventies (Cooper and Whelan, 1973), and constant monitoring throughout the decade indicated no sign of an improvement (Murphy and O'Brolchain, 1971; Murphy and Fitzgerald, 1973; Murphy and O'Luanaig, 1975; Maguire, 1979). In 1975 Irish expenditure on research and development was running at about one-quarter of the EEC average and at about one-sixth of that prevailing in the US. (O'Farrell, 1986, p. 16). This is not an impressive picture. Yet the stark truth is that Irish industry's expenditure on research and development during the nineteen-seventies grew substantially more slowly than the volume of output, so the situation actually represented a decline in research and development intensity on an already low base (Kennedy, Giblin and McHugh, 1988, p. 245). Some of the reasons for this situation, and its consequences for Irish economic development, are attested to by Kennedy, Giblin and McHugh, when they remark (1988, p. 261) that:

> The prospect of developing a large food processing industry was hampered by, among other things, the unwillingness of the farmers who controlled the processing co-operatives to forego any short-term advantage on the price of their products with the result that the co-operatives were starved of development funds..

Statements like the one just quoted are suggestive. If nothing else they point to the possibility that development is being hindered by an entrepreneurial orientation towards productive activity which sees it, not as means to the end of longer-term growth and development, but rather as a source of income to be maximised in the short-term and expended for non-productive purposes. In all this points to a second, and more general, possibility: namely, that productive activity may be valued below non-productive activity, and that commitment to the former may be scaled down in order to maximise the value in the latter. Perhaps this is why so many Irish entrepreneurs were satisfied with 'a nice, neat little profit ... without much growth'.

Available evidence that touches on commitment levels and the moral sphere lends support to the proposition that many Irish entrepreneurs are not as committed to business development as they might be. According to Fogarty (1973, p. 98), for example,

> A man with an interest in a number of small businesses would still like many of the people he deals with "to be there in the morning before a quarter past ten", and to keep their lunch break to something shorter than 12.30 to 2.30:
> O.K. they want to work a five-hour day: don't spread it over eight or nine hours and hold everybody else up as well.

A business man who had returned to Ireland after gaining his early business experience in Britain had some particularly scathing comments to make about the attitudes and practices of those with whom he had to deal in the course of the conduct of his Irish operations:

> I have been rather horrified in fact, since I came back to Ireland, at the low moral values here. I am not speaking of sexual matters, I mean generally. People make appointments which they do not keep, which, in fact, they make glibly with no intention of keeping. Business people will make promises which they can't keep, and they seem to think that they are doing you a favour by making the promises, that this is as far as they are expected to go. What I would call the Protestant work ethic is badly needed here .... I wonder if it is based on religion, or upon the education they have got which is so religious here? .... That is why Ireland needs the North [Northern Ireland] like a sore needs an antiseptic (quoted in Fogarty, 1973, p. 97).

The reference to Northern Ireland - and to the Protestant work ethic, of which more anon - is interesting in that it points to one of the cultural variables which we shall be examining in later chapters. And the individual who made these comments is not alone in comparing business standards in Northern and Southern Ireland in a way that does little to flatter the Southern Irish entrepreneurial community:

> We're very close to the border here, you know, and there are some very good business people across in the North ... They got into a lot of new ideas ... I think they're harder workers anyway .... You know around here we're moving a lot earlier than people in other parts of the country, we start work a lot earlier ... and put more

effort into the day too. I'd say it's a lot of influence too from people coming across the border ... Living as close to competition, we've only got to make one slip at all and we're lost: there's no restriction against stuff coming across the border (quoted in Fogarty, 1973, p. 89).

Like it or not, comments like these suggest that the rather easy-going and lax attitudes they describe are widespread throughout the Southern Irish business world - if more morally effective and committed entrepreneurs operated in the South, their competition would either force the lackadaisical ones out of their lethargy or out of business altogether. That moral laxity and easy-going attitudes to work and to business are indeed widespread is confirmed by Professor Michael Fogarty, whose comments on his interviews with entrepreneurs were reported in Chapter 1, and are worth repeating here:

One of the most disturbing features of these interviews was how often informants came back to the thesis that what families, schools, the Church, the social system and the business system itself have failed to produce in Ireland is people with the basic virtues of honesty, integrity and hard and purposeful work. (1973, pp. 96-7).

It is, of course, true that the evidence we have culled from Fogarty's interviews refers to a situation that prevailed in the early nineteen-seventies. We should not, however, jump to any hasty conclusions about the extent to which Irish entrepreneurship may have changed in the interim. Complaints about the absence of honesty, integrity and hard and purposeful work are not lacking in the nineteen-eighties (O'Farrell, 1986, p. 160). And neither is a considerable body of evidence that forces us to conclude that continuity, rather then change, is the order of the day in Irish entrepreneurial circles.

In this conclusion we are supported by an erstwhile director of the Irish Management Institute, Brian Patterson, who, in the course of many years involvement in the education of Irish managers, came to the conclusion that, 'while some Irish management teams are second to none ... the other end of the spectrum is appalling' (quoted in O'Toole, 1987). There are a small group, he went on say, who are international in outlook, but there are far too many who retain the view that 'the home market will do well enough'. The Irish home market is similar in size to Lancashire. So Patterson wants to know: 'What kind of company would say that they were going to satisfy the Lancashire market?' Clearly the answer must be: not one that cherished any kind of expansionist ambition that was worth talking about. Given all this, the fact that eighty per cent of 'Irish' manufacturing exports in the non-food sectors are the products of foreign owned firms should come as no surprise.

Many of Ireland's good managers are, it has to be said, running companies which are none-traders. Since their virility symbols consist in expansion through the acquisition of foreign-based non-traders, rather than in diversification into the Irish-based production of internationally-traded goods and services, their contribution to Irish economic development is somewhat limited. Much the same can be said of other large Irish companies who operate in traded sectors; too often these confine their activities to low value-added basic commodity processing; according to the Industrial Development Authority their investment in new products and in research and development continues to date to be low by international standards and when set against the development needs of the economy (Bell, 1987); their failure to take advantage of the opportunities offered through grants, tax incentives and access to new markets continues to be 'a major factor inhibiting Irish industrialisation' (Kennedy, Giblin and McHugh, 1988, p. 214).

Generally speaking the records of smaller Irish companies are no better than those of their larger counterparts; in the view of a leading Irish investment banker they set their sights below their full potential for expansion; they are not vigorous enough in analysing markets or the competition; they are not effective enough in overcoming production and marketing problems that cost them profitable opportunities for growth (Lattimore, 1989). The Industrial Development Authority confirms these views; notwithstanding an impressive package of grant and tax incentives only one-third of IDA supported small companies employ more than ten people, a fact which 'points to absence of an international outlook ... characterised particularly by a lack of investment in new products for export markets' (IDA, 1986, p. 14).

With reference to the orientations and activities of Irish entrepreneurs, therefore, history does seem to be repeating itself. This seems to be especially true with reference to the coming of the Single European Market in 1992. For example, in commenting on a survey of small and medium sized companies' preparedness for the increased opportunities, and competition, that will come in 1993, Downes (1991) reported that:

> Small companies in Ireland are optimistic about the future of their companies with the approach of the Single European Market in 1992, but they do not think it relevant to prepare for it.

This is a situation which Mary Bennett, President of the Chambers of Commerce of Ireland, finds 'very alarming' (quoted in Downes, 1991), and which Paul Skehan, a director of the same organisation, finds disturbing; Irish firms were making assumptions about the Single Market without having any real knowledge of the subject; only seven per cent of the companies in the survey described their state of awareness of the market as 'detailed and very specific' (Downes, 1991). The reasons for the sense of alarm and disturbance revealed here are not far to seek; the Single Market could create bigger problems for Ireland than for any other member of the EC; the advent of the Channel tunnel will place the country at a distinct disadvantage, making it the only European state not directly connected to the mainland. It is interesting to note in this connection that when asked about the major constraints impeding their capacity to export, fifty-four per cent of the companies taking part in the Chambers of Commerce survey mentioned the cost of travel to European markets, fifty-three per cent mentioned transport costs, forty-seven per cent communication costs and forty-five per cent distribution costs. Yet seventy-one per cent of the companies asked did not see any advantage in entering into joint marketing and distribution agreements with other Irish companies, agreements which could hardly fail to have a significant positive impact on relieving the cost impediments they identified (Downes, 1991). The complacency and failure to reorganise in the face of changing conditions which the textile manager complained about in the early seventies are evidently still very much a feature of Irish entrepreneurial life in the nineties.

If we pause to consider the evidence presented so far it seems impossible to do other than conclude that Irish entrepreneurs have not, in the main, answered Lemass's call. On the whole the picture that emerges from a review of their practices and performance is one that leaves the impression of an easy-going, complacent entrepreneurial community, too many of whose members are content with a neat little profit made on the home market, and too few of whom are interested in taking on the challenge of developing new products for new markets in the internationally-traded goods and services sectors. As in the seventies, therefore, frustration continues to be the lot of the growth-oriented entrepreneur, as this exasperated outburst from a leading Irish entrepreneur, Fergal Quinn, demonstrates:

> Anyone with drive, with a truly innovative or entrepreneurial spirit cannot fail to be dragged down by the sheer torpor that characterises our society .... All of [which] reminds me of the Spaniard who asked the Celtic scholar if the concept of *manana* existed in Irish and was told: "We have nothing with quite the same sense of urgency" (quoted in Kerr, 1986).

The story about the Spaniard and the Celtic scholar is an old one, and no doubt apocryphal. Nevertheless, the fact that a leading Irish entrepreneur was driven to using it in 1986 to make a point about the business community of which he is a member confirms that Ireland is not blessed with an abundance of energetic, dynamic and committed entrepreneurs. Lemass may have issued his clarion call. Evidently few have chosen to answer it.

Meanwhile, down on the farm

Ireland's agricultural resources are considerable; there are almost seven million hectares of available land, forty-five per cent of which can be considered good farming land. Over ninety per cent of farms are owner occupied, and on very favourable terms; there is no land tax; the rates once levied on agricultural land were abolished when the Irish Supreme Court decided that they amounted to an unconstitutional attack on property. Agriculture remains Ireland's most important industry, accounting for over ten per cent of GNP and for over £3,000 million worth of exports, over a fifth of Ireland's total exports (Roche, 1989, p. 9). It is also significant in another respect; the food processing industry is unique among the major manufacturing sectors in that it is still overwhelmingly in Irish ownership and control. In contrast, the country's other major export earners - pharmaceutical, computer equipment and mechanical engineering - are almost exclusively foreign-owned (Roche, 1989, p. 9).

Since the nineteenth century Irish agriculture has become increasingly oriented to an extensive grass based production of beef and dairy products, being characterised by high levels of seasonality in production and inefficient resource use. Observers have long been struck by the easy-going attitude which Irish farmers adopt towards the productive resources at their disposal:

> Irish grass farming mainly consists in this, that Heaven causes the sun to shine and the rain to fall, and that Man sends the cattle to the pasture and gives himself no further trouble about them (Bonn, 1906, p. 38).

The quality of the resources available to Irish agriculture producers are eloquently described by Mr. G.A. Holmes, a New Zealand grassland expert:

> Let me say, first of all, that there is no area of comparable size in the northern hemisphere which has such marvelous potentialities for pasture production as Eire undoubtedly has. The depth of loam in the plains and valleys, the abundance of limestone, the normally mild winter, and the reliability and distribution of the summer rainfall combine to make ideal natural conditions for growing grass and for raising and fattening livestock. In 8 of the 26 counties I have seen old permanent pastures with a density, colour, composition, and grazing capacity superior to anything in western Europe, their quality being proved by the excellence of the cattle on them. In some of the same counties, and in all the others which I visited, I saw hundreds of fields which are growing just as little as it is physically possible for the land to grow under an Irish sky (Holmes, 1949, p. 8).

Holmes cannot, it seems, resist inserting a sting in the tail of his remarks; the quality of the resources is second to none, the quality of their use, evidently, leaves something to be desired.

From this evidence it would seem that down on the farm Irish entrepreneurs are just as easy-going as their counterparts in other sectors of the economy. The evidence presented to this point thus far is, of course, historical, but there is every reason to suspect that continuity, rather than change, is as much the order of the day in agriculture as it is elsewhere. An agricultural processor, thoroughly familiar with the farming community and its ways, commented scathingly in the nineteen-seventies:

> It is quite difficult sometimes to convince a farmer who has about fifteen productive hours in a week that it doesn't rate a forty hour salary .... Any fellow who will put in forty productive hours on a

farm will have in excess of any industrial worker, but most are only doing about a quarter to a third of a week's work. They take seventy hours doing it, but that's only beside the point (quoted in Fogarty, 1973, p. 98).

After all, as another critic observed,

The farmer has inherited his land, and therefore his capital is zero. He makes enough to live on, and he says his prayers, and it's beat into him every Sunday that he needn't give a damn about this life, it's the next one he's going to (quoted in Fogarty, 1973, p. 98).

Comments like these point ineluctably to the failure of Irish farmers to exploit effectively the valuable natural resources available to them. They also, rather obviously, suggest that attitudes to business are somewhat lacking in terms of the cultivation of any ambition that is directed towards growth and development. This is a situation which the price and income increases consequent upon Ireland's membership of the European community might have been expected to remedy. The years following the country's accession to EC membership were boom years for Irish agriculture; the switch from the low-priced UK market to the high-priced EC market resulted in a forty-five per cent increase in real prices received by farmers between 1971 and 1978, and farm incomes rose by over 400 per cent (seventy-two per cent in real terms) over the same period; land prices rose from about £100 per acre in the nineteen-fifties to £4,600 per acre in the middle nineteen-seventies - this was higher than the price of land in The Netherlands with its vastly more productive agriculture (Coogan, 1987, pp. 142-4). Increases in prices and incomes of the magnitude described might have been expected to bring about a significant change in the productivity of the resources employed in Irish agriculture. In all, however, their impact does not appear to have been too inspiring:

It is depressing at times to see the vast amount of land that is wasted in Ireland. Rushes and bushes grow wild on fields, where, with a bit of care and attention, these are easily controlled. Often, such owners are clamouring for more land. Applying fertilisers would improve the grass and provide not alone good grazing, but good quality food which would reduce greatly the cost of buying expensive feedstuffs in winter (Cullen, 1988).

From this last observation it is obvious that, even in the late nineteen-eighties, many farmers still had a very lax attitude towards their land and businesses; they did not treat the land well; areas of grass were starved of lime and fertilisers in places where their application would allow for a near doubling of the stocking rate (Cullen, 1988). Attitudes to planning are also somewhat lax, notwithstanding the grant incentives that are available and the fact that, for some farmers, it is a requirement of the farm modernisation scheme; for every farmer that is planned, evidently, there are two or more who are not planning or who are only minimally planning (Sheehy, 1978). After all this the findings of the National Farm

Surveys conducted by the Rural Economy Research Centre, as summarised by Boyle (1987, p. 4) should come as no surprise; quite simply it reports 'that the average farm in the National Farm Survey sample is reckoned to be operating at a level of technical efficiency which is 40 per cent below "best practice"'.

There are, however, other significant senses in which Irish farmers fall below what their customers, and even the law, might regard as 'best practice'. Here, for the first time, we confront in detail what we referred to earlier as the moral aspect of Irish entrepreneurship. For example, the farmers have been warned that the use of illegal hormones, growth promoters and antibiotics could destroy their £2,000 million a year beef industry. This warning was issued by the Irish Veterinary Union (IVU), whose members estimated that up to seventy per cent of cattle slaughtered in meat factories had implants of illegal substances supplied by black market racketeers (Dargan, 1987). These substances appear to be smuggled into Ireland by the truckers who export the meat, to the point at which there is 'a massive black market in hormones which appears [sic] to be readily available' (Ryan, 1988a). It is interesting in this connection to notice that the farmers, instead of abandoning their illegal activities, condemn the veterinarians for 'damaging the industry' by calling attention to them; in the words of one veterinarian 'telling the truth is [it seems] worse than living a lie' (Dargan, 1987). What particularly infuriated the IVU, was the evident failure of the authorities to enforce the law effectively:

> We have no desire to harm the industry by publicity, but we will not accept a situation where we see the law being openly abused and where our members are being asked to turn a blind eye to illegal acts. The buck stops here - which in this case is the stamp of veterinary certification (Flaherty, 1987).

The IVU also attacked the Farmers' Organisations for refusing to condemn the use of implants. They were no less critical of the meat factories, the operators of which appeared to be encouraging farmers to implant while, at the same time, using the 'Green Ireland' image when exporting (Ryan, 1988a).

The enthusiasm of the farmers for cultivating easy profits *via* the employment of illegal substances which could damage their industry contrasts strongly with their failure to remedy animal health conditions, the persistence of which could also put their industry in jeopardy. The failure to eradicate Mastitis is a case in point here; it was estimated, in 1987, to be costing the country £50 million a year, more than £20 per individual cow. In all forty per cent of Irish milk fell below the projected EC Mastitis control standards (Flaherty, 1987).

No other country in the world has such a poor record in eradicating Bovine TB as Ireland (Dillon and McKenna, 1990). This is notwithstanding an eradication programme which cost the state £1 billion between 1954 and 1985 (Coogan, 1987, p. 147). Part of the reason for this failure lies with the traditional cattle production methods employed by Irish farmers; Irish cattle move up to five times in their lives compared to

38

only once in other countries (Dillon and McKenna, 1990) - a situation defended by trade interests who, of course, benefit from the frequent sales which Peter Dargan, the general secretary of the Irish Veterinary Union, claims are a major factor in the failure to stamp out TB and brucellosis (Dooley, 1989). Failure, however, is also due to the exploitation of loopholes in the scheme by unscrupulous farmers. Coogan (1987, p. 148) describes the situation:

(a) The scheme allowed the farmer, not the department [of agriculture] to nominate his own vet; (b) The department paid, not the vet who did the testing, but the practice which employed him. This resulted in a buddy-buddy relationship between the farmer and the man who owned the practice. A tip-off to the farmer that early testing had showed up reaction in his herd enabled him to dispose of it to an unsuspecting customer - a butcher, say, or another farmer - before the follow up testing could be carried out.

With the connivance of unscrupulous vets, therefore, Irish farmers frustrated the eradication of Bovine TB, and did so in the interests of short-term profit and by putting contaminated meat into the human food chain. Long-term costs will, as always, have to be paid; from 1992 it is likely that all reactor meat sold in the EC will have to be heat treated, something that will result in heavy losses to Irish farmers.

It is very difficult to interpret the evidence presented so far as depicting a farming community that is animated by an anti-traditionalistic, development-oriented spirit. On the whole the evidence seems to point in another direction: namely, to low levels of commitment to progressive, productive effort, and what is potentially worse, to a desire to increase incomes by resort to ethically - or at any rate legally - questionable, and potentially very damaging, expedients in preference to raising the effort-efficiency threshold. Short-term greed, combined with a tolerance for a situation which discloses high levels of inefficiency, waste and slovenliness are clearly a very poor basis for modernisation, diversification and for the development of the food industry, which is, of course, ultimately dependent on agriculture.

Development in agriculture and the food industry is, it must be said, also hampered by the farmers in other ways; as we saw above the development of the food industry was frustrated by farmers who sought to maximise their short-term gains by exacting the highest possible price for the milk which they sold to the processing cooperatives which they controlled, thus starving these organisations of funds which were needed for development (Kennedy, Giblin and McHugh, 1988, p. 216). Short-term income was thus maximised at the expense of long-term development, and maximised, what is more, in circumstances in which, as we have seen, real farm incomes had risen substantially due to the higher consumer prices that prevailed after Ireland's accession to the Common Market. In many cases the increased income was used to support high levels of borrowing by individual farmers, who did not always use the borrowed money exclusively for productive investment. In fact, as Coogan (1987, p. 144) puts it: 'Costly home improvements were effected.

The eating-out habit spread and overdrafts mushroomed'. Above all, however, the old habits and business methods persisted. Coogan provides us with a graphic account of these methods, and their consequences:

> The simplest thing to produce on a farm, and the most lucrative, was a bullock. All a farmer had to do was to glance at the beasts every day, take a few elementary precautions such as dosing and ensuring provision of fodder, and he made money. Why bother with the exhausting uncertain business of planting vegetables? If he did bother he often had that ingrained rural Irish attitude that contracts and fixed prices are dangerous snares set by the purchaser to trap the poor producer. If someone offered a better price for his crop, he blithely sold at the eleventh hour, thereby disappointing either a wholesaler or a vegetable processor who might go bankrupt or at least go elsewhere next year. This would leave the farmer with the following year's crop on his hands, and create boom/glut situations in which many farmers washed their hands of vegetable production altogether. As a result a steady tide of Israeli, Cypriot, Dutch, Portugese, Polish and even Canadian and American vegetables found their way into Irish shops and supermarkets. Since the end of the 1970s shoppers have been able to rifle through countless packages of West German and Dutch chips and frozen vegetables in the freezer compartments of Dublin supermarkets without finding any Irish brands (Coogan 1987, pp. 144-5).

Coogan's thoughts here point up the following important issues. Firstly, the over-concentration of Irish farming on the meat and dairying sectors; seventy-five per cent of total production is accounted for by meat and dairy products, and eighty per cent of the acreage devoted to tillage is used for the production of cereals, fifty-nine per cent of which is under feeding barley, showing a high level of tillage-dependence on the meat and dairying sectors (Roche, 1989, pp 11, 79). Secondly, Coogan exhibits the way in which the 'ingrained rural Irish attitude' to contracts at fixed prices has hampered the development of food processing industries which provide markets for the products of a diversified agriculture. All this is important, again, for two reasons. The first of these has to do with the fact that much needed industrial development is hindered, while the second is concerned with the fact that the meat and dairying sectors are acutely dependent on intervention and export subsidies provided under the rubric of the CAP. The Irish current affairs magazine *Hibernia* described the situation graphically, when it responded to a controversy generated by the reporting of Irish Radio and Television's agricultural correspondent. *Hibernia* had this to say:

> Irish farmers were producing beef and dairy products that could not be sold at any price ... the fairy godmother in Brussels was no longer prepared to pay for massive stock-piles that eventually would have to be dumped ... Irish agriculture has been built on false foundations and on false promises. Now the October 1986 cupboard is bare, there is no more money to pay for surplus products. Irish

farming was exposed on national television for what it really is - a massively laid-back lifestyle which has been cushioned and comforted for years, and which now has no hope of getting cash for the bulk 'f its wares (quoted in Coogan, 1987, p. 130).

Fortunat ly for the farmers they have the support of the Irish government, the efforts of which have so far been successful in resisting far reaching reforms of the CAP. For all that, however. *Hibernia's* point is a well taken one. Irish farmers are not, of course, the only ones who depend on the CAP. Nevertheless, the implications of CAP reform are potentially greater for Ireland than for any other EC country for two main reasons: First, because of the importance of agriculture in the economy as a whole; in Ireland it accounts for ten per cent of GNP compared with a European Community average of 3.5 per cent. Secondly, because in 1989 thirty-eight per cent of Irish beef and forty-seven per cent of Irish dairy products were sold in non EC markets. If these exports were deprived of EC price support, i.e. if they had to be sold at world market prices as the US and the Cairns group are demanding through the GATT, Irish farm income would decline by some £900 million per annum, that is it would fall to some forty per cent of its present levels (IFA, 1990, pp. 61-2). The failure to diversify, therefore, means that Irish agriculture is sitting on a time bomb; the stark truth seems to be that it is too dependent for comfort on a price support system which is increasingly coming under attack by forces within and outside of the European Community. If these forces ever prevail Irish agriculture could face a catastrophe.

It is not, of course, only the farmers who are in danger from over-concentration on the meat and dairying sectors; the Irish food processing industry is also vulnerable since the composition of its exports reflects the concentration, a factor which makes it equally dependent upon intervention and EC export subsidies. The problems of the food industry, however, do not end here. For example, the unwillingness of the farmers to remedy the high seasonality of primary production (with a peak-valley trough of 14:1 as against an EC norm of 2:1) has militated against the development and marketing of profitable high value-added food products with short shelf lives that are vital to the development of an effective food industry (Kennedy, Giblin and McHugh, 1988, p. 261). Bad business methods have also hindered progress on this front. Not for the first time Coogan (1987, p. 145) points to the customer-alienating activities of some vegetable growing cooperatives:

Potatoes, for example, were (and often still are) sold in sacks made of thick, brown paper. These, when opened revealed muddy, ungraded potatoes. Often under a layer of large tubers, were many small ones which ought to have been fed to pigs. The European counterpart was and is made of mesh or plastic, so that the shopper can see the properly graded potatoes that are on offer.

Comment on this sort of malpractice seems superfluous. Much more, however, stands to be revealed.

41

Failures, fraud and frolics

Activities like those of the potato producers just described have undoubtedly frustrated the industrial development of Ireland. And they are indicative of the sort of conduct which has provoked progressive, developmentally-minded entrepreneurs to complain about the low standards of quality, reliability and honesty which they saw as all too prevalent in Ireland (see Fogarty, 1973, pp. 81, 89-91, 97-100; Gorman and Molloy, 1972, p. 90; O'Farrell, 1986, p. 160). Thus a textile manufacturer admitted to Fogarty that unreliability had left 'a trail of disaster' behind it in an export market (1973, p. 80); while an agricultural processor complained:

> We still have to live down the total dishonesty of those who sold meat in England ... the bad quality ... heifers sold, bought and delivered genuinely for three weeks, and then the cows ... and ... any trick of the loop work (quoted in Fogarty, 1973, p. 90).

Researchers have been struck by the adverse comments of foreign customers about the 'variable quality', 'lack of consistency' and 'unreliability of supply' of Irish beef exports (McKinsey, 1977, p. 33). In the words of one export customer: 'The Irish industry was not particularly careful in meeting the product specifications of the various markets involved' (quoted in IDA, 1977, p. 69). According to the same source (IDA, 1977, p. 70) the trading standards of Irish suppliers were evidently 'consistently poor', something that did nothing to enhance the possibilities of developing the food industry. That quality continues to be a problem in food, and in industry more generally, is not difficult to demonstrate; the chief executive of the Irish Quality Control Association reported, in 1987, that the beef industry still had a long way to go and stated that seventy per cent of the food firms and manufacturing companies who applied for the Association's 'Quality Mark' in 1986 - twenty-six years into the new era - failed to meet the required specifications (quoted in Mulligan, 1987); surveys carried out in 1986 and 1988 confirmed that Irish lamb had a poor reputation for quality in its principal export market (Ryan, 1988b); a leading Irish businessman, Denis Brosnan, opined that, in tourism, Irishness was 'the antithesis of quality' (quoted in Donohoe, 1986). In all Irish industry was said to be losing £910 million a year because it was not exercising adequate quality control, a loss which the investment of a mere £70 million would evidently have reduced by more than fifty per cent (Reynolds, 1987).

The additional evidence presented in this section shows that the activities of the Irish entrepreneurial establishment are damaging to development, not only because they involve insufficient attention to the development of new products and markets, but because they allow for existing markets to be inadequately serviced with respect to standards of quality and reliability. While some of the problems here are due to lack of experience and effective quality management, it is hard to avoid the conclusion that many are due to deliberate unscrupulousness and thus touch directly on what we referred to earlier as the moral aspect of entrepreneurship in Ireland. The example of the heifers cited above was one instance of unscrupulous dishonesty and fraud. It is, as we shall now show, by no means an isolated case.

The range of ethically irregular activities engaged in by members of the Irish entrepreneurial community is as long and complex as its effects are often damaging. For example:

> For years the existence of a significant number of local abbatoirs who neither respect hygiene or veterinary regulations nor pay associated levies, undermined the efforts of licensed slaughterhouses to compete effectively on home and export markets (Jordan, 1988).

Another instance of the damage caused by unscrupulousness is provided by the bakery industry. Here illegal bakeries, who violate planning, tax and health laws, have captured twenty per cent of the Irish confectionery market. As a result twenty-two legitimate bakeries went out of business between 1985 and 1987 (Howick, 1987).

Sources in the Irish furniture industry claim that many shops refuse to buy from manufacturers unless they get the products VAT free; they do all their business in cash. As a result manufacturers who want to avoid building up a store of illegal cash have to obtain their supplies VAT free, and since this cannot always be done, end up, sooner or later, having to 'cook the books' (McAlease, 1983). One furniture manufacturer expressed surprise that the tax authorities did not move in on evasion: 'in this industry everyone knows when you pass wind, it is fairly clear who is doing it and where the furniture is going' (quoted in McAlease, 1983). Tax evasion is also widespread in the bloodstock, clothing and building industries (McAlease, 1983).

In all only 33.1 per cent of Irish employers pay the income tax they collect from their employees under PAYE into the tax authorities on time, and only twenty-four per cent of traders are punctual in paying in the VAT which they collect from their customers - the comparable British figures are ninety-five per cent and sixty per cent respectively (ITOU, 1987). When one discovers that thirty-one per cent of employers and thirty-six per cent of traders still have not met their liabilities after six months, it becomes obvious that unscrupulous Irish business people are using the tax authorities - and the employees and customers from whom they collect the tax which they should have passed on - as sources of working capital (ITOU, 1987). The unfortunate Revenue Commissioners - and the taxpayers - have become, in effect, Ireland's newest bank, making interest-free loans to unscrupulous business people; although interest is formally charged on arrears only about one-eighth of it is actually paid (ITOU, 1987).

Tax evasion in Ireland has reached chronic proportions; it has arrived at the point where 'only mugs pay their taxes', and at which tax officials suspect that the government's manifest unwillingness to deal with the problem is conditioned by the fact that many of the biggest evaders are leading supporters of the political parties (McAlease, 1983; ITOU, 1987). The general situation is well described in a report from a Parliamentary Committee of Enquiry:

Businesses which have tried to observe the law have been decimated e.g. hotel, electrical retailers and motor trade etc. In some cases they have been forced out of business by the activity of unscrupulous competitors who ignore their VAT or declare only part of their sales transactions .... As the state machinery is ineffective in controlling this form of unfair competition many retailers face the prospect of going out of business or joining the black economy. Retailers are also affected unfairly by competitors who do not officially exist i.e. those who operate retail outlets without incorporating their businesses, registering for VAT; operating the P.A.Y.E./P.R.S.I. for employees or paying tax (*Oireachtas Eareann*, 1984, p. 16).

Between 1979 and 1983 the Special Enquiry Branch of the Revenue Commissioners discovered some 23,000 unregistered businesses - a feat performed by a unit employing only twenty people (*Oireachtas Eareann*, 1984, p. 17). It is, perhaps, not surprising that the *Oireachtas* Committee on Small Business felt 'that the question must be asked as to what would be discovered if greater resources were made available in this area' (*Oireachtas Eareann*, 1984, p. 17). The inference is obvious: given more officials the Special Enquiry Branch would have discovered more than a mere 23,000 unregistered businesses. Revenue Officials often need to be quick as well as numerous to get their hands on unscrupulous operators; in the words of one frustrated tax official 'businesses are opening and closing like lightening to avoid us' (quoted in McAlease, 1983).

Many of those Irish businesses which do register - and which, therefore, exist 'officially' - are shy about submitting annual returns to the company registration authorities, as the law requires them to do. Speaking in 1987 the then Minister of State at the Industry Department described this situation as 'scandalous':

> The data has been inadequate and woefully out of date and this has deprived the business community and the public generally of an essential basic safeguard against abuse (quoted in O'Morain, 1987).

Notwithstanding a promised drive to increase the rate of returns, the situation does not seem to have improved; in 1990 over one-half of the 180,000 registered companies were behind time with their returns - twenty per cent were up to a year behind, while the remainder were three or even four years late with their submissions (Doheny, 1990). As an official at the Companies Registration Office put it, this presumably means that, of the 180,000 Irish companies, 'the majority are not respectable' (Doheny, 1990).

It is quite clear that the easy-going ways of the Irish entrepreneurial community extend beyond the low levels of commitment mentioned earlier; members of that community are evidently quite happy to play fast and loose with the tax authorities and the law - not only breaking the law themselves, but forcing their customers and competitors to do likewise in order to survive competitively. All this was quite clearly facilitated by the Government's somewhat easy-going response to the issues of law enforcement and tax collection; everybody in the furniture industry evidently knows who is doing the evading, but is allowed to go on; the Audit Unit of the Revenue Commissioners - a crack anti-evasion team - was abolished and its members redeployed to other duties, notwithstanding the fact that it had collected £6 million in unpaid tax in 1986 and £10 million in 1987 (Irish Press, 1988); nearly £10 million worth of health contributions owed by farmers were unlikely to be collected, as indeed were large sums of evaded VAT, because the Revenue Commissioners did not, and would evidently not be given, the resources to collect them (Irish Press, 1987).

Unscrupulousness towards the tax authorities is by no means confined to the corporate sectors; individual tax morality among the farmers and the self-employed is also very low. In fact the Irish have been described as 'a nation of tax dodgers' (Halligan, 1986). In 1986, for example, the total assessed as outstanding from all sources amounted to £3,883 million, of which £1,578,000 was accounted for by income tax and £97 million by social insurance charges. In all it was estimated that only £205 million of the income tax and £41 million of the social insurance charges would be collected (ITOU, 1987). Even allowing for excesses in the estimates these figures represent evasion on a massive scale - the total income tax yield for 1987 was £2,721.7 million (ITOU, 1987). Figures like these lend ample justification to the claim that Ireland's 100,000 self-employed people are engaging in fraud on a massive, multi-million pound scale (Buitlear, 1988). They also go some way towards validating the claim that Ireland is suffering from a crisis in morality; from a corruption of public values which has contributed to a crisis in the state's finances (Halligan, 1986). The government's answer to the massive levels of evasion of personal income tax - a system of self-assessment - is, to the views of the tax officials, no solution at all; individuals' self-assessments will, they estimate, be subject to audit once every 50 years, something that amounts to offering tax evaders 'a new bonanza ... a new tax, the PWYW - the pay what you want tax' (quoted in McLoughlin, 1990). Available evidence suggests that these strictures are justified; the first 153 audits on self-assessed returns yielded unpaid taxes of £1,057,000. Unless these audits were carried out on very untypical taxpayers, their results do not auger well for the success of self-assessment.

Whether the Revenue Commissioners were goaded into action by comments like these it is impossible for us to say. Nevertheless, in 1991 they established a small 'hit squad', 'designed to tackle Ireland's tax evaders in a sector by sector blitz' (Nally, 1992). Reports of the squad's activities tell us something about the nature and extent of evasion, not least in the 'pub trade'. This trade accounts for 8.5 per cent of Ireland's GNP; it is famous for its creative accounting, and according to the head of the squad has evaded tax to the tune of £100 million a year since 1988 alone (Nally, 1992). Evasion methods employed in this trade include the following: the sale of alcohol smuggled into the country from Northern Ireland - in the Spring of 1992 500 barrels a week were being smuggled into the West of Ireland alone; deliberately underestimating the number of pints in a keg; the non-reporting of, often considerable, bonuses derived from long-term agreements to sell the products of particular suppliers; the non-reporting of profits derived from free kegs and free gifts from suppliers; and fraud on purchases from wholesalers which are paid for in cash. Several of these evasion tactics are facilitated by the fact that suppliers' and wholesalers' invoices do not identify the publicans being supplied. This makes evasion on free and cash based transactions relatively easy for the publicans concerned. The Revenue squad admit that they do not know how much potential revenue is disappearing *via* cash sales, but it is 'the biggest single scam', constituting 'a trade within a trade'; it is a simple matter for a publican to dip into his till, pay for purchases in cash and keep the entire profit from the subsequent retail sale of the drink (Nally, 1992). Suppliers are now being required to record customers' names on invoices and to provide the Revenue with adequate records as part of a general tightening up of anti-evasion procedures. Large settlements, some for six figure sums, are being reported, and more are expected (Nally, 1992).

Stimulated no doubt by cross-border differentials in taxes and prices and EC payments, smuggling across the border between Northern Ireland and the Republic constitutes a significant, and no doubt profitable, activity for some members of the Irish entrepreneurial establishment. As with all illicit activities it is, of course, impossible to provide exact estimates of the nature and extent of the trade, but it is extensive and covers a wide range of products. As we have seen alcohol figures prominently on the lists of smuggled products, and Irish customs authorities were reported as being privately critical of the Licensed Vintners' Association for not doing enough to control its 'rogue members' (Kelly, 1987). Water is evidently also smuggled *vice* beer; publicans have been sold water by smugglers, instead of beer and stout, though perhaps understandably they have not complained about it to the police or customs authorities (Cork Examiner, 1988b).

According to the Irish Customs Service fuel oil smuggling is a multi-million-pound business, and televisions, videos, microwaves, cookers and other electrical items are also smuggled widely (Beach, 1988; Colley, 1989). Wheat and egg smuggling has also been engaged in, to the detriment of legitimate producers in the Republic of Ireland who can be undercut in their own markets by the lower prices at which the smuggled products are available: in 1987, for example, the Irish Farmers' Association called on the Customs to prosecute millers who handled smuggled grain (Spain, 1987); and egg producers in the Republic were likewise driven to demand a 'clampdown on egg smugglers' (Leitch, 1987). Needless to say cattle also figure prominently in the list of smuggled commodities. Some idea of the extent of this trade can be gathered from the following headlines, chosen randomly from Irish Newspapers in the late nineteen eighties:

'30,000 Cows Smuggled a Week' (*The Sunday Press*, 30 November 1986).

'Dawn Seizure of Smuggled Meat Breaks all Records'
(*Irish Independent*, 23 January 1987).

46

'Customs Seize 1,360 Smuggled Cattle'
(*Irish Independent*, 10 February 1987).

'Cattle Smugglers on the Run' (*Irish Press*, 24 February 1987).

Irish smuggling has, on occasions, been accompanied by a certain amount of unpleasantness between smugglers, their supporters and the police and customs officers. Gun battles have been reported on, at least, two occasions (McArdle, 1987; Beach, 1988); and smugglers were reported to have warned customs' officials that they would 'ride shotgun' to protect their consignments (McArdle, 1987). Farmers have also caused trouble from time to time; on one occasion they mobbed customs officials who were trying to seize 1,800 gallons of smuggled petrol - the customs unit had to be rescued by the police (Evening Herald, 1988). Evidence suggests that meat factory personnel have also been subject to intimidation; fearing reprisals they refused to process cattle seized from smugglers until the Department of Agriculture forced them to do so (Burke, 1987).

The Irish tax authorities are by no means the only victims of the fraudsters in the Irish entrepreneurial establishment; as we have seen, with reference to the cattle trade, customers have also suffered from fraud which the Irish industry has had to live down. Suppliers of white goods and electrical products, among others, are suffering so badly from fraud that four leading white goods and electrical suppliers have had to take special steps to try to remedy the situation. The firms concerned are GEC (which distributes Hotpoint products), Dimpco (which acts for Belling and Hoover), EID (distributors of Electrolux, Zanussi, Tricity and Bendix appliances) and Novum Limited. These companies are concerned about what is known in Ireland as the 'Phoenix syndrome'. As the term 'Phoenix' perhaps implies, this refers to a situation in which the proprietors of limited liability companies run up debts, liquidate their companies to avoid payment, and simply establish a new company unencumbered by any liabilities. A representative of the 'gang of four' describes the situation they are confronting:

> In our business it's a case of caveat vendor, not caveat emptor. It is time we tackled the mavericks. In many cases firms have collapsed with big unpaid debts and the owners have gone on to re-emerge trading in the same business, sometimes in the same premises (quoted in Kiberd, 1988).

The four firms mentioned have suffered so heavily from syndrome operators that they have combined to rationalise their credit control policies, to try to ensure that they do not give

> £500,000 to £1 million credit to a shop which is no more than a leased hole in the wall with an owner who owns nothing but a nail to scratch himself with (quoted in Kiberd, 1988).

The companies do try to avoid supplying those who start up again.

47

However, the fact that their products are distributed through wholesalers sometimes makes this difficult and so works to the advantage of the fraudsters. The Revenue Commissioners and other trade creditors have also lost heavily as a result of the 'phoenix syndrome'; many of those who go bankrupt and start up again also owe the unfortunate Revenue Commissioners large sums of money.

Conclusion

With the 'Phoenix syndrome' we bring our general review of the practices and performance of the Irish entrepreneurial establishment to a close. In providing the review we have tried to present the record of Irish entrepreneurs 'doing for themselves' in order to show something of the spirit of Irish entrepreneurship. On the whole the evidence makes it difficult to argue with those Irish entrepreneurs who suggested that the institutions and processes of socialisation in Ireland had failed to produce people with the basic virtues of 'honesty, integrity and hard and purposeful work'; disagreeable though this judgement may seem to many - and it is, to remember, an Irish judgement - it is amply justified by reference to the conduct which we have had to describe. For all that, however, we must be careful. It is not, as we made clear in Chapter 1, our intention to make moral pronouncements about the behaviour we have recorded in these pages; that is an activity which we are happy to leave to others who may consider themselves better qualified than we are to take the moral high ground. Our interest in the behaviour we have reviewed is purely technical. Given the nature of our 'vocations', it must necessarily remain so.

From the technical nature of our interest in the conduct of Irish entrepreneurs it follows that the question we must ask is, not 'Is the conduct morally good or bad?', but, 'Is it conducive to the achievement of the economic development?' Any answer to this question, and any judgements derived therefrom, must rely on technical and not at all on moral criteria. It is perfectly possible to specify the kind of entrepreneurial action which Ireland needs if it is to achieve the levels of economic development to which its people seem to aspire; given the small size of its home market its entrepreneurs need to become involved in the internationally-traded goods and services sectors; given Ireland's natural resource base - principally its agricultural potential - they need to raise productivity and add value to the natural products that are available; they need to develop new products for new markets, and, given the nature of the competition and the standards demanded by consumers, they need to attend to quality, to enhance reliability and to eschew those activities which can alienate customers and thus destroy opportunities for themselves and for others operating in their economy. When it is measured against these specifications, the behaviour of Irish entrepreneurs does not, in the main, seem to be the sort of behaviour that conduces to the achievement of economic development; they have not attacked opportunities lying in the internationally-traded goods and services sectors; they have not increased the value-added to the natural products of their country, being mainly content to continue in the traditional patterns of low value-added commodity trading; they have not developed new products for new markets, but have been happy with a nice, neat little profit derived from operating on their traditional home markets; they have clearly also failed to service existing markets effectively through cultivating appropriate standards of quality and reliability; they have shown a capacity for unethical and imprudent dealing which has damaged their own reputations, the commercial reputation of the country, hindered the operation of other units operating in their economy, and, through tax evasion, damaged the Irish state. On the whole, therefore, the spirit of Irish entrepreneurship seems to rest in an easy-going, complacent attitude to economic activity which amounts to a 'sheer torpor' and which is too-often combined with unscrupulous and unethical dealing. Either way the result is the same: the cause of Irish economic development is not advanced, indeed, it is often frustrated and hindered. No other conclusion seems possible on the strength of the evidence presented here. And, as we shall see in Chapters 3 and 4, there is a good deal more of such evidence to be encountered.

3 Irish entrepreneurs do more for themselves

Introduction

In this chapter we want to move from the general to the particular; having outlined, in general terms, the practices and performance of the Irish entrepreneurial establishment, we want now, through the media of selected case studies, to examine Irish business methods in a little more detail. Thanks mainly to the secrecy in which Irish entrepreneurs do for themselves only a limited number of cases are available for study in detail. Nevertheless, those that are available are powerfully illustrative of certain aspects of the spirit of Irish entrepreneurship, and are therefore worth the attention they are about to be given. If nothing else they will help us to provide some good exhibitions of the art of money-making, Irish style, and to show the close connections that exist between the Irish entrepreneurial and political establishments. In all, therefore, this chapter will enable us to build on the ground covered in Chapter 2 and thus help us to appreciate more precisely in what matter the Irish entrepreneurial problem consists.

Those who thought out and implemented the Irish development strategy did so with a view to creating increased employment through industrialisation. Given the small size of the Irish home market and the low levels of exporting engaged in by Irish industry, which was mainly confined to low value-added, basic commodity exports with low entry barriers, this required Irish entrepreneurs to force entries into the internationally-traded goods and services sectors, selling either new products or, where appropriate, upgrading their existing product ranges and, with reference to the commodity sectors, adding far more value to the products than had hitherto been the case. If Irish entrepreneurs had attended to these matters with some degree of energy, the country's development prospects might have been enhanced immeasurably. As we saw in Chapter 2, however, they did not, in the main, do anything of the kind, but persisted in their traditional patterns of activity in an easy-going spirit - a 'sheer torpor' in the words of one of their number - that was punctuated by orgies of damaging unscrupulousness in connection with money-making. This last point is quite significant and suggests that the evidence presented in Chapter 2 needs to be interpreted with care. We say this because the fact that Irish entrepreneurs may be easy-going, lax and wasteful in their approach to the exploitation of resources and in their attack on opportunities lying in the internationally-traded goods and services sectors should not be taken to imply that they are either uninterested in money-making, as such, or lacking in the skills and talents that are appropriate to the generation of profits. As this chapter will perhaps show, the problem is not one of a lack of interest in 'turning a buck', but lies rather in the directions in which that interest is pushed and in the methods that are used to develop it.

Property, politics and planning: money for nothing

In the course of preparing this book the authors interviewed an economist working for an agency concerned with promoting the industrial development of Ireland. Reflecting on the inadequacy of home grown industrial developers, the economist made some remarks about those who had done well out of the new Ireland:

> I mean your friendly local millionaire in this country usually has two sets of interests. Usually it's very significant property interests, which is typically where he has made his money, and typically having made it, what he does is put it into bloodstock; which is nothing, it doesn't offer security whatever it offers, put it that way, it's an incredibly high risk activity which is hugely developed in this country ... its the portfolio balance between the office block ... which gives a guaranteed rental income, and then what [they] can afford to play a little bit more riskily with other factors.

It is time to see how some of these 'friendly local millionaires' made their money. As will become evident not a few of them made it quite literally 'for nothing', or, at least, for very little indeed.

In March 1989 the Irish High Court decided to put Dublin County Council into receivership. The grounds for this extraordinary decision lay in the Council's refusal to pay £1.9 million compensation to a company called Grange Investments. Grange Investments was controlled by two Mayo-born property developers, by names Tom Brennan and Joe MGowan. Brennan and McGowan were large scale builders and developers, whose claim against Dublin County Council had more than a touch of the ironic about it; Dublin County Council had been involved with more litigation with them over the years, over breaches of planning regulations and unfinished estates, than it had with any other developer (McDonald, 1989, p. 87). An especially notorious example of their work could be seen at Kilnamanagh in County Dublin; advertised as a garden suburb with shops, services and plenty of open space, the estate was left in 1979 as an unfinished mess, with unmade roads, faulty houses, unprovided services and with the open spaces often consisting of little more than piles of builders' rubble.

In an ideal world the County Council would have been able to force the hands of Brennan and McCowan by denying them planning consent for future developments until the mess at Kilnamanagh had been cleared up. However, they could not do so because, as McDonald (1989, p. 88), points out, 'like many large builders they operated through a myriad of front companies, each one set up to carry out a specific development and forming a distinct legal entity'. They became the biggest house builders in Ireland, and, of course, acquired their stud farms in proper order. Building houses, however, was far from being their only money-making expedient.

Dublin County Council was not, after all, put into receivership; it paid Brennan and McCowan their £1.9 million and continued the hopeless task of trying to plan the development of the County for the local affairs of which it was responsible. The not inconsiderable sum which the unfortunate taxpayers had to donate to the two developers was paid out as compensation for losses which the County Council occasioned them by refusing planning permission to build houses on land which they had acquired in the Swords area of Dublin County. Ireland's constitution evinces a profound respect for the rights of property, and so does the country's Local Government (Planning and Development) Act which was passed into law in 1963. Under Section 55 of this Act developers are entitled to claim compensation for any reduction in the value of their land which results from a planning authority's refusal to grant planning permission. There are some exceptions; as outlined in Section 56 of the Act these include situations in which development is premature because the land is unserviced, is likely to cause a health or traffic hazard, is precluded because the area is subject to a special amenity order or because the development would impede a view or prospect of special amenity value or seriously injure the amenities and reduce other property values in the vicinity (Carr, 1987).

In Ireland primary responsibility for planning lies with the Local Authoritity; builders and landowners are required to obtain planning permission for all developments, though they can, in cases of refusal, appeal local authority decisions to a planning appeals board (*An Bord Pleannala*). Given the rights to compensation enshrined in the 1963 Act it is obviously of the utmost importance that Planning Authorities - and, where it is involved, the appeals board - cite non-compensatable grounds when refusing, or upholding a refusal of, planning permission. If non-compensatable grounds are included local authorities are protected against claims. If not they are wide open under planning laws that have been described, and with come justification, as 'a speculators' charter' (Carr, 1987).

In refusing Grange's application for planning permission to build on the Swords site, Dublin County Council specified non-compensatable grounds for its rejection. Brennan and McCowan then took the matter to the Planning Appeals Board, which upheld the County Council's refusal. In doing so, however, the board failed to specify the non-compensatable grounds cited by the County Council and so left the County authorities open to a claim for compensation which Brennan and McCowan duly lodged. The official who signed the planning appeal board's decision was Daniel Molloy (McDonald, 1989, p. 88). Not long after this event Molloy signed another appeals board decision concerning a company in which Brennan had an interest. As on the first occasion Dublin County Council's refusal was upheld, but the non-compsensatable grounds given by the council were omitted rendering that body once more open to a claim for compensation. A claim for £2 million was promptly entered against it (McDonald, 1989, p. 88).

Molloy was appointed to the Planning Appeals Board by Ray Burke, the *Fianna Fail* minister with responsibility for local government. As well as being a government minister, Burke was a member of Dublin County Council and an auctioneer who had a close business relationship with Brennan and McCowan; he acted as agent for the hundreds of houses which they sold in the Swords area; their accounts indicate that they paid him some £15,000 in fees for services in connection with 'planning'; one of their company's built his house, which was designed by their architect, John Keenan, who was later appointed to the Planning Appeals Board by Mr. Burke. McDonald (1989, p. 88) describes the impact which the activities of this energetic *Fianna Fail* minister had on the Irish planning process.

Almost single-handedly, Mr. Burke undermined public confidence in the impartiality of the planning process by his last-minute appointment to Board Plaeanala after Fianna Fail's defeat in the general election of June 1981, and November 1982. On the first occasion, just hours before Garret FitzGerald's first government took office, he named three new members of the appeals board - John P. Brennan principal architect for Brennan and McCowan, Daniel Molloy a Belfast-born businessman and Michael Cooke, a bye-law inspector for Dublin County Council, who had worked as a quantity surveyor for Brennan and McCowan. Later, during the interregnum between Fianna Fail's defeat in November 1982, and another FitzGerald-led Coalition government taking office, Mr. Burke named two more members of the board - Patrick Malone, Fianna Fail's director of elections for Laois-Offaly, and his own constituency adviser, Mr. Lambert, a one-time travelling salesman. Pointedly, he declined to continue the tradition of appointing a senior official from the planning division of the Department of the Environment. Mr. Burke justified his appointments on the basis that they would help to clear the backlog of appeals, but the Irish Planning Institute pointed out that what was really needed was more planning inspectors rather than new board members. Dick Spring, who took over as Tanaiste [Deputy Prime Minister] and Minister for the Environment in December 1982, also believed that Board

Plaeanala - which was set up in 1977 to 'take politics out of planning'- had suffered a major setback, and he was determined to do something about it.

Spring, eventually, did do 'something about it'; in 1984 he sacked the Fianna Fail appointed board and replaced amid considerable controversy.

We are not in a position to assert that any improprieties were involved in the decisions to which we have had cause to make reference; we are merely describing what happened and we are not imputing anything to anybody. Nevertheless, the circumstances we have described are singular; individuals, Brennan and McCowan, were handed down planning decisions which enabled them to make huge claims against a local authority by a board, the membership of which included two people who worked for them, and which was constituted through appointments made by a government minister who acted as their paid agent in land, housing and 'planning' transactions. The fact that Burke felt free to make these appointments at all tells us something about the close relationship between politicians and certain types of business people in contemporary Ireland; it is a close, cosy relationship which is open to abuse on a large scale. More than this we cannot assert, though we can note that the Burke appointed planning board performed another service for Brennan and McCowan; just eleven days before they were removed from office, they facilitated Brennan and McCowan's sale of a Dublin city site to John Corcoran's Green Property Company. Green wanted the site, which was recognised as having special amenity value, for office and residential development, but their application for planning permission was turned down by Dublin Corporation on the grounds that the existing character of the area should be preserved. In a decision which many regarded as inexplicable, the Planning Appeals Board reversed the Corporation's decision, thus clearing the way for Brennan and McCowan to sell to Corcoran (McDonald, 1989, p. 88).

Corcoran and Green Property Company had a somewhat chequered career in the property development sector. Aided and abetted by an architect called Stephenson, a leading member of *Fianna Fail* and a friend of Charles Haughey, they forwarded plans for a huge office development in the St. Stephen's Green-Hume Street area of Dublin city. This involved the purchase of some fine Georgian buildings, some of which were privately owned and two of which were in state hands. Stephenson was able to arrange that the state would give up the two properties it owned to facilitate the development, for which planning permission was granted by Dublin corporation (McDonald, 1985, p. 82). When the proposed sale of the two state properties was announced, however, conservation interests raised an outcry. Under pressure the government stated that they would not dispose of the houses until all interested parties had been consulted, and actually promised that they would not be sold at all if Dublin Corporation decided to preserve the area as Georgian (McDonald, 1985, p. 83).

Dublin Corporation subsequently designated the area for preservation and refused Stephenson planning permission for an extended scheme which would, of course, have involved the destruction of properties in the preservation zone. An immediate appeal was lodged and the *Fianna Fail* Minister for Local Government, Kevin Boland, who, after a public enquiry, overruled the Corporation and granted permission for the development. Notwithstanding appeals from conservation groups the government broke its earlier promises and disposed of the two properties to Green; the development could now go ahead.

Conservation groups now took direct and radical action; they submerged the Green Company in a sea of protest and actually occupied one of the Green-owned properties in Hume Street to protect it against the predations of the developer. Corcoran, apparently, was most upset; the story has it that he had to be nursed through many sleepless nights by the architect Sam Stephenson (McDonald, 1985, p. 97). After some delay and procrastination Corcoran recovered his nerve and decided to act. What happened is well described by McDonald (1985, pp. 97-8):

> Bill Kavanagh, who ran an outfit called K-Security ... was hired to do the dirty work. At the height of a long cement strike, he placed an innocuous-looking advertisement in one of the evening papers offering idle construction workers £25 each for a day's work. At 4.30 a.m. on Sunday, 7 June 1970, K-Security's newly-recruited goon squad, fifty-strong and armed with pick-axes and a battering ram, smashed down the hall door of [the occupied house]. On the premises at the time were four stalwarts of the occupation .... Three of them made for the cast-iron balcony on the first floor where they screamed and shouted and made such a din that all the lights in the Shelbourne Hotel came on. They were grabbed by the goon squad, many of whom were also shouting and roaring, and dragged down the stairs over broken glass and barbed wire before being kicked out the door. Meanwhile [the fourth member of the group] had escaped with a list of supporters' telephone numbers and, after finding a working telephone kiosk, she began ringing everyone to raise the alarm. Less than an hour later Garret FitzGerald and many others were at the scene and so was a large force of Gardai. K-Security's goons had attached a chain to the balcony from a lorry and they were ready to pull the house down. As more and more supporters descended on Hume Street, they were prevented from carrying out this summary execution and, in any case they hadn't got a demolition licence. By sheer force of numbers the Hume Street protesters managed to regain possession of the house and, after a lot of jostling and some nasty incidents, the hired goons eventually withdrew leaving their 'day's work' unfinished.

This resort to brute-force evidently did not harm Corcoran's reputation; he went on to build 90,000 square feet of office accommodation on the site which he let for, what was at the time, the stupendous rent of £3.50 per square foot. In order to achieve his ends, however, he had to compromise; the offices had to be built in a style that maintained the existing character of the streetscape - fake Georgian.

The splendid environment of St. Stephen's Green provided another example of property development, Irish style. A Roman Catholic religious order, the Sisters of Charity, owned five fine Georgian houses, in which they operated a hospital. On moving the hospital to another site they sold the houses to the British-owned Lyon Group, one of whose Irish directors was Sean Lemass - the erstwhile *Fianna Fail* prime minister who, to remember, called the new breed of entrepreneurs to the centre of the Irish stage. Notwithstanding the fact that the houses were listed for preservation, an obliging *Fianna Fail* minister granted outline planning permission. Fearing a repetition of the Hume Street affair, however, Lyon did not proceed with their original plan; their development, in fact, restored two of the houses and replaced the other three with faithful replicas (McDonald, 1985, p. 102).

In 1974 the Dublin property market suffered a setback and Lyon went into liquidation; their building operations were finished by their bankers and the final product was christened Sean Lemass House. Corcoran picked up some of Lyon's land holdings and went on to purchase his stud farm and Sean Lemass House was eventually purchased by another *Fianna Fail*-connected property developer called John Byrne. Kerry-born Byrne originally made money out of dance halls, and moved into property in the early years of the Lemass boom when he established an outfit called Carlisle Trust. His first venture into office building in Dublin was an edifice called O'Connell Bridge House; this provided 45,000 square feet of office space and no car parking space at all. The absence of the latter is significant because, at the time, Dublin Corporation's regulations specified that developers had to provide one car parking space for every 500 square feet of office accommodation. Yet the Corporation waived their car parking regulations, and their height regulations, in favour of Byrne. As McDonald (1985, p. 36) remarks, 'it is difficult to explain this strange turn of events other than that it came about by political influence'.

Byrne usually had no difficulty in finding state tenants for his office blocks, until, that is, he acquired the above-mentioned Sean Lemass House. Try as he might Byrne could not find a state sponsored organisation to take this property; he first netted the Department of Fisheries, and, after they pulled out, hooked the Department of Posts and Telegraphs until they also withdrew.

> Wherever he turned he found himself facing a brick wall. And this wall, it transpired, was the Minister for Finance George Colley. He personally vetoed any and all proposals to lease Sean Lemass House because he was convinced that his arch-rival Charlie Haughey had a stake in Byrne's property empire. At the time Haughey was serving in the same cabinet as Minister for Health and Social Welfare (McDonald, 1985, pp. 263-4).

Political influence helps, but is clearly not without its limitations when political rivals are animated by spite. For once Byrne was beaten and after eighteen frustrating months he sold the property at a nice, neat little profit of £1 million.

The purchaser was one Patrick Gallagher, son of the legendary Matt Gallagher. Matt Gallagher was an intimate of Byrne, and, when he died in 1974, Byrne became a sort of surrogate father to young Patrick and taught him the tricks of the property trade. Young Patrick turned out to be an apt pupil; he became a prodigiously successful developer in his own right and also went into the fringe banking business. The Gallaghers, father and son, were well connected politically; they were a *Fianna Fail* family and were especially friendly with Charlie Haughey, who sold his Grangemore estate to Matt in 1969. This was a controversial deal because Haughey took advantage of a provision in a recent Finance Act - which he, as Minister for Finance, had initiated - to avoid tax on the £200,000 windfall produced by the sale (McDonald, 1985, p. 285). Suitably enriched Haughey was able to purchase a 200 acre estate and develop his bloodstock interest, a passion he shared with his good friend young Patrick, who, incidentally, surpassed his fellow 'friendly, local millionaires' by actually acquiring a racecourse.

Like Byrne and Matt Gallagher, young Patrick experienced little trouble in finding state tenants for his growing collection of office blocks. He did, however, occasionally have trouble getting his projects started; like Corcoran he was not immune from the attentions of 'do-gooding' protesters who objected to the destruction of historic buildings which his development projects not infrequently necessitated. On one famous occasion a group of architectural students occupied a building in Molesworth Street (Dublin) with a view to preventing its demolition. Gallagher met this challenge with considerable originality; he drove to the site in his Rolls Royce and agreed to the students' demands before calling a press conference at which he announced that he was laying-off 300 building workers. If nothing else this ploy roused Gallagher's employees; within a short time workers from a number of Gallagher sites were picketing the student-occupied building with placards saying 'Save our Jobs'.

Gallagher's ingenious ploy, however, did not succeed in removing the students, so he resorted to more conventional methods and obtained a court order against them. Thereafter his originality reasserted itself:

at one o'clock the following morning, as [the students] held a meeting to decide what to do next, the demolition workers attached a hawser line to one of the high chimney stacks and pulled it crashing through the roof. Then, while the helpless students were held back by 'security men' with half-starved Alsatian dogs, Gallagher's minions moved to complete their work of destruction. According to an eye-witness report in *The Irish Times*, 'the demolition workers swarmed over the old building and looped their hawser line around the massive end wall and onto a big tracked digger. The digger backed off, its great jointed neck reared back, it lifted off its tracks, but the building would not give ... A large group of Gardai arrived, and late-night diners watched the machine wearing itself out trying to bring the wall down, but it would not budge'. Eventually, the building - which Gallagher's representatives had told the High Court was in a dangerous condition - had to be chipped away bit by bit before the site could be cleared for development (McDonald, 1985, pp. 225-6).

If these futile attempts to demolish a building were faintly amusing, the eventual collapse of Gallagher's property and fringe banking empire was not - and the latter did not have to be 'chipped away bit by bit', but came tumbling down without any urging from a 'big tracked digger'. The crash came in 1982 when Gallagher's banks put his property empire into receivership; they were owed, in all, some £30 million. Gallagher's fringe bank folded along with his property business, as it was bound to do given the manner in which it had operated. Most of the deposits taken by the Gallagher-owned bank were loaned at low interest rates to Gallagher's property business. These loans were secured by a debenture and floating charge on Gallagher's properties and assets. However, these expedients were effectively worthless because they applied to assets that were already mortgaged to the other banks with whom Gallagher was dealing. When the Gallagher-owned bank collapsed, therefore, there was a shortfall of £4 million and the liquidator had no alternative but to tell the High Court that Gallagher's bank been 'operated and run by the directors with a scandalous disregard not only of the Companies Act but of the Central Bank Act' (quoted in McDonald, 1985, p. 271). The fraud squad was called in.

Gallagher was never brought to trial in the Irish Republic. The Northern Ireland authorities, however, had no hesitation in moving against him as his sister-banking operation in the North also collapsed; he was charged and pleaded guilty to false accounting and the theft of £100,000 and was eventually sentenced to a term of two years imprisonment. Gallagher's guilty plea makes the decision of the Republic's Director of Public Prosecutions not to proceed against him all the more extraordinary, but the decision was allowed to stand. Nor was any explanation offered for the fact that it took six years from the date on which the High Court ordered the liquidator to hand over his report to the DPP for the matter to be investigated to the point where the decision not to prosecute was handed down. And the Gallagher case is by no means unique. International Investments Limited, a fringe bank operated by a Corkman called George Finbar Ross went broke in 1984 leaving about 900 people in both parts of Ireland minus some or all of their savings. As with Gallagher, Ross was charged in the North but not in the Republic, a circumstance which provoked an Ulster Unionist MP, Roy Beggs, to write to the *Taoiseach* demanding the authorities in the South appoint an inspector to examine ILL's operations. The reply he received was not reassuring; once more the matter had been referred to the fraud squad; once more the police sent the file to the DPP; once more he decided not to prosecute. And so, the reply continued,

> In the circumstances the Minister for Industry and Commerce does not consider that the appointment by the courts of an inspector under the Companies Acts would serve any useful purpose (quoted in Seekamp, 1992).

Far from satisfying Beggs, this reply provoked him to further correspondence in which he put a very pertinent question to the Republic's authorities:

You may be aware that as a result of an investigation by the RUC [the Northern Ireland police], a person has been charged with conspiracy to defraud depositors with International investments Limited .... Does this decision reflect the efficiency of the RUC, or the extent of political interference from political leaders in the Irish Republic on the ability of the Garda [Irish police] to reach the same conclusions (quoted in Seekamp, 1992).

Beggs's question, of course, cannot be answered with certainty in connection with either of the cases mentioned; we have no information concerning Ross's political connections, if any; we have no way of knowing whether or not Gallagher's close connections with Haughey protected him from prosecution in the Republic. What we can say, however, is that there is evidence which suggests that political interference in the Republic's judicial process is not unknown.

McGowan versus Nangle is one case in point. Nangle was a member of the Irish police force and brother-in-law to a *Fianna Fail* minister, by name Sean Docherty. In December 1981 Nangle assaulted McGowan in a public house in Blacklion in County Cavan in the Irish Republic. McGowan made a formal complaint, refused attempts to 'buy him off' and the case was set for hearing in September 1982 (Joyce and Murtagh, 1983, pp. 240-1). On the morning of the hearing McGowan was arrested by the Northern Ireland police and held as a suspected terrorist. Evidently this was done by special request of the Republic's special branch with the obvious motive of preventing him from attending the hearing; there were no grounds for suspicion of terrorism, and he was released later in the day. He was, however, prevented from attending the Court and so the case against Nangle had to be dropped (Joyce and Murtagh, 1983, pp. 245-7).

The same minister apparently had a habit of intervening with the normal course of 'due process' in the Republic's jurisdiction. For example,

Docherty's attempts to have a Garda recruit from his constituency passed out from training although he failed his final examination, did not succeed after the instructors threatened to strike. Many guards in his constituency believed that they were unable to do their jobs because people knew that if they were charged with a criminal offence there was a chance the charge would be dropped and even where convictions were made in the courts, it was known that a high number of petitions to Docherty for a reduction in sentence were successful (Joyce and Murtagh, 1983, p. 275).

On 28 February 1982 two members of the Irish police raided a public house, Kearney's, in the town of Boyle, County Roscommon, in which a number of individuals were engaged in a bout of illegal, after-hours drinking. They reported the matter to their inspector who told them to prosecute and noted his decision in the case file. In the meantime the owner of the public house, one Kearney, appealed to Docherty - who was now the Minister for Justice as well as being a TD (MP) for the Boyle area - for help. Thereafter the inspector reversed the decision to prosecute, giving as his reason that 18 February was election night and that it was not policy to prosecute after-hours drinking on election nights (Joyce and Murtagh, 1983, pp. 128-9). The local sergeant, Tom Tully, was not amused by this change of heart; he had experienced Docherty's interference in the past - Kearney had succeeded in avoiding prosecution on a similar charge in 1980 - and so he protested strongly on this occasion (Joyce and Murtagh, 1983, p. 129). On 28 July 1982 Tully was ordered to transfer from Boyle to County Cavan. He subsequently appealed against the transfer and when his appeal was rejected took legal advice with a view to fighting the matter through the courts. In an affidavit he cited five cases to support his claim that,

> I am the victim of a vicious piece of victimisation at the hands of the Minister for Justice and some Garda officers because I would not yield to political pressure to square serious violations of the law (quoted in Joyce and Murtagh, 1983, p. 237).

Tully was subsequently persuaded to pursue his case through the Garda Review Body rather than through the courts. He did so, and, much to Docherty's chagrin, succeeded in getting the transfer overturned.

The cases just reviewed do not, of course, prove that Gallagher and Ross escaped prosecution in the Irish Republic because of political intervention in the judicial process. What they do, however, is enable us to suggest that suspicion of political interference is far from groundless, and those who entertain it are not living in some fantasy world of their own devising. In this connection it should be remembered also that there is more than one way of structuring political interference in judicial process: political authorities, for example, can restrict the capacities of enforcement agencies to function effectively by denying them access to the resources which they need. With reference to the Irish case it has to be said that referring a case to the fraud squad is a procedure that is likely to prove about as frightening to the fraudsters in business as a rap across the knuckles with a bunch of shamrock. While the squad has been successful in clearing up social welfare and mundane cheque frauds, it has not been able to make a serious impact on more complex and serious cases like those involving Gallagher and ILL. Unlike the UK Serious Fraud Office, which has a multidisciplinary team of accountants, lawyers and police personnel, the Irish Squad is staffed by rank and file *Gardai* who lack specialist expertise (O'Toole, 1990). In consequence the Squad has neither the resources nor the expertise to cope with complex fraud cases which are increasingly part of the Irish business scene (Magee, 1988; O'Toole, 1990). Officers charged with the investigation of frauds are known to be frustrated by the lack of resources that are available to them, and, indeed, by the antiquated state of Irish law, including the laws of evidence which apply in fraud cases (O'Toole, 1990). Leaving aside altogether the questions relating to direct political interference, the truth is that Irish politicians have not provided the *Gardai* with the personnel and resources needed to deal with fraud. We cannot, of course, assert that their motives lie in protecting their friends from effective investigations -

though, as we saw in Chapter 2 allegations of this sort have been made with reference to tax evaders. Nevertheless, the failure to upgrade the law and to give the fraud squad resources which are more adequate to the demands being made on it show remarkable complacency in the face of a growing problem.

There is another aspect of property dealing in the Irish Republic that deserves mention in these pages, if only because it provides a clear demonstration of how to make money for nothing. In the nineteen-seventies Dublin was probably the fastest growing city in Europe; the population of the Dublin subregion grew from 745.047 in 1966 to 1,003,164 in 1981 (Brunt, 1988, p. 151). Accommodating this large increase in population required large programmes of local authority and private housebuilding, and included the construction of three large new towns in the subregion. The planning process, however, left a good deal to be desired:

> In Britain, the first step to be taken in any 'new town' scheme would be that all of the land required would be designated by an Act of Parliament and then taken into public ownership, at prices often not much more than its existing value as agricultural land. This, together with the establishment of a special commission to oversee the enterprise, gave planners effective control over the design, layout and scheduling of the entire development, with land being released in stages to the private sector for approved housing or industrial schemes. No such commission was established [for the Dublin 'new towns'], perhaps because of over-weaning respect for the rights of private property or, perhaps, because the government never took the matter seriously enough. The EC study consultants conclude that the absence of an overall development agency, with specific powers and functions and with a designated budget to oversee the implementation of the strategy was 'a major weakness'. What happened, therefore, was little better than *laissez faire* planning, hardly planning at all. Colours were inked on a map and, at the stroke of someone's pen, the landowners in possession of parcels zoned for development made a fortune. And if some found themselves on the wrong side of the lines drawn by the planners, they could always enlist the support of friendly county councillors to have their land rezoned (McDonald, 1989, pp. 78-9).

Under Irish planning legislation elected local authorities, who employ the professional planners, have formal control over the planning process and can, therefore, materially contravene zoning patterns determined by the professionals and have land rezoned from one use to another. The procedures involved are quite simple: landowners who want their land rezoned need to persuade councillors to propose and second a motion for rezoning which is put to the council, voted on, and adopted or rejected as the case may be. When Dublin County Council's first development plan was adopted in 1972, the area experienced its first rezoning scandal as councillors from both *Fianna Fail* and *Fine Gael* pushed through motion after motion riding roughshod over the objections of the Council's professional staff. Ray Burke, whom we met earlier in the chapter, was involved in the rezoning, once more in connection with his old friends Brennan and McCowan; Burke tabled motions to have agricultural land which they had bought rezoned for development thus 'immeasurably increasing its value' (McDonald, 1989, p. 80). Again in 1979 and 1982, when the plan was reviewed and then redrafted, councillors cheerfully ignored the advice of their professional planners in their rush to facilitate those who owned land and who wished to enrich themselves by effectively doing nothing. Included in one of the rezoning motions was land belonging to a *Fianna Fail* councillor and TD, Liam Lawlor; Lawlor had bought the land for £170,000 some months before it was put through the rezoning process, a process which increased its value to around £500,000 (Millotte, 1990h). In all the council voted to rezone some 3,000 acres of land, and, therefore, to enrich a number of interested individuals in the process.

Lawlor and many others were not, however, to be allowed to realise their profits on this occasion; the scandal gave rise to a public outcry against the Council, which reversed almost eighty per cent of its rezoning decisions; Lawlor lost his seat in Parliament in the 1982 general election, and the leader of *Fine Gael* put pressure on local councillors belonging to the party not to vote for rezoning against the objections of the professional planners (McDonald, 1989, p. 81). No such pressure appears to have been exerted on *Fianna Fail* councillors; between 1985 and 1988 forty-five contraventions of the County Plan were adopted by the Council, twenty-one of which were contentious and passed only because - more often than not - the *Fianna Fail* majority voted solidly in favour of them (McDonald, 1989, p. 85). *Fianna Fail* unanimity here gave rise to the suspicion that the party was applying the whip on planning matters - this is illegal, since in planning matters the council is regarded as acting in a quasi-judicial capacity (O'Loughlin, 1990). So occupied did the Council become with rezoning matters that, for a time, practically no other business could be considered; planning motions must, by law, go to the top of the agenda, and there were often so many that the council simply had no time to consider any other business.

What these orgies of money-making did was to enable a small coterie of politically well connected people, and sometimes politicians, themselves, to make substantial profits. They also, of course, gave rise to the occasional scandal, made the lives of the planners difficult, deprived local taxpayers of large sums of money and hampered Dublin County Council's capacity to conduct its business in a normal and orderly way. What they did not produce, however, was anything in the nature of permanent jobs and self-sustaining economic growth in an economy and society that needed both desperately. Again no moral judgement is implied in this statement; it is a simple technical observation. Construction jobs are, by the nature of the building trade, temporary. To put matters somewhat crudely, when the project is finished the friendly millionaire retires to his stud farm and the workers retire to the 'dole'. Such, it seems, is an essential part of economic development Irish style.

How to buy a building

The case we are now going to examine is a complex one that aroused considerable controversy In Ireland. It concerns *Telecom Eareann* (TE) Ireland's state-owned telecommunications company and its attempts to purchase a site on which to provide itself with a new corporate headquarters building. At some point in 1989 it seems to have occurred to TE's chairman, Michael Smurfit - also chairman and chief executive of the multinational Smurfit group - that TE needed a new building. He raised the matter at a board meeting on 9 July and thereafter contacted two firms of auctioneers, one of whom showed him round a site occupied by a bakery called Johnston, Mooney and O'Brien (JMOB). Smurfit was enthusiastic about the site and became resolved that the telecommunications company should acquire it.

Late in 1988 a man called Dermot Desmond set up a company called United Property Holdings (UPH). As chairman and chief executive of National City Brokers (NCB), Desmond was a prodigiously successful stockbroker, and, like many of those who have figured in this record so far, an intimate of Charles Haughey. Desmond's foray into property was occasioned by an upturn in the Dublin property market, and his company's first acquisition was a building in central Dublin occupied by TE. In November 1988 Desmond instructed an auctioneer to offer JMOB £4.4 million for their site. The tender was accepted and a deposit was paid by NCB on behalf of UPH, though the sale was not completed by the tender date as UPH was evidently not in possession of adequate funds (Cooper, 1992a).

In December 1988 Desmond wrote to Smurfit asking him to invest £100,000 in UPH. In response Smurfit took a private stake and arranged for the Smurfit group pension fund to invest £400,000 in UPH convertible preference shares (Cooper, 1992a). UPH now set about rebuilding its equity base and arranged for auctioneers acting on its behalf to circulate potential purchasers of the site, which it did not yet own, with a brochure. A solicitor called Noel Smyth evidently saw the brochure, visited the site, and, in May 1989, told the auctioneers that he was interested in acquiring it on behalf of certain unnamed parties which he said he had in mind. Who these parties were we do not know. What we do know, however, is that Desmond instructed Smyth to offer UPH through one of its directors Kevin Barry - although Desmond set up UPH he was not a director - the sum of £6.3 million for the JMOB site, an offer that was made on 19 June 1989. In other words, as Cooper (1992a) puts it:

> Dermot Desmond was asking a solicitor to offer £6.3 million for a property which a company set up by Desmond was seeking to acquire for £4 million.

Safe in the knowledge of this £6.3 million offer, UPH was now able to complete its purchase of the JMOB site - it was purchased from the receiver as JMOB was now in liquidation. Its directors were confident Smyth would complete his purchase, the fruits of which would enable them to repay the loans obtained in the process of rebuilding UPH's capital base. UPH's directors did not know that Smyth was acting for Desmond, though Barry evidently did know that Desmond was helping Smyth to raise finance but considered it to be none of his business (Cooper, 1992a). Four other buyers were known to be interested in the site, though UPH decided to stick with Smyth in spite of the fact that the company's solicitor was expressing doubts about Smyth's ability to come up with the money.

Desmond and Smyth were evidently having difficulty in raising the £6.3 million needed to buy the site from UPH; they had to try several banks and, at the end of the day, Desmond had to arrange for mezzanine finance to be provided. The High Court inspector examining the whole affair could not help remarking that:

> The evidence from the banks is significant because it shows the understanding of each bank of the representations made by Desmond and/or Smyth in relationship to the ownership or proposed ownership of the purchasing company (Chestvale), and also shows the banks understanding that at least as early as July/August 1989 consideration was being given to Telecom becoming an occupier of the JMOB site (quoted in Cooper, 1992a).

In doing the rounds of the banks Desmond and/or Smyth seem to have provided different banks with different information. For example, in discussions with Trinity Bank,

> Desmond mentioned the names of Telecom and Cablelink on a 'for example type basis' as the sort of companies which might relocate to a new corporate headquarters on the site. The lending executive at the bank also wrote the names of Magnier and McManus on one of his memoranda. Asked why he said that he had been given those names by Desmond as an example of 'the type of people he either knew or dealt with or could deal with'. It was not mentioned specifically that they were becoming involved (Cooper, 1992a).

According to the internal memorandum drawn up by Lombard and Ulster, however,

> The borrowing company will either be Fitzwilliam or a wholly-owned subsidiary thereof. The beneficial shareholders of the borrowing company will be as follows: Dermot Desmond, Larry Goodman, Michael Smurfit, J.P. McManus and Smyth .... It is expected that Bord Telecom will apply for planning permission for 100,000 square feet of office space to meet its own requirements on an enlarged site incorporating part of the JMOB lands ... Bord Telecom will be a potential purchaser for the office portion of the development which the promoters value, with planning, at £8 million (quoted in Cooper, 1992a).

In the meantime Smyth was trying to raise funds from the Bank of Ireland. In the process of discussions he informed the bank's representative, Michael Moriarty, that the project was a personal venture with Desmond, McManus and Magnier (Cooper, 1992a). Irish International Bank was also told that Desmond, McManus and Magnier were involved; when an official of the bank questioned Desmond's dual role as vendor and purchaser Smyth informed him that Desmond wanted to sell while others in UPH did not, and that to keep the peace in UPH his (Desmond's) role should not be disclosed (Cooper, 1992a). The bank which eventually provided finance for Chestvale, Ansbacher, also noted that the shareholders in Chestvale were Desmond, McManus and Magnier (Cooper, 1992a).

In the meantime Desmond had introduced a man called Doherty to the business; he later claimed to be the sole beneficial owner of three companies involved in what was becoming an increasingly convoluted series of transactions: namely, Chestvale, Delion and Hoddle. Doherty was interested but could not afford the building, so Desmond brought in mezzanine finance. This was provided by a friend, Colin Probets, who operated an Isle of Man registered company called Freezone. Desmond had a long standing relationship with Probets, from whom he obtained the £60,000 which he lent to Conor Haughey, Charles Haughey's son, for the refurbishment of the older Haughey's yacht *Celtic Mist* (Cooper, 1992b). Probets contributed £1 million, which, together with a sum of £3 million from Ansbacher Bank, enabled Smyth to pay UPH £4 million in August 1989, thus enabling the latter company to settle its accounts with the receiver.

The company for which Smyth was acting was evidently a company called Chestvale. Chestvale as yet had made no written agreement to purchase the site and Desmond is said to have offered it to an English property company for £6.3 million. Meanwhile negotiations with banks were proceeding, with Smyth informing one of them,

> that a Cypriot company Delion would have a deposit of £2 million in Jersey, or with the Bank of Ireland, with a guarantee in favour of Chestvale. [The bank] was informed that both Delion and Chestvale were owned one-third each by Desmond, Magnier and McManus and that they were the beneficial owners of the property to be sold (Cooper, 1992a).

Smyth also informed this bank about the proposed sale to TE and the bank officials dealing with the application for funding recommended acceptance to their superiors. According to Cooper (1992a) the recommendation,

> described Delion, the proposed borrower, as being a Cypriot Company owned by 'Desmond, Magnier and McManus'. It said that Chestvale was to become a subsidiary of Delion, as UPH was about to sell it to Delion.

The recommendation further noted that UPH was 'owned mainly by Desmond, Finnegan and Smurfit' (Cooper, 1992a). Desmond was, therefore, according to information given to the banks, involved in all three companies, The High Court inspector's report notes the bank's concern at this and other points:

> The bank's own memoranda at the time note concern at the dual roles of various parties including Desmond and Smyth .... in addition to this express reference to the dual roles, it would appear that concern was also expressed by the managing director of Bank of Ireland in relation to the dual role of Smurfit. Dr Smurfit appeared on the credit application form as being a shareholder in UPH, whose property was ultimately being bought by Telecom of which he was chairman. Moriarty's evidence [Moriarty was a bank official dealing with the matter] is that in a conversation that he had with the managing director of the bank at the end of March or early April 1990, the managing director expressed surprise at the connection of Dr Smurfit in this way (Quoted in Cooper, 1992a).

We left Michael Smurfit in 1989 on a visit to the JMOB site, about which, to remember, he waxed enthusiastic to the auctioneer who organised the visit for him (Cooper, 1992a). Sometime in October or November 1989 Smurfit contacted Desmond, expressed his interest on behalf of Telecom and asked Desmond to find out if, by whom, and for how much, the property might be for sale. Desmond then contacted Smyth and advised him to ask a price of £10 million for the site. On meeting Smurfit on 29 November, however, Desmond informed him that the vendors only wanted to dispose of 4.5 acres, the asking price of which was going to be £7.5 million. When Smurfit asked Desmond who the vendor was he was told that it was a company called Chestvale which was acting through Noel Smyth.

On the following day Smurfit wrote to Desmond saying that, although he would have liked the full 6.8 acres, he was willing, subject to his board's approval, to offer £7.5 million for the 4.5 acres that were available. On the same day he wrote to TE's chief executive, Fergus McGovern and sent him a copy of his letter to Desmond. Given that his understanding was that Smurfit was only investigating possibilities, the chief executive was evidently surprised to find that matters had progressed to the offer stage. Nevertheless, Smurfit wrote to McGovern again on 5 December suggesting that the two men visit the site in advance of TE's next board meeting. According to Cooper (1992a):

> Desmond told McGovern that he had a previous involvement in the site and the Telecom chief executive formed the impression that this interest no longer existed. The only information about the vendors given was the name of Chestvale and that the principals were clients of Noel Smyth.

The matter was discussed at a TE board meeting held on 15 December - even though some board members were seemingly unaware of Smurfit's offer - and an architect, who happened to be a close friend of Smurfit's, was appointed to do some appraisal work on the site. On 9 January McGovern informed Desmond that TE wanted the whole site but thought that the asking price of £10 million was a little too high. Desmond returned with a suggested price of £9.4 million. Evidently he 'saw himself as an honest broker who wanted to make buyer and seller happy with the deal' (Cooper, 1992a).

Desmond's 'honest brokering' did not, however, begin with his response to McGovern's offer for the whole site; he had, to remember, Smurfit's original offer of £7.5 million for the 4.5 acres which had been put on the table on 30 November 1989. Desmond wasted no time in drafting a reply to this offer: he told Smurfit that he was unable to advise him on the matter, 'because we disposed of this property to Chestvale'. He did, however, offer to use his influence with Chestvale on behalf of TE.

Given that, according to information given to the banks, Desmond owned a stake in Chestvale, UPH and Delion, we may safely presume that he had some influence to use. Given also that TE was being touted as a potential purchaser of the site, in attempts to persuade the banks to provide finance, we may presume that he was quite willing to use that influence on behalf of TE, and that he was no less keen to act as an 'honest broker' dedicated to securing the mutual happiness of buyer and seller, especially since, according to the information available to the banks, he had stakes in all three of the companies involved in the sale to date. Clearly a tangled web was being woven around the activities of Desmond and Smyth. Tax considerations, if nothing else, were to necessitate some further elaborations.

The 'game plan' for dealing with the tax arrangements was seemingly devised by an accountant called Bourke who worked at a stud farm owned by Magnier. According to Cooper (1992a) it involved an 'Irish company (presumably Chestvale) being owned by "Offshore Limited" which would be owned by "L"'. The Irish company was to borrow £3 million on a back to back arrangement between Offshore's bankers and another Irish bank and another unnamed company was to be registered in Cyprus to be owned by a trust or guarantee company referred to as 'LIC'. The identities of 'L' and 'LIC' have not, so far as can find out, been established. Nevertheless, as we saw above, a Cypriot registered company, with suitable financial guarantees, did make a timely arrival on the scene. This was the Delion company, which, if the information which Smyth is said in the inspector's report to have given to a bank is correct, was owned one-third each by Desmond, Magnier and McManus. It is a reasonable speculation that Delion was 'Offshore Limited' for it was to acquire the Irish company Chestvale, also owned, according to evidence in the inspector's report, one-third each by Desmond, Magnier and McManus. Before the sale to TE was concluded yet another company was to become involved.

This was a company known by the name of Hoddle. Hoddle was a shelf company controlled by Noel Smyth's firm which commenced trading in April 1990 when it entered into a contract with Chestvale to purchase the JMOB site from Delion who had agreed, on the same date, to purchase it from Chestvale, the consideration being that Delion would take over all Chestvale's liabilities. The transfer from Delion to Hoddle did not take place on the same day, but was arranged on 3 May 1990 at a price of £9.3 million. Four days later Hoddle sold the site on to TE for

£9.4 million. At the time of the sale Hoddle did not have a bank account, so the proceeds were lodged in an account controlled by Delion. The Inspector's report concluded that the beneficial ownership of Hoddle was in the same hands as the beneficial ownership of Delion, which was, of course, owned by the owners of Chestvale meaning that Desmond had an interest in all four companies involved in a transaction in which £5.4 million was added to the value of a site in less than a month. This is, perhaps, the most singular aspect of the whole series of transactions. Although Smyth made UPH an offer for the site in June 1989, the Inspector's report states:

> It would appear that no written agreement was signed by Smyth or his clients with UPH at least until April 1990, even though one of the apparently most important reasons for acceptance of Smyth's offer was his perceived ability to meet the closing deadline with the liquidator of JMOB (quoted in Cooper, 1992a).

The Inspectors report continues to outline the mystery:

> Even in the latter part of July (1989), when the UPH solicitor was expressing concern at Smyth's delay, Barry [the director of UPH dealing with the matter] does not seem to have sought information as to the financial capacity of Smyth's clients to comply with their part of the agreement, save that he seems to have relied on assurances by Desmond that Smyth would perform (quoted in Cooper, 1992a).

Desmond's confidence was amply justified: Smyth did perform, but only when the Telecom contract was, for all practical purposes, firmly in the bag.

We must be careful here and state firmly that we are not imputing any impropriety to anyone; the Inspector's report, on which our account relies, reveals some questionable business practices but does not impute blame to anyone. Nor are we in a position to do so. For example, the beneficial ownership of the companies involved has not been proved to have been with Desmond, Magnier and McManus, although the Inspector can show that their names were mentioned to the banks in that connection - McManus and Magnier have, in fact, denied beneficial involvement, so presumably their names were given to the banks without their knowledge or consent. Pat Doherty has claimed to be the beneficial owner of Hoddle, Delion and Chestvale at all times that are relevant to the transaction. But was he? The Inspector's report reveals that relevant share transfers were made somewhat later than the relevant times; the Hoddle shares were not transferred to him until 30 September 1991 - eleven days after he made his claim to the ownership of the company; the shares in Delion were not transferred to him by Smyth until 10 October 1991.

Even if, as much of the evidence suggests, Desmond, Magnier and McManus could be proved to be the beneficial owners of Hoddle, Delion and Chestvale, this would not demonstrate them to be guilty of any impropriety. Any such demonstration would require proof that they were acting on 'insider information' and were in possession of secret assurances that TE would buy the site from them. Smurfit might, of course, have been the source of such assurances; he had, as we have seen, a stake in UPH and thus stood to profit from the deal; he was also friendly with Desmond, Magnier and McManus - he was, along with Desmond and McManus, the latter is a well known gambler and bookmaker, involved as a director of an ill-fated enterprise called Classic Thoroughbreds; he did take an unusually close interest in the purchase of the site - something that should be weighed against the fact that his post in TE was a part-time one, 'a purely honorary duty on behalf of his country' (Cooper, 1992a). None of this, however, proves anything against Smurfit; it does not establish that he knew that Desmond was acting through UPH, the company in which he had an interest - as we have seen he claims to have been under the impression that Desmond was not; it does not demonstrate that he knew that any of his friends had interests in Hoddle, Delion or Chestvale; it certainly does not prove that he colluded with them in the slightest degree, or behaved with any impropriety in connection with the convoluted series of deals associated with the purchase. Those involved in the transaction, whoever they were - and their identities will probably never be conclusively proved, may thus have been taking a commercial risk with large sums of their own and others' money; the whole chain may have been set up as a gamble that TE or some other buyer would take the site on suitable terms.

It has to be said, however, that those involved in the sale would have been most unlikely to find a buyer willing to purchase the site in the way TE did. Indeed some of the circumstances surrounding TE's acquisition of this very expensive site are so extraordinary as to be almost unbelievable; at the time of their purchase they had no planning permission for any development on the site; they commissioned no detailed valuation of the site from independent sources; they have never provided any good reason in justification of their claimed need for a new corporate headquarters. Unfortunately for TE planning permission was subsequently refused, and the refusal was upheld on appeal. In consequence they are now the proud possessors of £9.4 million worth of 'White Elephant'.

Press revelations concerning the TE affair gave rise to a public outcry and led to the appointment of the Inspector whose interim report provides much of the information on which our account is based. The Inspector, it has to be said, received less than full cooperation from many of those he needed to interview in the course of preparing his report and his enquiries were delayed by the initiation of nine separate High Court actions (Kennedy, 1992). Nevertheless, the Inspector has managed to piece together some account of the money trail that followed TE's payment of the purchase price. Of this, £1.8 million went to UPH, while a further £2.43 million went into Freezone's account in a Dublin bank. £956,118 was paid to Banker's Trust New York from two Delion accounts. The account into which these monies were paid was evidently held in the name of Montezuma. When the Inspector asked Desmond about this he was told it 'was the name of an Aztec king' (quoted in Maher, 1992). The address for the New York account was Allied Irish Banks, Channel Islands, an account which the Inspector thinks may be the mysterious. J.

& B. McMahon account, the ownership of which he has been unable to determine. Again when Desmond was questioned about the ownership of this account he told the Inspector that 'he didn't know, that it was just another name not that of real people' (quoted in Maher, 1992). £1.3 million was subsequently withdrawn from the Freezone account and used to repay a sum which Desmond borrowed from two individuals to meet a demand from Allied Commercial Trust which was suing him in connection with an investment it made in Financial Coursewear Limited, a company owned by Desmond's private company, Dedier. Desmond clearly had some control over the Freezone account; he withdrew £400,000 in cash; payments totalling £470,430 were made to his firm NCB; a payment of £80,000 went to Dedair, among others detailed in the Inspector's report. On 11 October 1991 - two days after the appointment of the Inspector - the balance of all monies in Delion's account were transferred out of Irish jurisdiction. It went into an account held in the name of P.J. Doherty in Allied Irish Bank in Jersey.

Back on the 'home front' some of the leading actors in the drama have had to 'write themselves out' of a few scripts; Smurfit had to resign as chairman of TE; Desmond resigned as chairman of *Aer Rianta* (the Irish Airport Authority) - to which post he was appointed by Charles Haughey - and his company NCB was asked to suspend work that it was doing in connection with the possible privatisation of TE. As we mentioned above Desmond is a very successful stockbroker, whose success in winning state contracts has aroused suspicion among the stockbroking fraternity that he is an object of political favouritism; he has worked for *Aer Lingus* (the Irish state airline) and for other state sponsored bodies involved in transport, the distribution of gas, electricity supply and, not least, TE itself (Cooper, 1992b). His work for *Aer Lingus* was also touched by controversy; a confidential report which he prepared concerning one of its subsidiaries, Irish Helicopters, fell into the hands of another of Charles Haughey's sons, Ciaran, whose firm Celtic Helicopters was Irish Helicopters principal rival and who also worked as a consultant to Ryanair, a private sector airline in competition with *Aer Lingus* - it was claimed that a junior executive of NCB supplied the information without the knowledge of his superiors (Cooper, 1992b). It was one of Ciaran Haughey's helicopters that brought Bernie Cahill, the chairman of the Irish Sugar Company - then state owned - to Charles Haughey's home in May 1990; the older Haughey was then prime minister of the Irish Republic and is said to have ordered Cahill to appoint Desmond's NCB to handle Irish Sugar's impending privatisation, even though the company had a long standing and satisfactory relationship with another stockbroking firm. Irish Sugar is, however, another story. As we shall see it is very much another case of Irish entrepreneurs 'doing for themselves'.

Sugar, not spice, but the money is nice

On 1 September 1991 details of action being taken against a firm of solicitors in Cork were published in an Irish Newspaper. The plaintiff was one Christopher Comerford, the Chief Executive-Managing Director of a company called Greencore. The case was brought in the matter of the disputed ownership of a mysterious Jersey-based company called Talmino; Mr. Comerford was claiming a £2.1 million stake in the company, through the agency of a loan note, which had been acquired in trust for his four adult children (Riegel, 1992). Comerford's action stands at the heart of a tangled web of corrupt and illegal activities, which yielded substantial profits to those who engaged in them. Untangling the web is, as we shall see, no easy matter. Nevertheless, an attempt to unravel at least some of the strands of the weave is worth the effort; as with the other cases reported in these pages, it tells us much about the sort of characters that inhabit the upper echelons of the Irish entrepreneurial establishment.

The roots of the affair we are about to describe lie deep in the history of the quest for Irish industrial development. In December 1926 the Irish Sugar Manufacturing Company was established to develop an Irish sugar industry. ISM was a private enterprise operation, which, with the aid of generous government grants and subsidies, put its first plant into operation in 1926. Despite government aid, however, the company could not operate profitably and by 1933 its position had become unsustainable. In that year the Irish government established a state company called *Comhluct Siucre Eareann Teo* (Irish Sugar Company), which took over the ISM operation and built three more plants as part of a determined drive to make state-sponsored enterprise succeed where private enterprise had failed.

And succeed it did. By 1935 its factories were processing some 70,000 tons of sugar and by 1940 its profits had passed the £300,000 mark, while, over roughly the same period, the number of farmers involved in beet growing increased from 27,700 to over 50,000. In 1946 the company began a diversification programme; it established an agricultural machinery division, went into limestone and subsequently launched a determined bid to develop the Irish food processing industry through its subsidiary Erin Foods, which, among other things, helped to pioneer the accelerated freeze drying process. In addition the company established the first national soil testing service in Ireland, provided its growers with technical advice, fertilisers and other aids, not excluding specialised machinery of its own design, and invested heavily in research and development activity. In all it was an effective operation designed to foster the rational development of Irish agriculture and its related food industries.

Despite, or perhaps because, of its manifest success, the activities of the company were constantly hampered by a weak and ineffective private sector and its alliances with politicians who were happy enough to place restrictions on state enterprise at the behest of the private sector. M.J. Costello, the company's general manager, voiced his frustration in a letter to the Industrial Development Authority written in 1957:

> It is fully realised that there would be an outcry from existing [private enterprise] producers if we were to go into competition with them (quoted in ICTU, 1986, p. 13).

The general manager's protests were in vain, though he continued to articulate the resentment felt in the company. Thus, in 1962 he wrote to the Department of Finance in the following terms:

> [T]his company has been compelled to carry out the development of food processing under handicaps whereas any other industrial development would be encouraged by financial aid ... the government's policy that this business will be grant-aided if it is run by or jointly with outside [private] firms, but will not be grant-aided if run by us, imposes a competitive disadvantage .... I think that we have shown satisfactory evidence that the sugar industry is one which has not only a chance of, but a great chance of expansion .... I think it is tragic that any doctrinaire consideration should result in its being handicapped or denied the assistance offered to others (quoted in ICTU, 1986, p. 13).

The 'doctrinaire considerations' to which Costello's letter adverted were, of course, the pro-private enterprise prejudices of the Irish political and entrepreneurial establishments which were hindering the development of his company's operations; it was denied access to the grant-aid available to companies operating in the private sector and was precluded from selling more than ten per cent of Erin Food's production on the Irish market in case it competed too effectively with private enterprise producers. It was through the 'doctrinaire prejudice' described by Costello that the seeds of the Talmino affair were sown and, indeed, germinated. As we shall now see they produced a singular crop.

The fact that Irish private enterprise was incapable of developing the country's sugar industry did not mean that it was unable to derive profits as a result of the state company's undoubted success. *Comhlucht Siucre Eareann Teo* (CSE) was a monopoly supplier of refined sugar to the Irish market. For some strange reason, however, it did not behave as a monopoly supplier; it did not handle its own distribution, but allowed a consortium of private enterprise wholesalers, acting through a company called Sugar Distributors Limited (SDL), to share the profits derived from its activities by allocating its distribution to them. This seemingly 'irrational' situation was allowed to persist - even though in 1975 CSE acquired a fifty-one per cent stake in SDL - to the obvious advantage of a private sector which played no part in the development of the industry; CSE allowed SDL to continue to make substantial profits, which between 1985 and 1991 amounted to some £9 million.

The dates 1985-1991 are significant here because they mark the duration of one Christopher Comerford's reign as chief executive of CSE, which was privatised in 1990 and now trades as Greencore. Comerford, as we have seen, is currently disputing the ownership of the Jersey-based company called Talmino against the claims of three other individuals, by names, John Murphy, Charles Lyons and Thomas Keleghan, to the beneficial ownership of that company. Lyons and Keleghan are significant actors in the drama which is about to unfold; Lyons was a Greencore executive and Keleghan was an SDL executive for over twenty years, and the former was, additionally and in company with another actor in the drama - one Michael Tully at the time the Company Secretary to Greencore - a director of a company called ISM Investments, which happened to be a subsidiary of SDL, which, to remember, was fifty-one per cent owned by Greencore (Gallagher, 1991). Tully, Lyons and Keleghan had, however, further interests which need to be reported here; they were, along with Charles Caravan the managing director of Odlums and a Greencore executive, shareholders in a company called Gladebrook. In 1989 Gladebrook bought out the forty-nine per cent private enterprise stake in Sugar Distributors Limited from the consortium of wholesalers which owned it for a total consideration of £3.3 million. This, in itself, was an interesting transaction; only £1.6 million was paid directly by Gladebrook, the balance was paid through a special dividend distribution by SDL itself.

If the plot to date seems complicated, it is about to become even more so. What we are confronted with so far is a situation in which four individuals, Tully (the Company Secretary of Greencore and a director of ISM Investments), Caravan (a Greencore executive), Lyons (a Greencore executive and a director of ISM Investments) and Keleghan (an SDL executive) had, through their company Gladebrook, acquired forty-nine per cent of SDL a company which was fifty-one per cent owned by Greencore for the consideration described above. Not the least interesting feature of this convoluted transaction was the manner in which it was financed. Gladebrook paid the consortium who owned the forty-nine per cent of SDL £1.6 million and the balance was paid in the form of a special dividend of £1.7 million from SDL itself. There is, however, more to the matter because the £1.6. million which Gladebrook actually paid was partly financed by a loan of £1 million from ISM Investments. To render matters as simply as possible the situation is as follows: ISM Investments (directors, Tully and Lyons) a subsidiary of SDL (of which Keleghan is an executive) which is fifty-one per cent owned by Greencore (of which Tully is company secretary and Lyons, Keleghan and Garavan are executives) makes a loan of £1 million to Gladebrook (in which Tully, Lyons, Keleghan and Garavan are the shareholders) to buy a forty-nine per cent stake in SDL. More SDL itself financed a further £1.7 million of the purchase through a special dividend. Now Greencore was a majority shareholder in SDL, so no special dividend could have been paid by SDL without the express approval of its majority shareholder, of which Tully just happened to be company secretary and Comerford managing-director and chief executive. It is clear, therefore, that the board of Greencore, of which Tully and Comerford were members, was willing to facilitate Tully and his associates (none of whom, as we have seen, was in any case unconnected to Greencore) to buy a minority shareholding in a Greencore subsidiary through their company Gladebrook. The board of Greencore facilitated them further when, a year or so after their purchase, it agreed to buy their stake in its subsidiary for a price that yielded Tully and his associates in Gladebrook a profit of some £7 million. We are now back with Talmino and Comerford's claim to the beneficial ownership of the company. Talmino owned a twenty-five per cent stake in Gladebrook, so whoever owns Talmino can claim a nice slice of the £7 million profit which Gladebrook made on its extraordinary transaction. Comerford, needless to say, did not declare his claimed ownership of Talmino to his board, the board which must have sanctioned the special dividend payment by SDL which helped to finance Gladebrook's purchase and, through its subsequent purchase of Gladebrook generated the profit of which Comerford now clearly wishes to claim a share.

As in the case of TE, the exposure of the dealings connected with the Sugar Company's outright purchase of its subsidiary gave rise to a good deal of public disquiet; there were calls in the Irish Parliament for the profits to be refunded and two separate enquiries were instituted into the affair. So complex were the issues to be investigated, however, that the enquiries came to different conclusions about the ownership of Talmino; one held that Comerford was the beneficial owner while the other vested ownership elsewhere. One of the enquiries pointed to potentially serious breaches of company law on the parts of those involved and there was some talk of prosecutions, though, so far as we know, no proceedings have yet been instituted against any of the parties involved.

What is principally of interest here, however, is not what happens to those involved, but rather what they did and what their activities tell us about the orientations of the Irish entrepreneurial establishment. The activities which we have described have to be seen against the background of the changed circumstances which the Irish sugar industry has had to confront following Ireland's accession to EC membership. Briefly these involved the removal of protection and the imposition of production quotas, conditions which exposed the industry to possible competition in its home market and placed limits on its possibilities of expanding through the manufacture of its traditional product - refined sugar. As a result, if the industry is to contribute to Irish economic development, it will have to rationalise and diversify its product range. Rationalisation has already begun; two of the company's four sugar refining plants have been closed, with dramatic economic consequences for the small towns in which they were situated. Diversification, however, remains to be pushed forward, and will, of course, require investment. It is only when this background is considered that the activities we have described are thrown into full relief. Instead of being concerned to lead their group of companies forward into a new era, some of those concerned with running them used their position and influence to get the group to finance their private purchase of a portion of a subsidiary company and a year or so later further exerted influence in persuading the group to purchase that share at a price that was so inflated as to yield them a profit of some £7 million. The point must be, of course, that the sum in question could have been put to other uses; it could, for example, have been used to assist in funding a diversification programme. Instead it has passed into the pockets of some well placed operators who will use it for their own purposes, whatever these may be. Again we make no moral judgement here. our judgement is a technical one and rests in the observation that the 'loss' of these funds is no help to a company facing the sort of future Irish Sugar is facing. The activities of those involved, therefore, have contributed nothing to Irish economic development.

Conclusion

In this chapter we have tried to present some case studies of Irish entrepreneurs 'doing for themselves'. Those readers who feel disposed to question their typicality or representativeness should read the material against the background provided in Chapter 2, which suggests that, while they may be more spectacular than many, the cases should not be regarded as exceptional in terms of the orientation to money-making disclosed in them. Here we have seen politically well connected members of the Irish entrepreneurial establishment 'doing for themselves', in fact doing extremely well for themselves, while at the same time contributing little or nothing to the promotion of self-sustaining economic growth which their economy and society needs if it is to develop and solve its social problems. In pointing to the close and cosy relationship that holds between elements of the Irish Republic's economic and political elites, the evidence presented here suggests that the relationship is also open to abuse; we have seen planning decisions reversed in a speculators' favour by a public board responsible to a minister who had a commercial relationship with the speculators, and whose appointments to the board concerned included individuals who were ex-employees of the speculators; we have seen evidence of failures to prosecute a politically well connected individual on a charge to which he had pleaded guilty in another jurisdiction; we have seen evidence that the state is willing to overlook violent acts undertaken by, or on behalf of, politically well connected individuals; we have seen that it is reluctant to give the fraud squad the powers, personnel and resources it needs to tackle fraud in the jurisdiction; we have seen, in Chapter 2, a state that seems reluctant to attack the problem of tax evasion at the individual and corporate level, a reluctance which, as we mentioned, gave rise to the suspicion that it stemmed from the fact that the evaders, many of whom were known to the authorities, were politically well connected; we have seen a state that is reluctant to amend its planning laws to protect near-bankrupt local authorities from the predations of politically well connected property speculators claiming compensation, or to legislate against rezoning from which so many, including sometimes politicians and their relatives and friends, make a lot of money at the expense of rational planning. In short we have seen a state that is manifestly willing to countenance forms of money-making which, if they are not corrupt, border on the corrupt, and which certainly do nothing to assist in achieving the development to which so much lip service is paid. In short we see a state that exhibits many of the characteristics of Myrdal's soft state, an institution which is more typical of the third world than of the first. As summarised by Goldthorpe (1975, p. 145) this kind of state exhibits, and thus fosters a social climate distinguished by:

> 'a lack of social discipline'; deficiencies in law enforcement; disregard of the rules by public officials at all levels, and their collusion with powerful persons whose conduct it was their duty to regulate. In particular, 'tax evasion by the affluent is colossal'.

When read against the background of the evidence presented in Chapter 2, the material in the present chapter accentuates the sense of paradox to which a careful reading of Chapter 2 must give rise. We say this because the 'sheer torpor' exhibited in the listlessness of the Irish entrepreneurial approach to resources and opportunities might be taken as a simple reflection of some anti-materialist ethic, orientation towards which directs people away from too much engagement in profit-hunting. While such an ethic seems to exist in Irish society - the Dublin managers mentioned in Chapter 1, for example, seem to reflect it in the sentiments they expressed - it is one that is clearly qualified because the 'torpor' is broken by orgies of unscrupulous gain-seeking which, if anything, reflect a robust, prudentially and morally unregulated materialism.

The paradox is, however, more apparent than real. We can see this if we consider Max Weber's characterisation of economic traditionalism. Weber coined this term to describe the ethos of business people whose commitment to economic activity was limited; he applied it to people who did not see business as a field in which activity was to be pushed to its utmost limits, but rather as a field to be cultivated moderately, in terms of the amount of disciplined work and effort to be devoted to it, and in a spirit of satisfaction with existing markets, standards and techniques, so long as it enabled them to enjoy the standards of living to which tradition had accustomed them. Traditionalists, therefore, were a sleepy and undynamic lot when it came to the application of disciplined work and effort; they felt no special commitment to economic activity and to productive work and effort; they lived off the economy rather than for it, and so did not care how they made their money so long as they made it. Given this it followed that their sleepy and undynamic orientation towards disciplined work and effort was not incompatible with an amoral unscrupulousness when it came to the pursuit of gain; the fact that a greed for gain does not stimulate people to become active, committed and disciplined workers does not mean that it will not drive them to feats of unscrupulousness, as in the case of Weber's (1930a, p. 57) example of 'the Dutch sea-captain who "would go through hell for gain, even though he scorched his sails"'. Certainly the evidence suggests that Irish entrepreneurial action exhibits these traditionalistic orientations, and we want to find out why this is so. Before we try, however, more evidence to the point can be presented.

4   Food industry frolics

Introduction

In conversation about their country's failure to achieve economic development Irish people frequently advert to Ireland's lack of natural resources as one of the factors responsible for its comparatively underdeveloped condition.   There is, it has to be said, some truth in this observation, though it is far from being the whole story.   It is certainly true that Ireland lacked the deposits of coal and iron on which the heavy industrialisation which many countries achieved in the nineteenth century was based.   Nevertheless, the country had some of the best agricultural land in Europe and was by no means unfavourably placed in terms of achieving industrial development through the processing of her agricultural products.   Unfortunately for Ireland the record of her entrepreneurs in this area is not a good one; Irish food processing remains in a comparatively underdeveloped state, relying, in the main, on low value-added commodity exports in beef and in a very limited range of dairy products, which are, at the present time, very heavily dependent on intervention and export refunds from the EC.   In this chapter we want to look at some case study material from the food industry.   As with the cases reviewed in the preceding chapter, the material to be examined here involves some complicated trains of events.   Nevertheless, it is also revealing as to the extent to which attempts to develop an industry can be frustrated by the entrepreneurs who are operating in it.

Our cases in this chapter will be taken from the meat processing industry.   The common opinion among those 'in the know' is that fraud is widespread in that sector of Ireland's food processing industry.   Arriving

77

at a reasonable estimate of its extent is, however, difficult; the companies themselves are secretive and the Irish government is very reluctant to come clean about the issues. European and Irish taxpayers, and often the customers, are the principal victims of the fraudsters in the meat industry who profit widely through making fraudulent claims relating to intervention, aids to private storage (APS), export refunds and through the shipping of sub-standard meat. As an agent for the EC the Irish Department of Agriculture is responsible for administering the refunds - which can be of the order of £2,500 per tonne - and for ensuring that the rules are kept. Yet as O'Keeffe (1990b) points out:

> Most of the rules have been broken by many companies at various times. The Court of Auditors of the European Commission reported in 1987 on problems such as export refunds being paid on goods which never left the EC; grossly inadequate examination of beef exports and superficial examination of a few cartons; no defrosting of packaged meat to check its status; and exports through non-approved ports with no official records of examinations.

As we shall now see the evidence available provides ample justification for the concerns expressed by the Court of Auditors.

A pig in a poke

Ireland produces some 2.1 million pigs per year, about one per cent of the EC total. The effective development of the industry has been limited by the small home market and by the fact that its products are uncompetitive in export markets when pitted against those of Denmark and The Netherlands, Europe's largest and most cost effective pig meat producers. Traditionally Irish pig meat production has been in the hands of small, often family owned, processing units which have relied on the home market, with some limited exporting of cured Wiltshire side, on a commodity basis, into the UK market. Practically nothing was done to enhance the international competitiveness of the industry; animals were finished at low weights resulting in a poor meat yield, and this, combined with poor marketing, kept prices low against a background of high input costs.

High feed costs have, in fact, been the major problem confronting the Irish industry. Feed costs account for about three-quarters of the total cost of producing pigs, and the simple truth is that the Danes and the Dutch enjoy significant advantages over the Irish in this vital region. These advantages derive from the superior organisation of Dutch and Danish production; Dutch production is concentrated near the port of Rotterdam and can take advantage of cheap bulk imports of tapioca, which, together with soya, accounts for well over half of Dutch feed and thus reduces the industry's needs for more expensive cereal-based products; Danish production is cereal-based, but has the advantage of a highly efficient compounding industry and extensive use of cheap on-farm compounding (Roche, 1989, pp. 68-9). In Ireland, by contrast, the compounding industry is inefficient and in need of rationalisation, and on-farm compounding has not been developed on the Danish pattern. Irish producers rely heavily on dairy by-products, something which may be responsible for the low feed conversation rate that is the rule in Irish production (Roche, 1989, p. 68).

As with all meat products pig meat can be traded either as a commodity or in more fully processed forms. When traded as a commodity the meat is sold in sides to wholesalers or retailers who further cut and process it for themselves, something that makes commodity trading a low value-added activity as far as the first processor is concerned. Alternatively first processors can add value themselves; they can produce the meat in fully processed form, ready for retail sale form and dispose of it direct to retailers in modified atmosphere packs which can be sold direct to consumers. Pork is particularly suitable for trading in this fully processed form; it does not suffer from the loss of bloom which shortens the shelf life of similarly processed and packed beef, and producers have accordingly moved away from commodity trading and towards the production of fully processed consumer products. The Irish industry has, however, been slow to follow this pattern; the bulk of Irish pork is still exported as a low-margin commodity product (Roche, 1989, p. 71).

Export markets for pork are substantial and thus offer significant opportunities for the development of Irish production; Germany, for example, imports about 500,000 tonnes per year, while Italy and France import 480,000 tonnes and 360,000 respectively. Japan, however, is by far the most lucrative market, importing up to 250,000 tonnes a year and offering prices up to three times higher than those available in Europe. At present Ireland has a very small share of these markets; its exports to Japan, at 4.000 tonnes a year, are negligible when compared to the 100,000 tonnes a year that come from Denmark (Roche, 1989, p. 75).

In 1988 the Industrial Development Authority announced an ambitious strategy for the development of the Irish pig meat industry; the programme had an investment target of £140 million, aimed to increase exports by some £350 million and to create around 5,000 new jobs. Among others a company based in the small County Monaghan town of Ballybay seemed set fair to play a leading part in the development of pig meat production in Ireland. In 1981 a family called McCabe founded a pig processing plant in the town. On the whole this seems to have been a successful enterprise; it attracted the interest of a leading Danish food company (ESS Foods) who took a minority stake in it and helped it to develop a thriving export trade, not least in the lucrative Japanese market. As a result of its success the company outgrew its original plant and set about the construction of a new state of the art production unit. Ballybay Meats opened this new plant in April 1989. It was built at a cost of £6 million, employed 170 people and was claimed to be the most modern pig meat processing unit in Europe. Grant aid was, of course, provided on a lavish scale; the totals, from European and Irish sources, amounted to some £4 million, around two-thirds of the total cost of the plant.

Ballybay Meats, however, did not fulfill their original promise. After only nine months of operation their plant was in the hands of the receiver. In all the company's debts amounted to some £10 million; £3 million was owed to the Ulster Investment Bank - who sent in the receiver; £2 million to pig producers; and £4 million to other creditors, including £600,000 to an Irish government agency (RTE, 1991a). This, however, was no ordinary bankruptcy.

When the receiver moved in on 5 January 1990 the first discovery he made was that the computer had been wiped clean of all accounts; some records were eventually discovered - in a rubbish skip - after the receiver was given an anonymous 'tip-off' - and hard disc copies existed, on which, however, to quote the receiver: 'an exercise had been done' (RTE, 1991a). Leaving the accounts for the cold store the receiver made another interesting find; the store contained nearly 8,000 made up, wrapped boxes which were clearly ready for dispatch. According to the labels the boxes contained neck fillet, and the total consignment would have been worth well in excess of £300,000, if only the boxes had contained anything. And they did not contain anything; when opened and examined each and every one of them was found to be empty (RTE, 1991). Somewhat bewildered, the receiver asked one of the McCabes for an explanation and was told: 'It was not illegal'.

Illegal or not, it soon became clear that the receiver was not the only party interested in looking into the affairs of Ballybay Meats; the Irish Department of Agriculture was 'sniffing around', so were the Irish customs, the fraud squad and even the Danish police. As usual the Irish authorities were unwilling to provide information about the nature, scope and reasons for their investigations; as in all other cases where fraud is suspected the authorities kept their own counsel. ESS Foods was, however, more open about the reasons for the involvement of the Danish police; according to their managing director the Ballybay plant was used to stamp and repack cheap European pig meat in forged copies of boxes used by the Danish slaughterhouse, Royal Dane Quality (O'Keeffe, 1990a). Understandably ESS was very unhappy about the forgery; the firm had a high reputation for quality and did not want it compromised by the sale of low quality meat masquerading as its product, especially on the US market where the forged product was evidently sold. Ballybay Meats has denied the Danish allegation, though evidence of documentation bearing Royal Dane Quality stamps has been found at their plant (O'Keeffe, 1990a).

Fraud and forgery notwithstanding, the receiver was confident that he could dispose of the plant as a going concern, save 170 jobs for an area that needed them badly, and provide the European and Irish taxpayers, who had between them 'subscribed' some £4 million towards the costs of the plant, some return on their 'investment'. And why should he not have been? He had, after all, an almost new, 'one owner', £6 million, state of the art plant in pristine condition which prospective buyers could have obtained for around £2 million. A week before the plant was put out to tender, however, someone threw the proverbial spanner into the receiver's works with a vengeance. What happened is best described by the person responsible for security at the plant:

> 20-25 people, some of them wearing combat jackets, balaclavas, carrying sort of truncheons, chains, came into the premises [and]

just literally took it over (quoted in RTE, 1991a).

The occupying group included former workers at the plant and would only speak to members of the McCabe family. Subsequently George McCabe, the former managing director of the company, held a rally at the plant gate at which he claimed that both his family and his company were the victims of a malicious campaign of vilification (RTE, 1991a).

From the outset the objective of the occupying forces was clear; it was not to defend the jobs or to secure better wages and conditions, but was intended, rather, to deter all prospective buyers from tendering for the plant in order to ensure that the McCabe family, and only the McCabe family, could buy it back from the receiver. And the stratagem worked: Although the receiver obtained a court order against the occupation force, no commercially viable tender for the plant was received. To the receiver's view this was a direct and unambiguous result of the occupation.

Although they were compelled to leave the plant as a result of the court order, the defenders neither stood down from action stations nor left the field of combat to the enemy; they placed a permanent picket on the plant and were clearly determined to hold the line until the individuals who ran the plant into bankruptcy could get their hands on it again. A systematic and sustained programme of intimidation now began; the lives of the receiver and his staff were threatened; the hotel at which they were staying received threatening telephone calls; the receiver's car was followed bumper to bumper in an attempt to further intimidate him - the driver of the following car - a former employee of the company was fined £100 for dangerous driving as a result (RTE, 1991a). The same former employee later threatened to cut a security guard's throat, along with the former secretary to the managing director, who announced, in the hearing of a police officer, that she would burn the security guard and his family out of their home; offences for which the individuals concerned were subsequently fined £2 (RTE, 1991a). And the trail of intimidation did not end there, as a representative of the company responsible for security at the plant testified:

> About an hour-and-a-half after [the threats against the security guard] some of them arrived at my house. They were in a car. I'd been actually driving from town, I was driving home, I had my son with me when I pulled into the driveway. The car followed me in, a number of people emerged from the car, approached me, one of them made some threats, talked about the incident that happened earlier and again I was told to leave Ballybay and to have no more to do with it (quoted in RTE, 1991a).

The same individual who harassed the receiver in the car case and threatened to cut the security guard's throat was involved in this incident and was once more arraigned before the awful majesty of the law; the district justice presiding at his trial told him that 'he stepped way out of line' and adjourned the case for a year (RTE, 1991a).

Threats against the receiver, his staff and the security people were not, in themselves, enough to secure the defenders's objective; if the plant was to be preserved for purchase by the McCabes alone, all other potential buyers had to be discouraged from bidding for it. Once again, therefore, the defenders resorted to intimidation. One potential buyer, a leading Irish food company, was warned off in no uncertain terms. In a public statement they revealed:

> Within 24 hours [of visiting the plant to inspect it] two of the executives had been contacted, one on his car phone. They were told that if they bought the factory they wouldn't be allowed to operate it. It was made clear to them that this was a family business and that the McCabes should get it back - nobody else would be allowed to run the factory. It was stated that this approach had the full support of the people of Ballybay (quoted in RTE, 1991a).

Another company believed to be interested in the plant, also made public the warning they had been given:

> Early in 1991 an unfounded rumour arose that an executive of [this company] was about to purchase the Ballybay plant. He was told that if he bought the factory he would not be allowed to operate it. It was made clear to him that this was a family business, and that the McCabes should get it back and that nobody else would be allowed to run the factory (quoted in RTE, 1991a).

Evidently the people of Ballybay were initially sympathetic towards the McCabes, and, therefore, presumably willing to give some support to the pickets 'protecting' the plant. As time passed, however, and the plant stayed closed, this support began to dissipate, as the loss of 170 jobs in a small town like Ballybay (population about 3,000) was commercially damaging to local business interests. The local chamber of commerce became restive about the situation, as did many of the townspeople, who were also beginning to become concerned about the reputation of the town. Needless to say, the receiver was also becoming increasingly irritated; he had a virtually new, ultra-modern plant worth £6 million on his hands, and even at the 'bargain basement' price of £1.4 million, there were no takers. Clearly the defenders, and those backing them, had every reason to be pleased.

The affair dragged on through 1990; in November of that year a person, or persons, unknown, blocked the entrance to the plant by dumping a load of rubble in front of it, and the circle of intimidation widened to include members of the chamber of commerce and anyone else in the town who dared to speak out against what was happening - one person is known to have received a death threat, another had a dead mouse and a pair of Rosary Beads pushed through his letter box. The chamber of commerce organised a token demonstration and went to remove some of the rubble and were confronted by the McCabes and their supporters. Minor scuffles ensued, though there were no arrests.

By 1991 opinion in the town had swung heavily against the McCabes and those picketing the plant; Ballybay was becoming something of a national scandal and its people wanted to see the plant back in operation. Local *Fianna Fail* politicians also came in for criticism; the area had two *Fianna Fail* TDs (members of the Irish Parliament) and one Senator, none of whom seemed willing to speak out against the intimidation - the McCabe family were prominent members of the *Fianna Fail* party. This silence was roundly condemned, not least because one of the TDs was a minister, who might have been expected to behave in a responsible fashion. One local notable was in no doubt about this:

> I'm particularly disappointed with Rory O'Hanlon, a minister whose got the power to be able to act ... he's got the big stick ... he doesn't seem to be interested about it ... its killing the community, definitely killing the community (quoted in RTE, 1991a).

In April 1991 the receiver lost patience and finally secured the removal of the rubble that was blocking the entrance to the plant amid growing optimism and reports that a potential buyer had paid it a visit. Nothing daunted, however, some person, or persons, unknown put in a replacement load of rubble overnight, so the citizens of Ballybay woke up the following morning to find the *status quo ante* well and truly restored (RTE, 1991b). Following this the receiver announced that he was giving serious consideration to breaking-up the assets and selling them off piecemeal, whereupon the McCabes made the following astonishing move: They offered to buy the plant, which to remember cost £6 million and which they had run into bankruptcy with debts totalling £10 million, for £500,000 (RTE, 1991b).

Like Queen Victoria the receiver was not amused: he rejected the offer out of hand, though he was willing to sell to the McCabes provided the price was right. The Industrial Development Authority, The Irish Farmers Association - representing the pig producers to whom Ballybay owed £2 million - and, by now, many of the local people were opposed to the McCabes getting their hands on the plant. In any case the plant's export licence was revoked early in 1991, thus precluding its operation. As usual the Irish government made no public statement about the reasons for the revocation of the licence, though we can safely assume that the licence would not have been withdrawn if everything had been above board in the operation of the plant. The local *Fianna Fail* TDs, including the government minister, remained very reluctant to come out against the McCabes. At a public demonstration in Ballybay the minister, Mr O'Hanlon, stated that he wanted the plant reopened under 'credible management', after which the following exchange took place:

> Interviewer: But the Minister for Agriculture actually announced ... that he had revoked the export licence for the company under the McCabe management and is seriously concerned about some of the irregularities that seem to have been going on there. Given that situation in which a cabinet colleague of yours has expressed his concern, do you think it appropriate in this point of time that a bid from the McCabe brothers should be accepted?
> O'Hanlon: Yeah know, don't be puttin' words in my mouth. The

point is that I want to see credible management in it, and I underline credible management (quoted in RTE, 1991b).

The Minister for Agriculture, Michael O'Kennedy, was more willing to call a spade a spade in the course of a TV interview, parts of which went as follows:

Interviewer: Mr. O'Kennedy, should this man, George McCabe be allowed to buy that plant again?
O'Kennedy: Let me say in the first instance that I revoked the export licence for that plant in January [1991] for good and sufficient reasons. I won't restore any export licence unless I have good and sufficient reason for doing so, in the first instance. Now I've seen no public explanation from George McCabe or the McCabe family, any one of them, as to the reasons for the collapse so soon after the launch of the plant. Neither for that matter have I seen any public condemnation by the McCabe family of the intimidation which is clearly going on down there. I think that would help a lot, but let me assure you, as far as I am concerned, the licence is a pre-condition and it will not issue unless I am satisfied that not only the plant, but also the actual management of the plant is credible and acceptable.
Interviewer: And right now, would you regard George McCabe as a credible manager?
O'Kennedy: Well I've commissioned a report which is very detailed; and a lot of *Garda* investigations are taking place, and incidentally, police investigations in four countries. That's a matter, of course, for the police in the various countries and the law must take its course ... I am not prepared to engage in speculation at this point, there is no application [for an export licence] to me.
Interviewer: £4 million of taxpayers' money was involved in setting up that plant and we now seem to be in a situation where all prospective buyers, except for one, particular prospective buyer, are being frightened off; where the pickets are all in favour of one particular buyer, and where all that buyer is offering is half-a-million pounds, which the receiver says isn't enough, not by one-third is it enough?
O'Kennedy: That obviously is totally and utterly unacceptable ....
Interviewer: What's totally unacceptable?
O'Kennedy: A state of the art plant which was grant aided both by government, the IDA and by the European Community, as part of a major new rationalisation programme for the pig meat industry, which incidentally is going very well in other plants, that not only isn't operating, but that it is prevented from operating. That the people of Ballybay who clearly are entitled to have the opportunity for seeing their region and their employment restored, that they are being prevented from that by some disgraceful intimidation. And I find that I'd like to see that kind of intimidation is not only stopped, but publicly repudiated.
Interviewer: And to what extent do you think George McCabe was

responsible for that situation?

O'Kennedy: Well that's not a matter for me particularly to say. But I have to say that I found it strange on this particular programme, when in the face of all the facts, George McCabe actually said 'there is no intimidation; there is no evidence of intimidation'. We seem to be looking at two different situations. I heard the receiver; I saw that programme; I am aware of certain reports. Of course there's intimidation - disgraceful intimidation.

Interviewer: And how are you going to stop it? There are many people who say that the authorities should have gone in a long time ago to stop it.

O'Kennedy: Well I think in the first instance there are various responsibilities. I have mine as a minister on behalf of the government, and mine relates to the operation of the export licence and I've told you the conditions I attach to that. There is then the responsibility of the receiver. Incidentally, I hope that it won't be a break-up; that it will be an opportunity to restore that plant to effective operation.

The Ballybay case is, perhaps, the most spectacularly destructive example of Irish entrepreneurship that is available for review in these pages: A new, state of the art plant was run into bankruptcy in under a year, in very suspicious circumstances, and was kept closed for a long period by threats and intimidation, the purpose of which was patently obvious: namely, to see control of the plant restored to those who had run it into bankruptcy. The result was that heavy losses were sustained; the Irish and European taxpayers, who contributed massively to the plant's construction costs, lost; a share of a valuable export market was lost, with what damage to the credibility of Irish suppliers it is hard to say; pig producers, other suppliers and the banks lost; the workers lost, as indeed did the trade and commerce of a small town that depended heavily on the plant's contribution to its local economy. Ireland's commercial reputation must, of course, also have suffered; ESS Foods were none too pleased about the alleged forgeries carried out in the Ballybay plant, and could hardly be blamed if they were to become reluctant to deal with other Irish companies - and the same could be said for other foreign firms contemplating involvement with Irish producers.

The adventures of Mr Beef: a plan for development

Ireland's beef processing industry is renowned for its secrecy; it is dominated by private companies who are not required to publish details of their financial affairs and who are most reluctant to submit their activities to any kind of outside scrutiny, public or otherwise. Although there are about twenty processing companies presently operating in the trade, the industry is dominated by one company: Goodman International. This controls some forty-two per cent of Irish processing capacity and dwarfs its nearest rivals; the second and third largest companies control only sixteen and eight per cent of national processing capacity (Roche, 1989, p.

58). Goodman International reached its present standing as Ireland's - and indeed Europe's - biggest beef producer through the brilliant entrepreneurship of its founder Larry Goodman; he grew the company from virtually nothing to a point where its sales amounted to some £760 million by sheer acumen and unflagging work, and, through acquisitions in other sectors, built up a large empire in the food industry in Ireland and beyond. Controlling over forty per cent of the vital beef export trade, Goodman, and his company, were key players in the drama of Irish economic development. He was, indeed, Ireland's - if not Europe's - Mr Beef.

Leaving aside altogether the question of the close personal relationships between Goodman and leading members of Ireland's largest political party - *Fianna Fail* - the extent of his competence and the scale of his operations makes the Irish government's willingness to support his plans for the development of the Irish beef industry understandable. Goodman's now famous plan was first announced in 1987. Government support was to be forthcoming in the form of grant aid - up to £30 million from the Irish Industrial Development Authority and £30 million from the EC agricultural grant agency; section 84 loans - low interest loans available to manufacturing companies on the basis of tax breaks to the lending institutions - to the possible value of £120 millions; and new legislative provision that allowed tax relief on the full capital costs of investments in the food processing industry, including the IDA and EC grant components. Involving as it did the upgrading of six existing plants and the construction of four new ones, the plan was an ambitious one designed to yield over 650 new jobs. Given the general condition of the Irish economy and the prevailing high unemployment rate the enthusiasm with which the plan was greeted was understandable.

While the Industrial Development Authority gave its broad support to the plan it did enter some reservations about it; it was concerned about the level of EC funding being provided because this amounted to about half of the EC aid available to the Irish beef industry in a seven year period; it was also worried about the expansion of slaughtering capacity by 150,000 head when there was already overcapacity in the industry. Feeling that, in conditions of overcapacity, the construction of new plants would simply build up Goodman at the expense of his competitors, the IDA refused to sanction the construction of new plants. Discussions broke down and the company withdrew.

At this stage the government intervened and the IDA accepted the plans subject to a strict performance clause. The plan was then announced to the public in June 1987 at a press conference at which the Prime Minister and the head of the company were present. Special steps were then taken to ensure that the company could avail itself of the section 84 loans. Normally these were available only to companies that manufactured seventy-five per cent of what they sold, a stipulation that caused concern because if the company put more than twenty-five per cent of its sales into intervention it could be deprived of relief. By all accounts the Industrial Development Authority was successful in ensuring that section 84 loans would be available and a final draft agreement was signed by both sides in December 1987.

In February 1988, however, the company made an additional demand: it wanted the special performance clause removed from the agreement concluded with the IDA. The Authority reacted angrily and wrote to the head of the company reminding him that the clause was an integral part of the agreement. In March the head of the company met the Prime Minister at his private residence and the government agreed to drop the offending clause enabling a new grant agreement to be signed on 22 March 1988. Department of Agriculture and IDA approval was then given for EC funding to two projects and all seemed set fair for the development programme to get under way. The company, however, did little or nothing to activate the plan and ultimately demanded that the IDA underwrite the combined IDA and EC grants to the tune of fifty per cent of the total asset investment before it did so. The Authority could not agree to this and finally withdrew from the project in June 1990. No investment was made, no grants were paid, and so no development actually resulted from the great scheme. The company, however, obtained the considerable benefit of being able to draw down some £70 million worth of cheap section 84 loans.

The further adventures of Mr Beef: strange tales from the cold store

While the decline and fall of Goodman's development plan was unfolding, a train of events carrying accusations of fraud, fiddles and (political) favouritism was running through meat plants owned and controlled by his company. The train departed in 1986 and travelled in great secrecy for over two years until the first intimations of the nefarious doings of its operators reached the public when an opposition Member of Parliament raised the whole question of fraud in the beef industry in March 1989. Government response was rapid and predictable; the Prime Minister, speaking 'with a full sense of responsibility', accused the Member of attempting to 'sabotage the entire beef industry in this country', sentiments echoed later by the Minister for Agriculture who declared 'this kind of publicity can do untold damage to the international reputation of the beef industry' (quoted in Barry et al, 1989a). Fraud had, indeed, been discovered and penalties were agreed and accepted in secret by the company and the authorities. Clearly neither side wanted publicity. Ultimately, however, they were unable to prevent it; the veil of secrecy surrounding the Irish beef industry was to be lifted thanks partly to a British television broadcast in May 1991. The allegations carried in the programme were so potentially damaging that the government was forced to set up an Independent Tribunal of Enquiry.

A definitive account of the complex situation concerning fraud in the beef industry is not possible because the Tribunal has not concluded its deliberations. Nevertheless, firm evidence of large scale fraud does exist, of which some account can be given, always provided that we are careful to distinguish between what can be established as matters of fact, and what must remain, for now at least, matters of allegation only..

Ireland's beef export trade is very dependent on EC export refunds; nearly half of it is done with non EC countries, at world prices which are too low to make it viable without the refunds. Export refunds are administered on behalf of the EC by the Irish Department of Agriculture, and are paid against documentation specifying both the weight of the meat and its eligibility to attract refunds. Although checks are made, the system in place offers unscrupulous exporters opportunities to enhance their profits by two simple, though fraudulent, expedients: they can falsely overstate the weight of the consignments shipped on the documentation, that is they can claim refunds on meat which does not exist, and/or they can ship trimmings, which do not qualify for EC refunds, in boxes purporting to contain meat of the correct, refund-attracting, quality - thus defrauding the customer as well as the EC.

Late in 1986 Irish customs officials discovered both types of fraud taking place in cold stores owned by the Goodman company; in every case examined the weights recorded on the documentation were higher than the actual weights of the boxes to which the documents related, and twenty-seven out of a sample of thirty-nine boxes opened and examined were found to contain trimmings falsely represented as meat for which refunds were available (Millotte, 1991). Goodman's response was to deny responsibility for the fraud; it was put down to the activities of a sub-contractor who was responsible for the boning, boxing and weighing of the meat. Needless to say the sub-contractor rebutted this charge, counter-claiming in the process that Goodman employees re-weighed the meat before putting it into cold storage (Barry et al, 1989a). Since neither side has publicly elaborated on the terse contradictory statements reported, it is impossible to decide where the balance of the truth lies. Three points can, however, be made with certainty: First, fraud was definitely taking place. Second, it was the Goodman company that stood to benefit from it. Finally, an incident occurred during a subsequent customs investigation that is difficult to reconcile with the theory of sub-contractor responsibility. Goodman employees were allowed to assist the customs in the investigation, at which only customs officials and Goodman employees were present. In the course of the investigation a person or persons unknown altered the weights on boxes of meat in a clear attempt to hide discrepancies and so frustrate the purposes of the investigation. Since this is a serious offence, someone was taking a considerable risk in order to protect the sub-contractor. As Millotte (1991) points out, 'it was unlikely to have been a customs man'.

While the initial customs' investigation seems to have been rapid and effective - they knew they had uncovered a major fraud by March 1987 and submitted a report to the Department of Agriculture in September of that year recommending that the Goodman company be prosecuted and stating firmly that the weights were altered by Goodman employees as described above - subsequent enquiries were extremely slow; the Department of Agriculture did not call in the fraud squad until February 1988, and another ten months elapsed before the fraud squad obtained a copy of the customs' investigation report - rather obviously the essential starting point for the investigations (Millotte, 1992a). Even then only two officers were allocated to the case on a part-time basis to investigate what one of them described as the biggest fraud he had ever investigated (Millotte, 1992a). The officers, neither of whom had any previous experience of investigating beef frauds, conducted an investigation lasting two years and turned up nothing new. They finally reported to the Director of Public Prosecutions in January 1991, shortly after which it was decided that no prosecution should take place. As the senior legal assistant in the DPP's office put it in his report:

> Whatever hope there might have been in bringing home criminal responsibility for such activities, was effectively eliminated by the inordinate delay in completing the investigation and in particular in referring the matter to the Garda Siochana [the Irish Police] (quoted in Millotte, 1992a).

Slowness was , however, not the only feature of the investigation; it was also, it seems, somewhat confined in its extent. On 18 March 1987 Goodman asked for, and was granted, an urgent meeting with the chairman of the Revenue Commissioners, Seamus Parcear. At this meeting Goodman reiterated his claims about the sub-contractors, offered to forego the financial benefits of the fraud and pay the costs of the investigation - provided it was called off immediately (Millotte, 1991). Parcear informed Goodman that he had no power to call off the investigation, but he promised to bring Goodman's proposals to the attention of the then secretary of the Department of Agriculture, James O'Mahony. O'Mahony, however, had already met Goodman some two weeks before the Goodman-Parcear encounter, though details of the meeting have not seemingly emerged.

The customs investigation into the entire Goodman operation went ahead, although very few boxes of beef were actually opened and inspected. According to Millotte (1991) this happened because of an agreement between Goodman and the customs concluded at the end of July 1987, under the terms of which the investigation was curtailed in return for Goodman accepting the Department's method of calculating penalties. Given that twenty-seven of the thirty-nine boxes opened in the original investigation contained fatty trimmings masquerading as prime beef, the decision to curtail the investigation in this way must count as extraordinary. Nevertheless, the investigation was curtailed, so we shall never know what it might have revealed.

Although we shall never know what a comprehensive official investigation might have revealed about the Goodman operation, there are allegations, which, if they turn out to be proved, will show the operation to have been steeped in fraudulent practices, some of them, as we shall see, of a stomach turning variety. The allegations first surfaced in the British television programme (Granada, 1991) mentioned earlier, and most, if not all of them, have been repeated subsequently at the official tribunal. Most of the allegations were made by employees, and former employees, of Goodman's organisation, who saw his operations at first hand, and, indeed, were often directly involved in the frauds themselves.

An accountant who worked for Goodman summed up the approach of his company in the following terms:

> The philosophy of the company is basically profit maximisation.

You can only make so much money by doing it right, but it's so easy to make much more by abusing the system and all the factories did .... Mr. Goodman set the tone because he controlled the company very tightly (quoted in Granada, 1991).

Allegations made by the employee just quoted claim that Goodman's company abused the intervention system as well as the export refund system. The bases of the intervention abuse was as described earlier: falsification of documentation to misrepresent both the weight and quality of the meat being sold into intervention. The accountant can safely be allowed to continue the story at this point:

All intervention product has to be weighed in and the weights have to be recorder on a document called IB4 .... One of the ways of changing the weights was basically to reproduce an IB4. This would be a duplicate copy and what would happen is that the same details will be written down except that the weight would be increased by a certain amount of kilos. If there was any special notation such as signatures or other notations, or even blood on the original, this was put onto the duplicate (quoted in Granada, 1991).

The programme makers claimed to have copies of some IB4 forms, relating to intervention contracts from 1987. Some of these forms had been duplicated to show increases in weight of up to fourteen kilos for every animal.

Payment is also made on the basis of the quality of every animal. Quality is determined by a veterinary official employed by the Ministry of Agriculture who marks the carcase with an indelible grading stamp. Stamps are the property of the officials and they are kept under lock and key in each factory. If the allegations made are correct, however, it appears that the Goodman organisation had its own bogus sets of stamps, and that it used them to change the grades. According to another informant this was not an especially difficult operation:

It's very easy to change the grade ... with a knife you cut off the grade that's marked on the animal and you can then put any other grade you like on it (quoted in Granada, 1991).

Again the TV company claimed to be able to substantiate these accusations: It had obtained three bogus stamps from Goodman factories.

European taxpayers were not, however, the only victims of the Goodman company's allegedly fraudulent activities; customers suffered as well, receiving meat of questionable quality that was sometimes so bad as to be unfit for human consumption. In connection with one large Middle-eastern contract old frozen meat from intervention stores was subjected to a remarkable transformation: 'for a solid 18 months old frozen meat was turned into new' (Granada, 1991). Not for the first time someone who was involved can take up the story:

Informant: Some [of the meat] we noticed was dated as far back as

1974, that would have been thirteen years old at the time.

Interviewer: Did you rebox all of it?

Informant: Yes, all of it was reboxed as killed within the last week or two. Some of it was in pretty bad shape as well, it didn't look too good, some of it was turning green, some had been quite dirty, some of it was freezer-burnt, some had obviously been thawed and re-frozen it's er ... you could tell that by the colour of the bag that it's in, if the blood comes out it crystalises brown, even the top of the beef looks as if there was a fuzz on it.... No matter what shape it was in, it was all re-boxed (quoted in Granada, 1991).

When customers visited the plant measures were taken to conceal the re-boxing operations; the plant was cleaned up, the re-boxers were hidden away - sometimes they had to hide in the cold store to keep out of the way. Customers were thus deceived into thinking that they were getting high-grade meat for their money, when, in reality, they were being sold 'rubbish'.

Similar allegations were made by an ex-Goodman employee in the course of his evidence to the beef tribunal. According to this individual, as reported by Millotte (1992b), he himself engaged in an extensive range of illicit activities, including:

Cutting indelible "T" stamps off cattle from TB reactor herds and replacing them with EC health stamps so that the meat could be exported.

Breaking veterinary seals on meat containers and putting in illicit meat.

Switching low grade meat for high grade in the intervention system - and ineligible, low value cow beef for premium priced steer - defrauding the EC and enabling the factory to get the high price twice by selling the filched intervention product to UK supermarkets like Tesco and Safeway.

Extracting teeth from live cattle with a bolt cutter in order to deceive Muslim buyers into thinking that the cattle were much younger than they were - Muslims paid premium prices and wanted the best beasts. Clearly they did not always get what they paid for.

Regularly rerouting into the edible offal room livers that had been declared unfit for human consumption.

All these activities were carried on behind the backs of Department of Agriculture officials - including two veterinarians - who were responsible for monitoring production at the plant over the twelve year period in which the irregularities described went on. According to evidence given at the Tribunal, the officials did discover irregularities; they caught factory staff restamping TB reactors with EC health stamps. They did not, however, bring this matter to the attention of the Department of Agriculture. Instead they operated what one of the veterinarians, in evidence to the Tribunal, described as an 'in house agreement' with the factory management; whenever they detected false stamping of reactors they restamped the reactors with the required 'T' stamp, and, as a

91

punishment, put the 'T'stamp on an equal number of normal cattle. No further action was taken (Millotte, 1992b).

Two questions must now be asked: First, why did the investigation into the original 1986 fraud take so long? Second, why was the investigation into a fraud limited in scope seemingly after negotiations with the principal suspect? Like many good questions these are easier to ask than to answer. Nevertheless, the questions cannot be avoided; the evidence that the matter was not pursued with either vigour or effectiveness is too strong to be ignored.

The initial customs report recommending prosecution of the Goodman company was, to remember, given to the Department of Agriculture early in October 1987. It was first considered by an assistant principal officer in the beef division who recommended that penalties be imposed and that the matter be reported to the EC and to the fraud squad. These recommendations then went 'up the line' and reached the deputy secretary in January 1988, and he, in turn, reported the matter to the secretary James O'Mahony. For some reason O'Mahony arranged a meeting with a Goodman, either Larry or his brother. We do not know what transpired at that meeting. What we do know is that O'Mahony was on the point of retirement; he left the Department soon afterwards and subsequently became a director of a Goodman controlled company. O'Mahony's successor instructed Departmental officials to call in the fraud squad and briefed the *Taoiseach* (Prime Minister) on 25 January 1988 (Millotte, 1991). As we know the fraud squad took two years to complete their report.

It is obvious that the investigation into the Goodman affair was, at best, somewhat tardily conducted in terms of its speed and somewhat limited with reference to its scope. The slowness of the investigation might have been due to bureaucratic inertia and to the difficulties confronting the fraud squad, which, as we saw in the preceding chapter, is deficient both in the numbers and expertise of its personnel. Neither explanation is, however, entirely convincing: If the political will had existed to police the subsidies system, and fraud in general, then the inertia and the deficiencies in the fraud squad could have been remedied, and there remains, of course, the questions as to why the investigation was curtailed in negotiation with the prime suspect and why official reporting and penalty procedures were by-passed in favour of the cosy in house arrangements described above. Altogether these point to a lack of both political and official will to confront fraud in the beef industry.

There is evidence to suggest that this lack of political and official will to confront the problem was appreciated by the Goodman company and its employees. As one them, an accountant, put it:

> There was also a fear of being caught obviously in doing something that is basically illegal, but there was also a feeling that we were invincible, we had the right connections at the right places, that could basically control any investigation that could be put in place (quoted in Granada, 1991).

Recalling the reaction to the initial investigation in 1987, the same employee recalled that:

> There was a massive panic within the company and a plan was put forward as to how the damage could be limited. The plan was basically agreed between our people and the customs people at their head office that a certain sample of good meat would be selected for thawing out and investigation. This was a deliberate scheme to contain the damage because of the explosive nature of the investigation (quoted in Granada, 1991).

Viewers of the TV programme in which these allegations were broadcast were then treated to a sight of the masterplan which showed where the good boxes of meat, that the customs were supposed to open, were located.

According to the informant just quoted this plan did not work out correctly; seemingly local customs officials 'smelled a rat' and 'kicked up a fuss' about it, Nevertheless, it is clear from other evidence cited earlier that the investigation was neither rapid in its pace nor comprehensive in its scope. Its result was that the Goodman company had to pay a £1 million penalty in January 1989, although at one point the Department of Agriculture was considering a penalty as high as £10 million (Millotte, 1991). It was soon after this event that the veil of secrecy surrounding the affair began to be rent asunder.

As we saw it was an opposition member of the Irish Parliament (the *Dail*) who raised the matter with the *Taoiseach* and the Minister for Agriculture, requesting information and a debate on a number of occasions. His efforts attracted abuse and evasion; he was, to remember, accused of trying to sabotage the beef industry when he first raised the matter, and when he subsequently alleged that Goodman had been penalised the *Taoiseach* described his conduct as 'deplorable'. The clear implication of the government's riposte was that the opposition member was hopelessly wrong and that he should desist from future references to the beef industry and its troubles (Barry et al, 1989a). At the same time the Agriculture Minister went on to claim in a statement that 'all requirements of EC and domestic law are being adhered to', implying clearly that no irregularities had taken place, and so, by implication, vindicating the Goodman organisation. In the circumstances this proved to be incredible to some journalists, who, on pressing the Department of Agriculture, were given a crucially qualified version of the statement. This read:

> all requirements of EC and domestic law are being adhered to *by the state authorities* (quoted in Barry et al, 1989a, emphasis in the original).

In the light of the evidence even this statement is, at best, questionable. Nevertheless, the proverbial cat was at last beginning to emerge from the bag, though it took one more push - this time from the leader of the Irish Labour Party - before the opposition member's allegation that penalties had been withheld from Goodman was confirmed by the Minister for

Agriculture.

From all this it is quite evident that the Irish government were prepared to go to considerable lengths to protect the Goodman organisation from public exposure, in the process both the Irish Parliament and public were bombarded by misleading statements. It is also, of course, entirely possible that the government was trying to protect itself. It was, after all, bending over backwards to facilitate Goodman's plan for the beef industry; indeed it was doing so to the extent of providing £30 million worth of grant support from EC funds to a company that had been penalised to the tune of £1 million for defrauding the EC. And the government could not plead ignorance in extenuation of its behaviour. Although the *Taoiseach* denied 'official' knowledge of the affair in April 1989, he was, as we have seen, briefed about it by the Secretary of the Department of Agriculture in January 1988. Perhaps the matter slipped his memory, or might it have been the case that the briefing was somehow not an 'official' one?

The ultimate adventures of Mr Beef: crazy trading and a helpful government

Government support for the Goodman organisation was by no means confined to a willingness to provide it with lavish grants and protection from adverse publicity, if not indeed from the full rigour of the penalisation process. In March 1987 the *Fianna Fail* party returned to office and did the Goodman organisation a massive favour: they reinstated the export credit insurance scheme which had been suspended by the previous government - a *Fine Gael*-Labour coalition. This move greatly facilitated Goodman's activities in exporting meat to lucrative, but very risky, Middle-east markets, not least Iraq. Export insurance was reinstated and maintained against the urgings of the Insurance Corporation of Ireland (ICI), who acted for the government in insurance matters. Thus Mr. Frank Mee, ICI secretary, told the Beef Tribunal:

> our view was that there was a 50-50 chance of claims arising on the particular Iraqi cover. At that time there was a very tight budgetary situation in Ireland. You had hospitals being closed down for two or three million pounds. If claims arose it would be serious for the exchequer and we felt that, as a good agency who had to exercise prudence. We had to put our feelings on record (sic) (quoted in Millotte, 1992c).

In January 1988 Mee sent a detailed assessment of the risks associated with supplying Iraq to Finance Ministry officials. They could not have made comforting reading; oil revenue had fallen from $26 billion to an estimated $7.5 billion at a time when the country's external indebtedness amounted to some $100 billion. He also made no bones about stating that, in the opinion of ICI,

> the perceived success of Irish exporters in securing contracts in Iraq

is largely due to the unwillingness of other countries to supply goods to Iraq (Quoted in Millotte, 1992c).

In the circumstances Mee felt bound to express two conclusions: Firstly, that no further insurance cover should be provided on exports to Iraq. Secondly, that even the existing ceiling of £150 million on funds available was unjustifiably high. In spite of this professional advice, and it was repeated in substance the following September, ICI discovered that the Minister for Finance had sanctioned an additional $120 million cover for Goodman (Millotte, 1992c).

Questions about the export credit insurance scheme, however, go well beyond what the person on the Dublin omnibus might well regard as government recklessness in instituting and maintaining it in the face of the professional advice they were getting. There is also an awkward question concerning possible political favouritism in the distribution of the cover available, eighty per cent of which was given to the Goodman enterprise. According to evidence given at the Tribunal the initial £150 million available was kept in a secret fund, known evidently as number two account. This was not operated on a commercial basis, but was used to underwrite Goodman's exports when the Finance Minister, Albert Reynolds, believed them to be in the national interest. Millotte (1992c) sums the situation up as follows:

> While Goodman's competitors went to the ICI looking for export insurance for Iraq which it had no power to give, Goodman knew the secret: he went straight to the top.

To Desmond O'Malley - then in opposition as leader of the Progressive Democrats and later a minister in a coalition government which his party formed with the *Fianna Fail* - this amounted to 'blatant favouritism' - a charge which he has not dropped even though the Finance Minister against whom it was leveled, Albert Reynolds, became the Prime Minister of the coalition government in which O'Malley served. Other companies were certainly refused cover and put at a severe competitive disadvantage as a result; Taher Meats, for example, had to pay twenty-one per cent for commercial cover compared to the premium of one per cent at which government sponsored cover was available (Millotte, 1992c). Another company, Agra Trading, was also refused and suffered a thirty per cent cost disadvantage as a consequence (Morahan, 1992). Commenting on the case of another company that was refused cover - Halal - the chairman of the Tribunal opined that the refusal 'fits into the allegations of favouritism'; Halal was refused cover because it could not show a signed contract to supply beef to Iraq, a requirement that was not imposed on the Goodman company (O'Toole, 1992). It is, of course, a matter for the Tribunal of Enquiry to decide whether and to what extent favouritism was shown to Goodman. The truth is, however, that only one other company, Hibernia, was given access to cover under the state scheme; they received twenty per cent as opposed to the eighty per cent accorded to Goodman.

Once again, it seems, the Goodman company was given a special dispensation. And once again the special dispensation was abused. In this case the abuse was revealed through an investigation carried out by the consultancy unit of the Department of Industry and Commerce into a discrepancy between the official figures for beef exports to Iraq and the actual shipments made during the years 1987-88. In all this revealed that thirty-eight per cent of Goodman's total exports which were either insured or declared for insurance under the state-sponsored scheme had been sourced outside the state, and that a significant volume of the tonnage exported had been slaughtered and processed in plants located in England, Scotland and Wales (O'Halloran et al, 1992). The report stated that:

> examination of the documentary records and filing system used by AIBP [Anglo Irish Beef Processors - Goodman's company] indicates a highly efficient system for keeping all the documentary records in relation to each shipment. The existence of this system and the manner whereby the UK official documentary records in relation to beef sourced in the UK were kept, indicated that external sourcing of beef for exports to Iraq was an obviously well established company policy of which the management of AIBP would have been fully aware (quoted in O'Halloran et al, 1992).

Sourcing the beef outside Ireland was not, in itself, illegal - though it did little to promote the development of the Irish beef industry to which Goodman was ostensibly committed. Under the state sponsored scheme, however, only produce of the Republic of Ireland qualified for export cover, so Goodman's company should not have declared non-Irish beef for insurance under the scheme. In actual fact they did; shipments of UK sourced beef were given documentary certification as being of Irish origin and non-Irish beef was exported under Irish insurance. In the opinion of the Minister, Desmond O'Malley, this constituted 'a fraud on the state and the taxpayer' (quoted in Millotte, 1992c).

During the course of the investigation representatives of AIBP had assured the consultancy unit that all beef exported to Iraq was processed in the Irish Republic. At a subsequent meeting, however, an executive of the company admitted that over thirty per cent of its beef exports to Iraq came from Northern Ireland. As a solution to the problem he suggested that, since the total of beef exported to Iraq, including the non-Republican beef, exceeded the existing insurance cover, the Northern Ireland sourced shipments might be deleted and replaced by non-insured, legitimate shipments from the Republic (O'Halloran et al, 1992). Another cosy in-house solution, no penalties and, of course, no questions asked about what company policy would have been if the fraud had not been discovered!

As it happens no such easy salvation was available to the company on this occasion. By the end of 1988 the recklessness of the government in underwriting what would, without the insurance cover, have been reckless trading was coming home to roost; total exposure in Iraq amounted to £122 million, £51 million of which was seriously overdue (Millotte, 1992c). Iraq was taken off cover in January 1989, and, in the light of the frauds, Goodman's existing cover was voided in October of that year. Goodman immediately threatened legal proceedings and is currently sueing the Irish government for £160 million. And well he might, given that his exposure in Iraq amounted to some £200 million.

If the Irish government is to enter any defence against the charges of recklessness and political favouritism it can only lie in the articulation of a ministerial claim that what was done was done in the national interest and in the belief that Goodman was the only person capable of developing the beef industry and Irish agriculture along with it. We have already referred to his much vaunted plan for developing the beef industry, in which the *Fianna Fail* government reposed such hope, and to which they were willing to commit large sums in grant and other financial aid. As we have seen, however, Goodman's plan produced more procrastination than development, and there was, of course, the little matter of the export refund fraud on which the *Taoiseach* was briefed in January 1988. All the evidence suggests that Goodman was only interested in developing the Irish beef industry to the extent that it was taken to be synonymous with his own company's interests; he was not really interested in developing the industry in general, and in providing new jobs, but rather in building up his own power base in the industry at the expense of his rivals. There is, of course, nothing reprehensible about that; it is normal, competitive, capitalistic commercial practice. What is questionable, surely, is whether and to what extent it is legitimate for governments to commit taxpayers' money to assist a company to gain commercial advantages over its rivals. And that, whether the government fully appreciated it or not, is seemingly what happened. We have already seen some evidence in support of this argument; the IDA objected to that part of Goodman's plan to build new factories on the grounds that, in conditions of existing overcapacity in the industry, it might damage his competitors and presumably destroy as many jobs as it might create; the overwhelmingly privileged access which Goodman had to export credit insurance put some of his rivals at a competitive disadvantage in tendering for export contracts. If the Irish beef industry is to be developed on a sound footing what it needs is a greatly expanded capacity to produce high value-added processed food products which can be sold directly to retail outlets; at present only two per cent of Irish beef exports are fully processed, while forty-five per cent are in carcase form with bone in, that is to say they receive very little processing and have low added value.. In fairness to Goodman his plan envisaged development in the direction of increased processing, but nothing much was done about it. Instead Goodman proceeded to build his business by reckless low value-added commodity trading and an agressive policy of acquisitions rather than through the upgrading of his existing plant and product base. Critics have claimed that many of his acquisitions were spoiling operations designed to keep the competition out, and so reinforce his dominant position in the industry.

The misadventures of Mr Beef: boom and bust

Goodman's acquisitions became a cause of concern to the Irish Farmers' Association and ultimately to the Minister for Industry and Commerce in the *Fianna Fail*-Progressive Democrat coalition - the minister, Desmond O'Malley, was a Progressive Democrat; the farmers feared a growing

Goodman monopoly of the processing trade and were particularly concerned about the case of Classic Meats. Classic Meats is the third largest beef processor in Ireland accounting for some eight per cent of the country's export trade. Originally trading as Master Meats, the Company was owned by an Irishman, Paschal Phelan, and his Jordanian partner Zachariah Taher until it was sold to new owners in September 1988. Master Meats was bought by foreign investors and the transfer of ownership was approved by the government under monopolies and mergers legislation; the government was evidently under the impression that the company was close to liquidation and was assured that the investors intended to sell it in the near future (Godson, 1989b).

The circumstances of the sale were, to say the least of it, somewhat unusual and have given rise to litigation. In 1986 Phelan sold half of his shares in Master Meats to Taher and now alleges that Taher subsequently, and secretly, sold those shares to Goodman. Relations between Phelan and Taher were not always good, and in September 1988 Phelan offered to buy his partner's fifty per cent stake in the business. Under the terms of the original agreement between the two men, Taher could either accept Phelan's offer or make a higher counter offer for Phelan's own stake, in which case Phelan was obliged to accept the counter offer (Godson, 1989b: Nally, 1990). Phelan did not believe that Taher had the resources to take complete control of the company and so did not anticipate a counter offer. To his surprise, however, a counter offer was made and he had to accept it (Nally, 1990). On the following day Master meats was sold to the mysterious foreign investors who announced that they planned to sell off the company's plants.

If there was any suspicion about Goodman's surreptitious involvement in the takeover - and among farmers and people in the meat industry there certainly was - it must have hardened when the names of the three investors were revealed shortly after the takeover; they were all known associates of Goodman. Fearful about Goodman's growing monopoly power in the industry, the Irish Farmers' Association asked the then Minister for Industry to take steps to ascertain to whom the beneficial ownership of Master, now Classic, Meats belonged. This was not going to be an easy matter; the new owning company was registered in Liechtenstein under cover of that country's strict rules on secrecy, and the whole affair was so shrouded in mystery that the chief executive of Classic, Mr Quinn, asserted that even he did not know who the beneficial owner was (Barry et al, 1989b). Quinn's presence is, in itself, interesting in pointing up a possible connection to Goodman, and is certainly a good indication of the low moral standards prevailing in the Irish entrepreneurial establishment; Quinn worked as one of Goodman's managers for several years, and, while an employee of Goodman, was convicted of uttering forged documents relating to £168,408 of EC export refunds claimed in connection with Goodman exports. The trial judge described this as a 'venial' offence, and the Irish beef industry must share the view since it is obvious that a conviction for fraud is no barrier to employment at its highest levels. After a delay of seven months the government referred the matter of Classic (Master) Meats to the Fair Trade Commission, though in circumstances that angered the Farmers'

Association. In order to prepare their own submission to the Commission they asked it for details of the precise nature of the proposals it was to investigate and were refused on the grounds that the Commission could provide no such information without ministerial sanction. A subsequent request to the minister met with a response that was delayed beyond the deadline for submissions to the Commission and which the Farmers' Association described as 'dismissive and not treating the matter seriously' (quoted in Godson, 1989a).

The Fair Trade Commission failed to establish the beneficial ownership of Classic Meats; even it could not penetrate the veil of secrecy surrounding the whole question. Nevertheless, it did establish that Goodman was in effective control of the company and so went some way towards confirming the suspicions entertained in the beef and farming sectors. Pascal Phelan, one-time owner of Classic (Master) Meats was not surprised by the Commissions revelations: 'I have been consistent from the beginning about what happened. The farmers saw what happened with cartel prices this autumn' (quoted in Godson, 1989b). Phelan evidently sees the takeover as a Goodman engineered plot to eliminate him from the beef industry and is currently sueing Goodman for damages. Goodman has always denied that he is the beneficial owner of Classic. He does, however, admit to helping the Classic owners to find buyers for the plants they wanted to sell and to lending them some £20 million for working capital, without receiving beneficial ownership rights in return (Nally, 1990).

Subsequent investigations, however, revealed that, once more, the government seemed reluctant to allow the full facts to become public; they knew much more than they revealed. What they knew of was that a link existed between a secretive Liechtenstein registered, Goodman-owned company, by name Cork Company, and Classic Meats. The link was established through the director who 'tops the list' on the Cork Company's Liechtenstein registration documents. His name is Peter Marxer (Millotte, 1990d). It happens that Marxer is also a director of another Liechtenstein company called Tarsos Anstalt, which happens to be the company which acquired the ownership of Classic (then Master) Meats. This is what the Fair Trade Commission discovered, and what the government refused to make public - the facts were revealed in a newspaper article in September 1990. Once again, it seems, Goodman was to be protected.

By then, however, Goodman required protection from more than those farmers who were worried about the possible abuse of his dominant position in the Irish beef industry: the banks which had lent him large sums of money were becoming concerned about the prospects of ever seeing their money again. Most of Goodman's problems stemmed from the trade with Iraq which was so generously underwritten by the Irish government's insurance scheme. Payments from Iraq were small and late, yet Goodman had to go on supplying because putting Iraq on the stop list would probably have resulted in payments drying up altogether (Millotte, 1990c). As Goodman's problems deepened, the government became increasingly worried about the extent of possible insurance claims; the state's liabilities amounted to £110 million and claims looked increasingly likely. In January 1989 the government suspended the scheme, and, as we have seen, the Progressive Democrat industry minister, cancelled Goodman's existing coverage because of the frauds connected with the export of non-Irish beef. As a result Goodman was exposed in Iraq to the tune of some £200 million (Millotte, 1990c).

Goodman's problems were not, it has to be emphasised, a result of the Gulf crisis; they pre-date the Iraqi invasion of Kuwait and had come to the attention of one of his banks as a result of an investigation which began about a month before that event. The bank concerned was Allied Irish Banks (AIB), Goodman's second largest Irish creditor. Goodman made a perfectly normal request for an advance of working capital to finance the autumn kill; he needed about £200 million to finance his Irish operation, and some £50 million to finance the smaller British side of the enterprise (Millotte, 1990b). AIB sent in a task force and demanded detailed financial information on Goodman's operations before agreeing to any advance. Millotte (1990b) describes what happened:

> As the investigation proceeded, AIB senior credit manager, Ned O'Callaghan, soon realised he was dealing with a situation of crisis proportions. It has become apparent to the AIB team that Mr. Goodman's group of companies could not hope to service their accumulated debts, debts that are approaching £550 million and are owed to a range of international and Irish banks. With assets estimated to be worth £350 million, this leaves a gaping shortfall of £200 million.

In the circumstances AIB decided that it could provide Goodman with no further credit.

Goodman's borrowing needs were large. However, the scale of his operations, his financial muscle and his standing with the Irish government meant that he had little trouble in raising the credit he needed; his borrowings were spread across thirty-three banks in many countries, including Barclays in Britain, BNP in France, AMRO in The Netherlands and Commerzbank in Germany. According to Millotte (1990b) the bankers were watching the situation carefully; they were evidently worried enough to seek, and to be given, assurances from a senior Goodman executive that all was well with the company. When they discovered it was not, they refused Goodman access to the funds he needed to finance the autumn kill.

The extent of the Irish economy's dependence on Goodman's operations was starkly revealed when news of his difficulties finally became public in August 1990. One way or another he controlled nearly half of the country's slaughtering capacity and liquidation would have left tens of thousands of farmers without an outlet for their cattle - the sale of which often accounted for the bulk of their annual income. In these circumstances the failure of the Goodman companies would have amounted to a national catastrophe: Goodman had to be saved, or, at least, his companies had to kept in business and out of the hands of the liquidators. As was so often the case, the Irish government was evidently willing to oblige in the matter.

On 22 August 1990 Goodman met his worried bankers in London; he was in debt to the tune of some £550 million and several of the banks were determined to put his companies into liquidation. Goodman's financial adviser, Richard Hooper, requested a week's stay of execution, in order to put in place a rescue package which would offer the banks a better prospect of reclaiming their money than liquidation. As an incentive to the banks Hooper revealed the existence of the Liechtenstein registered Cork company and promised to make its assets available - it was reputedly worth £100 million pounds. He also assured them that he would seek Irish government financial assistance for Goodman International (Millotte, 1990f). At least one bank refused to play along with Hooper; the Dutch bank AMRO - to whom Goodman owed £30 million - decided to press ahead with liquidation (Millotte, 1990f). Clearly something had to be done about AMRO.

Something was done, though what was done is the subject of claims and counter-claims. These involved the EC Commissioner for agriculture, the Irishman Ray MacSharry, and the Dutch Minister for Agriculture, Gerrit Braks. What is not disputed is that MacSharry telephoned Braks on 23 August, the day after the London meeting with the bankers at which AMRO's threat to liquidate Goodman emerged. As a result of this call Braks contacted the deputy director general of the Dutch Agriculture Ministry and he, in turn, contacted AMRO whose managers then agreed to desist from their efforts to liquidate Goodman. This represented a remarkable change of heart by the bank; we have no evidence that they had, in the meantime, received reassuring information about Goodman's financial situation. The implications are, therefore, clear; MacSharry asked Braks to put pressure on AMRO to save the Goodman Empire and AMRO gave way under the pressure. Theodor Marious, a senior AMRO executive, confirmed this much in an affidavit, part of which stated that:

> following representations from a Dutch Minister for Agriculture (who stated that he had been asked to intervene) AMRO agreed to postpone action until after a further meeting of the bankers arranged to take place a week later on August 29 (quoted in Millotte, 1990f).

MacSharry has denied emphatically that he asked Braks to intervene on Goodman's behalf, and that he even spoke to Braks about Goodman at all; he claims that he telephoned to the Dutch Minister to talk about the problems of the beef industry generally and that he knew nothing of the Goodman affair beyond what he had read in the papers, though he did admit that he had consulted the Irish government before making the call (Millotte, 1990f). Braks's recollections about the telephone conversation are, however, at variance with MacSharry's; he asserted publicly that MacSharry spoke to him about Goodman, and told him about the pressure from the Dutch bank, though he stated, at the same time, that MacSharry 'was asking me to do nothing' other than to 'give my attention to the matter'. Millotte (1990f) suggests the obvious questions that arise concerning the MacSharry-Braks affair: First, why should MacSharry ring Braks, as opposed to any other EC agriculture minister, to discuss the problems of the beef industry? Second, why should he do so on 23 August? Unfortunately we can offer no definitive answer to these questions. All we can say is that contact was made and that pressure was put on AMRO not to liquidate. It might, of course, have been a coincidence, though if it was, readers may allow, it was a very singular coincidence indeed.

It was also a very fortunate coincidence; not only did it save Goodman from being bankrupted by AMRO, it was also the means by which his organisation was able to secure protection from the consortium of aggrieved creditors that were rapidly forming up around it. To see how this protection was secured we need to return to Ireland and to the peregrinations of Goodman himself. On the day on which the MacSharry-Braks exchange took place, it is alleged - and the allegation has never been denied - that Goodman helicoptered into the then Irish Prime Minister's home at Kinsealy near Dublin - the Prime Minister at the time being Charles Haughey. On that day also the Prime Minister talked to his Ministers for Industry, Finance and Agriculture and decided to recall the Irish Parliament from its summer recess and push through the Companies (Amendment) Act. The substance of this legislation is that it enables companies to obtain protection from their creditors by applying to the High Court for the appointment of an examiner to operate and restructure the company in conditions in which its creditors are precluded from applying for its liquidation. Getting AMRO to stay its liquidation proceeding was absolutely crucial here; the Irish constitution contains a ban on retroactive legislation, so if Goodman had been liquidated, or if court proceedings for liquidation had begun, his companies could not have obtained the protection that the amended companies legislation was designed to make available to him. Millotte, whose investigations have done so much to open up the Goodman can of worms to public view, can be allowed to describe the next crucial event:

> When Goodman's representatives met the banks again on 29 August they informed them that the restructuring package had been abandoned. There would be no government money and the Cork assets would not be made available. Instead Goodman would use the new Act, passed into law that very day, to keep his creditors at bay (Millotte, 1990f).

An examiner was appointed on 29 August to Goodman International and twenty-five related companies. Interestingly enough the Cork company was not one them.

The international banking community was not well pleased at this development; Goodman companies were now effectively beyond their reach and in the hands of an examiner over whose appointment they had no say, and over whose management of the company they had no control. Fears were also expressed in Irish financial circles about the hammering which Ireland's financial reputation was taking as a result of the affair; there was talk of German investors disposing of £1000 million of Irish government stock - a move that would have forced the government to raise interest rates by two per cent and of other possible 'punitive' measures being taken by international investors (O'Mahony, 1990). Resentment in the international banking community there certainly was; resentment about the nature of the legislation itself, and about what they clearly regarded as unprincipled financial behaviour which the Irish government clearly facilitated through its legislation.

Banking concern over the legislation arose at several points; the bankers did not like the ability of a company to appoint its own nominee as examiner without reference to the creditors, and hoped that the courts would interpret it in a way that enabled the examiner to act equitably with reference to creditors' interests. One banker went so far as to describe it as 'very draconian legislation which provides no comfort to any creditor' (quoted in Stanley, 1990). 'We're talking major mess here' opined another banker, reflecting on the uncertainty generated by the legislation, under the provisions of which, it seems, the examiner can either recommend a court to liquidate or force a reconstruction which no one creditor or group of creditors could veto. In the latter event the banks could be forced to take partial payment and to convert much of their debt into equity in the reconstructed company and would have no right to pursue either Goodman personally or all or any of his companies further.

Goodman himself has been criticised by the banking community for misleading them about both the extent of his resources and his willingness to commit to the discharge of his financial obligations to the banks. Goodman has assets which are not under the control of the examiner; the Cork company is one such asset, which, to remember, Goodman promised to put at the disposal of the banks at the first London meeting on 22 August. As one banker put it:

> It's effectively a poker game. Larry [Goodman] said in London he'd leave no stone unturned to support the banks in this crisis; now it's a question of trying to get him to turn the stones. There could be an additional net £20 million available from the Cork companies. That may not seem a lot, but it's the principle of the thing (quoted in Stanley, 1990).

What the bankers say they need is more information about Goodman's asset base. What they are concerned about, in addition to their other worries, is that it is not the job of the examiner to provide such information to creditors.

The significance of the Cork Company lies in the fact that it functioned as an umbrella for a variegated collection of Goodman interests, including Flushing Ltd and Murray Ltd, companies through which Goodman acquired his £160 million interests in UK based food giants Berisford International and Unigate. These shares were purchased with funds borrowed for what the banks assumed to be working capital (Millotte, 1990e). A senior executive of the West German Commerzbank spoke openly of his fears that Goodman would shift assets around to keep them out of the banks' reach. We are willing to help, he went on, but,

> We need open and honest revelations of all the connections between Goodman companies. We need more assets in the pot and we need

securities for our loans (quoted in Millotte, 1990e).

The same bank executive went on to make the staggering revelation that loans were made to Goodman on the assumption that he was personally liable for his debts. Goodman evaded this responsibility, however, by the simple expedient of transferring the ownership of Goodman International to a Channel Islands registered company called Kitlar, a move that came as a complete surprise to all but a handful of the banks with whom Goodman was dealing; he was after all, as the Commerzbank executive remarked, 'central to the national economy of Ireland, enjoying the trust and support of the Government. For most banks that seemed security enough' (quoted in Millotte, 1990e). Alas poor banks!

Further revelations, no less disturbing to the banks, were soon forthcoming. In an affidavit to the Dublin High Court in October 1990, the managing director of the Westdeutsche Landesbank (Ireland) Ltd (WLIL) stated that two of Goodman's transactions with the bank, involving Stg £12 million 'were in breach of contract and unlawful and constituted a misappropriation of the property of WLIL.' (quoted in Millotte, 1990g). According to WLIL, funds lent to Goodman for his usual business of beef production were used to cover his loss making investments in Berisford; the money borrowed from WLIL was seemingly transferred to a deposit account in the French bank BNP, which had lent Goodman £90 million to buy his Berisford shares. This was done, the German bank stated, because Goodman's arrangements with the French bank required him to deposit cash in the French bank to cover any falls in the Berisford share price in order to protect them from sustaining losses on their advance to Goodman. Goodman owned seventy million shares in Berisford, so he had to pay BNP £7 million for every ten pence fall in the share price (Millotte, 1990g). Between 2 July and 5 July Berisford's shares fell by nineteen pence. Under the terms of his arrangement with BNP Goodman had to deposit £13 million in order to cover this loss. This is almost the exact amount borrowed from WLIL on 4 July and 5 July. The Dutch Bank AMRO has also sworn a similar affidavit asserting that Goodman International borrowed heavily from it in June and July to cover its normal working expenses. Once more, however, Berisford's shares plunged and correspondingly large payments were made into BNP. If these sworn allegations are true Goodman was financing losses on Berisford by monies advanced on the understanding that they were to be used as working capital; the transactions were deceitful and unlawful, and, according to the Commerzbank official, were known to be unlawful before, during and after they took place (Millotte, 1991g).

At the time of writing the Goodman International group remains under the control of the examiner. The tribunal of enquiry into the beef industry continues its investigations and will, no doubt, produce its findings in due course. We cannot, of course, anticipate those findings in any way; we have no basis for doing so and can only report such evidence as is available to us through the tribunal proceedings and from the other sources indicated in the text. To date the evidence presented makes it difficult to avoid the conclusion that all is not well with the Irish food industry. The adventures of 'Mr Beef' have provided 'entertainment' of a a sort, but they have produced little in the way of economic development of the kind which Ireland needs. If anything, in fact, the opposite is the case; this adventurous character has left a trail of distrust and destruction in his wake, the full extent of which remains to be, if it ever will be, discovered.

Conclusion

If the Ballybay case was untypical by virtue of the prolonged campaign of intimidation associated with it, the Goodman case is also untypical though in a different respect; its untypicality arises by reference to the sheer scale of the operation of the Goodman companies. And this is the point: Goodman was not a small 'back street player' in the Irish beef industry; he was literally 'Mr Beef', controlling 'officially' over forty per cent of Ireland's processing capacity, and, as the affair of Classic (Master) Meats suggests, probably more. In addition to this Goodman enjoyed the close and sympathetic support of the Irish government; a support which enabled him to engage in reckless commodity trading, which sought to protect him from exposure, and which, at the bitter end, saved him from liquidation and from the demands of his creditors. As we have seen his activities have occasioned considerable disquiet among the international banking community, as indeed has the government's rather protective stance towards him. Ireland's commercial reputation has sustained considerable damage as a result.

Elements in Irish society are, it has to be said, aware of this. Strangely, however, their tendency is to blame the investigations that are taking place rather than the practices that are coming under investigative review. Ray MacSharry, Ireland's erstwhile European Commissioner, is a case in point. While still in post in the Commission MacSharry described the tribunal investigating the beef industry as a 'witch hunt' and described himself as 'sick, tired and disgusted' that such an investigation was taking place when there was a twenty per cent unemployment rate in Ireland.

> What disgusts me, and it really disgusts me, is the fact that we here in Ireland with over 20% of our people unemployed, seem to spend more time wondering about who is making money, who is making profits and how they made it.

What is even worse, however, is the fact that:

> We then set up investigations, enquiries and tribunals to bring down the very people who are creating tens of thousands of jobs and putting those jobs in jeopardy .... I am just sick and tired of tribunals, investigations and enquiries .... they are doing untold damage to this country at home and abroad (quoted in *Cork Examiner,* 1992).

MacSharry received support from an editorial in an Irish Sunday

Newspaper (*Sunday Business Post,* 1992). The *Post* agreed that the tribunal was investigating very serious allegations which had to be investigated, but clearly felt that a tribunal was an inappropriate forum through which to take the matter forward.

The combined forces of the gardai, the Director of Public Prosecutions and the courts system should be able to handle inquiries as this. The ability of the gardai to handle complex fraud cases has quite correctly been called into question but this should not be used as an excuse to bypass the present structures when a serious issue warrants investigation.

Nevertheless, the *Post* feels that the fraud squad should be strengthened and tribunals avoided because,

for a small economy dependent on foreign trade, the tribunal is sending the wrong kind of signals to our trading partners. Competitors of Irish companies in export markets are capitalising on these investigations in the marketplace, with potentially damaging results. Individuals with money to invest are wondering whether Ireland really has an enterprise culture which supports the creation of wealth and, as a consequence of this, new jobs.

MacSharry and his editorial supporter have, it has to be said, rather selective memories. In the first place, Goodman was not brought down by the tribunal; his enterprises got into trouble because of reckless commodity trading, an over-adventurous acquisitions policy that went wrong, and because he over-reached himself and provoked a government to void insurance cover for his reckless trading by making insurance claims which a minister deemed to be fraudulent, so any job losses that might result can hardly be blamed on the tribunal. Secondly, the tribunal was established as a result of allegations made in the Irish Parliament, and, more importantly because of the much wider audience, on a British television programme. The tribunal was thus established in order to save Ireland's reputation, not to damage it. It is very difficult to imagine, say a British company competing with an Irish meat exporter in a foreign market, saying to a potential customer:

Don't buy Irish because the anti-enterprise culture, Irish government has set up an a tribunal to enquire into allegations that you are being sold rotten meat by Irish companies, in order to protect you through its determination to maintain high standards in the Irish industry.

It is far more likely that the competition will be making use of the all too plausible allegations that Irish companies have sold bad meat, and that Ireland may not be such a good place to invest in because neither Irish companies, nor the Irish government, can be relied upon to maintain high standards of financial probity.

These thoughts make for a suitable point of return to the material covered in Chapters 2 and 3, especially since the present chapter brings our review of Irish entrepreneurs 'doing for themselves' to a close. The sentiments expressed by MacSharry and his editorial supporter might be read with the evidence presented in these pages concerning the Irish 'enterprise culture' firmly in mind. It is, indeed, a pity to bring down business people who create wealth and jobs. But who is doing it? What about the illicit businesses complained about by the parliamentary committee mentioned in Chapter 2? How many jobs have these destroyed? What about the illegal slaughterhouses? How many jobs were destroyed in that sector because legal operators simply could not compete? - and the same question could be asked about the operation of illegal bakeries. How many actual and potential jobs have been lost because Irish manufacturing firms pay inadequate attention to quality and reliability of supply, or because their marketing is weak and ineffective? How many actual and potential jobs have been lost because far too many Irish companies are satisfied with a nice little profit made on their small home market and show no ir .erest in growth?

We are not asking these questions in any spirit of moral indignation. We put them simply because asking them is a convenient way of summarising the evidence presented here and pointing up the impact of the entrepreneurship to which the evidence relates, and because they throw the views of MacSharry and his editorial supporter into some sort of adequate relief. MacSharry evidently feels that money-makers in Ireland are persecuted. Let us look at the record and see: What sort of persecution have those who made money out of Irish Sugar and TE been subjected to? What sort of persecution has been meted out to the operators of Ballybay, to the Gallaghers of Ireland, to the Phoenix syndrome operators, to the legions of tax evaders, operators of illegal businesses and politically-connected speculators who flourish in the Irish enterprise culture? None of these groups has any particular reason to feel persecuted; if anything, in fact, the tendency has been to protect them from too much exposure, as the facts of the Goodman case amply demonstrate. On the face of the evidence presented here it is hard to take seriously the idea that money-making is discouraged by an over-active state clamping down on the doings of Irish economic activists. If there is a problem, therefore, and there clearly is, its roots must lie elsewhere: namely, in the fact that the activities of Irish entrepreneurs are not generally productive of the self-sustaining economic growth which the Irish economy requires if the jobs which Irish society so desperately needs are to be created and maintained securely in the future.

One obvious consequence of these Irish entrepreneurial 'failings' is, of course, that the high hopes of the nineteen-sixties modernisers have not been fulfilled. The new economic strategy that we noticed in Chapter 1 did, indeed, achieve some initial success; gross product grew at an annual average of 4.4 per cent between 1960 and 1973; the decline in population was halted; industrial unemployment dropped below five per cent for the first time in the country's history and living standards began to rise. Most of the growth, especially in manufacturing, was, however, due to foreign direct investment into the Irish economy by overseas companies; by the mid nineteen-eighties foreign-owned enterprises employed some 80,000 people in Ireland, accounting for forty per cent of the country's total employment in manufacturing (Connellan, 1986). The contribution which foreign-owned firms make to the Irish development process is, in many cases, quite limited; about one-half of the value of their exports is made up of raw material and sub supply components which are imported into Ireland; their profits are repatriated on a large scale; they are, as we shall see, expensive to attract and ready to leave again when economic circumstances render their departure expedient. They have undoubtedly contributed to job creation on a very significant scale, but, in many cases that is as far as their contribution goes; it does not run much beyond the size of their annual wage bills and limited purchases of local materials. Foreign-owned companies are not, therefore, an unmixed blessing.

With hindsight we now know that the growth that took place in the Irish economy down to 1973 was deceptive. It was not due to any growing inherent strength in the economy, but to inward foreign investment and to the international boom conditions which were characteristic of the period. For the rest, however, the outlook was not so bright; endogenous Irish industry was sluggish and underperforming, and was not, as we have seen, showing much inclination to rise to the challenges of the times. In consequence the true weakness of the Irish economy became apparent again when the international boom petered out; many of the multinationals shut shop and departed; many Irish companies also went under; decline, followed by stagnation, set in once more.

We can trace the pattern easily enough through the growth of unemployment, which increased from 56,000 in 1961 to 61,000 in 1971, 126,000 in 1981 and 227,000 in 1986, since when it has been hovering around the twenty per cent mark. The dimming of the country's economic fortunes reflected in these figures did nothing to diminish the demands being made on Irish governments; they were still expected to create and maintain a modern infrastructure; they had to provide for an expansion in education and to maintain the kind of welfare system appropriate to a modern economy and society and had to take the cost of supporting the growing army of the unemployed; they had to finance the grant and tax incentives needed to attract foreign direct investment and to stimulate native entrepreneurs - corporation tax on manufacturing is only ten per cent and profits derived from exports are tax exempt. Irish governments could not finance these operations out of their current revenues and had to turn increasingly towards foreign and domestic borrowing. Along with unemployment, therefore, the Irish national debt grew; it increased from £414 million in 1960 to £1,480 million in 1973, £7,291 million in 1980, £14,773 million and £23,045 million in 1986, that is from sixty-four per cent of GNP in 1960 to 142.2 per cent of GNP in 1986 (Kennedy, Giblin and McHugh, 1988, pp. 89, 142).

Figures like these, of course, throw the activities we have described in the preceding chapters into graphic relief - not least the evasion of taxation in a state whose government clearly needs all the revenue it can get its hands on. They also show how the 'failure' of the Irish entrepreneurial establishment has created both a massive burden for the state or, more correctly, the Irish taxpayer - and a source of very safe profits for its members. A special study commissioned by the Department of Industry and Commerce tells us about the catastrophic costs involved. In the words of an Irish Newspaper(*Sunday Tribune*, 1992):

> The most startling [disclosure in the report] was the revelation that between 1981 and 1990 the state paid £1.6 billion (£1,600,000,000) in grants to private companies in order to create jobs, and that by 1990 this had resulted in just 7,000 permanent jobs. In addition tax reliefs of almost £3 billion (£2,980,000,000) were given.

From this it is easy to calculate that each of these jobs cost the Irish exchequer - again, more properly, the Irish taxpayer - a little matter of £654,285, a figure which, when European grant-aid is included, rises to around £750,000. Such is the cost of Irish entrepreneurial 'failure', as a result of which the Irish taxpayer has to shoulder the burdens of economic development, to the profit, it has to be said, of the entrepreneurial establishment whose efforts to bring about development have been so limited and unavailing; the government expenditure needed has to be financed by the massive borrowings referred to above, and this enables many members of the Irish entrepreneurial establishment to turn in a nice, neat and safe little profit from investments in government gilts.

5 The entrepreneurial problem: Questionable explanations

Introduction

Our objectives in writing this book thus far have been mainly descriptive; we have tried to set out the record of Irish entrepreneurs 'doing for themselves' with a view to exhibiting something of the nature and character of entrepreneurial behaviour in contemporary Ireland. In chapters 2,3 and 4, therefore, we presented a considerable body of evidence touching on the economic behaviour of entrepreneurs in contemporary Ireland. That evidence suggested that their approach to regular, continuous, value-adding enterprise was rather easy-going and complacent; too many were satisfied with a nice little profit without much growth; for too many the home market did well enough; there was clear evidence of a lack of attention to quality, of a neglectful approach to resources and opportunities and to a lack of ambition which, to remember, provoked one entrepreneur to protest about the sheer torpor which seemed to be a leading characteristic of Irish society. Alongside this, it has to be said, there was evidence of sheer money-making of an ethically unregulated kind in which customers, creditors and, not least, the Irish and European authorities were considered 'fair game' by unscrupulous operators whose activities did little to enhance, and arguably much to damage, their country's prospects of achieving economic development. What we have here are clearly patterns of commitment to economic activity which are limited and/or erratically, short-termist and ethically unregulated in terms of a certain 'devotion' to money-making. It is not so much the case, therefore, that the Irish are not interested in making money. The problem lies rather in the fact that their interest in money-making does not seem to have worked itself in terms of high levels of commitment to regular, continuous, productive work in value-adding enterprise which is prudentially and/or ethically regulated to the extent that it is planned, interested in long-term expansion and oriented to prudential and ethical standards of conduct which maintain confidence and thus sustainable relations with customers and significant others in the world in which it has to function. As we mentioned in the conclusion to Chapter 3 the behaviour of Irish entrepreneurs shows some correspondence with the behaviour patterns which Max Weber summarised under the rubric of economic traditionalism. From now on we shall use this designation as a summary term for the behaviour we have described.

Having outlined the conduct of Irish entrepreneurs our focus must now shift towards analysis and explanation of the behaviour we have described. From here onwards, therefore, our efforts will be directed towards answering the question: Why is it that Irish entrepreneurs conduct themselves as they do, and fail to cultivate alternative patterns of economic action some or all of which might be more conducive to the achievement of the social and economic development to which the Irish have come to aspire? As the title to this book perhaps indicates, the analysis it aims to provide is predicated to the view that the answer to the question just put lies substantially in the cultural values to which Irish entrepreneurs relate their economic activities. Much of the analysis that follows will, therefore, be directed to the task of determining whether and to what extent Irish cultural values have acted as 'determinants' of the economic behaviour of Irish entrepreneurs.

Our reasons for invoking culture as a possible explanatory variable are not far to seek; they are well expressed, in fact, by Karl Marx's (1934, p. 15) observation, 'Men make their own history, but they do not make it just as they please'. If Marx is right about this, and we see no reason to doubt that he was, then it follows that, although human beings are constrained by structures and circumstances i.e. by the sort of objective factors adverted to in Chapter 1, they are not so constrained as to preclude them from making an input into the history-making process through the agency of purposeful action. The fact that actors may not have unlimited scope to act, does not, therefore, mean that they have no scope to act purposefully in the creation of their destinies, and that is why our analysis will orientate towards culture as a potentially important variable. While making all due allowance for factors that limit the possibilities open to actors and which thus constrain and circumscribe action, we shall suggest that actors' orientation to the values of their cultures can influence their actions in those areas where they have scope to act.

The meaning of the term culture has, of course, been much debated by anthropologists and sociologists, and we do not propose to try to contribute to that debate in the pages that follow. In the first place we do not have the space. Secondly, since we cannot legislate for anybody else, we ought to be modest and confine ourselves to saying what the term means to us. When we use the term culture here we use it to refer to the whole complex of ideafacts and artifacts produced by a people in the course of its adaption to its natural and social environments. Concretely, therefore, cultures are congeries of values, norms, beliefs, customs, institutions, technostructures and forms of artistic expression which reflect the thoughts, feelings, actions and interests of peoples, and which, since the ideafacts form world views and the institutions and artifacts conditioning environments, come, in turn, to shape and mould the thoughts, feelings, actions and interests of peoples who are socialised into the shared evaluative, cognitive, institutional, technical and aesthetic standards which derive from them. It is through socialisation into these shared standards that human beings learn to endow their life situations and activities with meaning, and so achieve a self-understanding which enables them, together with others in their societies, to make judgements, inter alia, about what ends they will pursue, for what purposes, by what means, and with what prioritisation, when set in the context of other ends which actually or potentially compete for their attention. It is with the shared standards, especially the cognitive, evaluative and institutional standards into which the modernising generation of Irish entrepreneurs have been encultured that our analysis will be principally concerned; we want briefly stated, to find out whether and to what extent the culturally-given evaluative standards (values) to which they relate, and thus give meaning to, their economic activity have influenced their orientation to it. Tracing out the impact of these standards on the economic behaviour of this modernising generation will be neither an easy nor an uncontroversial matter. Nevertheless, we hope to be able to demonstrate that the cognitive, evaluative and institutional standards into which Irish entrepreneurs have been socialised have shaped and moulded their perceptions of their economic lives in ways that have significance for the problem we are dealing with.

Invoking cultural values in explanations of economic behaviour is, as we shall see soon enough, a controversial move and one that is viewed with disfavour by legions of economists, economic historians and other interested parties. For this reason, if for no other, we need to review elements of the opposition's case and to be extremely clear about the kind of claims we intend to make. These, as we shall see, will turn out to be circumscribed by an explanatory matrix which takes account of issues other than cultural values. We shall not, in other words, claim that cultural values provide the sole explanation of the conduct we have described, only that they form a significant part of any explanation that aspires to be comprehensive.

The controversy over culture

Marxists have usually tended to reject, or at least to be very sceptical about, assertions concerning culture as a determinant of economic interests and activities. We can see why this is if we accept that culture is produced by people in the course of their adaption to their environment. Adaption requires, as a first priority, that people organise production - crudely stated they must eat before they can think, pray etc.. From this it is a short step to the view that peoples' economic interests which, as a matter of the first importance, they must seek to promote and defend,

112

become the ultimate determinants of the cultures which they create and carry. All the components of culture are, therefore, seen to be influenced by, if not directly derived from, economic interests, arising as mere superstructural reflections of the economic base of a society. Culture, therefore, cannot determine economic interests because it is itself a 'product' that is determined by economic interests. It is not always clear that Marx and Engels were themselves so economically deterministic as to rule out all possibilities of independent influences emanating from culture. Most thinkers in the tradition to which their work has given rise are, however, extremely sceptical about such possibilities.

It was often said that, in arguing that the ideas of Protestantism, had a profound impact on the economic behaviour of capitalists, Max Weber was conducting a debate with the ghost of Karl Marx. For all that this may have been, there were, it has to be said, other ghosts at which Weber was also tilting. Weber was a child - albeit an aberrant child - of the German Historical School, which was characterised, among other things, by its rejection of the abstract, general theorising of the classical economists. The classical approach was rejected because those who followed it seemed to be uninterested in analysing the impact of culture on economic activities, holding these to be the result of motives that were universally present in people by virtue of their human condition. Adam Smith puts the case in the following terms:

> The principle which prompts to save is the desire of bettering our condition, a desire which, though generally calm and dispassionate, comes to us from the womb, and never leaves us till we go into the grave .... there is scarce perhaps a single instant in which any man is so perfectly and completely satisfied with his situation, as to be without any wish of alteration or improvement of any kind (quoted in Marshall, 1982, p. 24).

The influence of this point of view on the development of thinking about economic conduct is undoubted. As Marshall, (1982, p. 24) puts it, it resulted in classical economics developing as an approach to the analysis of economic conduct which the Historical School rejected on the grounds that it was,

> wholly dependent on a large number of empirically unverified assumptions about economic behaviour, notably that of the universal predominance of an income-maximising and self-interested 'rational economic actor'.

In arguing that the income-maximising and self-interested rational economic actor was the 'product' of ascetic Protestantism - a cultural phenomenon unique to the early-modern West - Weber was rejecting the classical view concerning the universality of the rational income-maximiser.

The implications of the line of thinking derived from political economy for the argument to be developed here are clear enough: If an income-maximising and self-interested rational economic actor is a universal, then differences in actors' orientations to economic life cannot be ascribed to the unique, individual value constellations of particular culture complexes; if actors behave differently in different culture complexes, it is not because the values to which they relate their economic activities differ as between the cultures - though they may, and often will, differ - but because the means-opportunity structures, i.e. the availability of capital and other resources together with a supply of viable economic opportunities to exploit, in which actors' income-maximising and self-interested orientations have to work themselves out differ as between the culture complexes under examination.   Thus if entrepreneurs in country A behave in ways that are more conducive to the achievement of economic development than entrepreneurs in country B, it is not because of any differences in the cultures of the two countries, but because the means-opportunity structures confronting entrepreneurs in country A are more propitious than those available to entrepreneurs in country B. Culture does not enter the picture.

As Worsley (1984, p. 41) sagely observes, however, the votaries of political economy are not alone in ignoring culture: those who reduce the study of society to social structure tend to do so as well. For our purposes this orientation can be exemplified by reference to the work of the world systems and dependency theorists. Although authors writing in these traditions exhibit differences in points of emphasis and detail, Wallerstein can be allowed to speak to what amounts to the general tendency of their work:

> We take the defining characteristic of a social system to be the existence within it of a division of labour, such that the various sectors or areas within it are dependent upon economic exchange with others for the smooth and continuous provisioning of the needs of the area. Such economic exchange can clearly exist without a common political structure and more obviously without sharing the same culture (Wallerstein, 1979, p. 5).

On this view clearly the world system is seen primarily as an economic system and actors within it are, before anything else, economic actors. Economic interests are thus held to be the primary and to be ultimately determinative of other social and cultural interests - an assumption shared with classical Marxism. It is, of course, true that cultural diversity is recognised; the world system contains numerous political and cultural subsystems. These, however, have to be analysed in terms of their 'organisational activity ... for the functioning of the world economy' (Wallerstein, 1979, p. 25). Analysis is, therefore, couched at the level of the system, toward the maintenance and integration of which its component subsystems are held to contribute functionally. There is no room for the analysis of purposeful human action and no need, in consequence, to invoke cultural variables in explanations of economic activity.

According to Wallerstein the present world system originated in Europe in the fifteenth and sixteenth centuries. From then onwards the more developed European capitalist nations used their superior capital, technical, productive and politico-military resources to subordinate other economies, often through the medium of direct colonial exploitation. Any independent development open to these economies was, therefore, arrested by capitalist-colonialist exploitation; such surpluses as they produced were transferred to the core, depriving them of funds for independent development; they were effectively confined to the production of food and raw materials, which the core countries needed, and which were exchanged for the core's industrial products, on terms dictated by the core economies, and were thus forced into a capitalist world system as dependent and subordinate partners. Development opportunities for the subordinated economies were thus severely restricted to the point at which they were arguably undeveloped by the predations of the capitalist-colonialist core (Wallerstein, 1979, p. 18; Frank, 1978, p. 11; Crotty, 1986). Formal decolonisation has not produced any fundamental change; the capitalist world system continues to be dominated by a group of core, industrialised countries, to which the economies of the semi-peripheral and peripheral, less developed and undeveloped nations remain subordinate to the extent that they are, in varying degrees, denied access to the means and opportunities to pursue independent courses of economic development. Any development of which these subordinated economies are capable is, therefore, development in dependence on the core-dominated world system. Dependence, according to Dos Santos, amounts to

> a situation in which a certain group of countries have their economies conditioned by the development and expansion of another economy, to which their own is subjected .... Dependency conditions a certain internal structure which redefines it as a function of the structural possibilities of the distinct national economies (quoted in Roxborough, 1979, P. 66).

Application of world systems type theorising to our problem clearly leaves little room for cultural explanations of entrepreneurial behaviour. If entrepreneurs in less developed countries appear to behave in ways that are not appropriate to development-achievement, their behaviour can be explained by reference to the claim that the operation of the world system has deprived them of access to relevant means and to a structure of development-appropriate economic opportunities. Their behaviour is, therefore, structured by their part in the division of labour in the world system, apart from the study of which it cannot be properly analysed or understood. Culture has nothing to do with the issue.

Theorising of the world systems type gained much of its credibility as a necessary corrective to the neo-evolutionary approaches of the so called modernisation theorists. As exemplified in the work of Rostow (1960) economic development is here envisaged as a process in which traditional societies transform themselves into the condition of modernity through a series of evolutionary stages of economic growth. Traditional society represents the first stage and is the baseline from which the process starts. Traditional societies are characterised by low levels of output and fatalistic value systems. In stage two - the so called pre-conditions for take-off -

the fatalistic values are replaced by ideas that emphasise progress and entrepreneurs emerge who mobilise capital, direct investment and set society off on the long haul towards development. These processes do not develop evenly throughout all sectors of an economy, so for a period modern and traditional sectors will coexist in a dual economy. Nevertheless, the development 'plane' has started to roll and moves to the third stage of its journey: take off. During take off the obstacles to development are finally overcome; entrepreneurial and political groups emerge and make development their first priority and industrialisation and commercialisation spread to all sectors of the economy, including agriculture. The drive to maturity follows as the fourth stage. This is characterised by high levels of productive investment, by a growing technological sophistication and dramatic increases in the wealth produced and available for distribution and, therefore consumption. High mass consumption and high levels of welfare are thus the defining characteristics of the final stage. Great Britain led the way in the unfolding of this process and was followed by other societies, notably the USA, which, for this school of thought, came to constitute the lead society and the most developed representative of modernity with its high rates of mass consumption, its democratic political system and its value system with its supposed emphases on openness, mobility, achievement, innovation and growth. In principle there is no reason why any society cannot follow the trail blazed by the lead societies, provided it is willing to break the shackles imposed by traditionalistic value systems and accept help from those who have developed already.

As our very brief account of the modernisation approach hopefully indicates, it makes some attempt to take account of entrepreneurship and the impact of cultural values in the development process. As Harrison (1988, p. 28) notes, however, the reference to culture is not unproblematic.

> Rostow's theory undoubtedly shares some of the characteristics of other modernisation theories. His unilinear approach to development, and to the idea that traditional societies not only had to change their economies but also their values and social structures, can also be found elsewhere. Indeed, it was but a short step from here to suggest, or to imply, that alterations in values could automatically lead to changes in economic structures. In other words: remove cultural blockages and somehow economic development would take care of itself, perhaps with the help of a modernising elite and a little diffusion from outside.

On this view clearly the principle blockages to economic development lie in cultural values, hence the corrective emphasis of the systems theorists on the blockages located in the structure of the capitalist world system. This corrective is, to our view, well and truly justified. Nevertheless, in applying it through an emphasis on the structural determination of conduct, the systems theorists divert attention away from purposeful, motivated human action and from any attempt to ascertain whether and to what extent that action can be influenced by the cultural values to which it is related by those performing it. Emphasising structural determination to the exclusion of cultural influences in this way seems to us to be quite as unjustified a proceeding as emphasising cultural influence to the exclusion of structural determinants; the fact that the conduct of entrepreneurs - and its consequences for development-achievement - can be structured by the nexus of means and opportunities available to them, does not rule out the possibility that the extent and direction of entrepreneurial motivation, and thus the manner in which available opportunities are exploited by entrepreneurs, cannot be influenced by the cultural values to which they relate their economic activity. What we need to do, therefore, is to adopt an attitude of analytical agnosticism towards the issues and to try to provide a framework through which we can examine them empirically by reference to the case we are studying.

Culture and entrepreneurial action: a framework for analysis

The point of departure for the analysis that follows lies in the view that entrepreneurial action, like all human action, is governed by four complex sets of conditions that apply to actors: namely, means, opportunities, motives and institutional constraints on conduct. It follows, surely as a first principle, that actors contemplating a course of action cannot put their programme into effect if they lack the means that are necessary to its implementation. In the entrepreneurial context, of course, the term 'means' refers to time, skills, capital and other resources, natural and otherwise, which it is the business of the entrepreneur to mobilise, manage and control. Given ample means, however, and the best entrepreneurial will in the world, it seems reasonable to suggest that actors can implement programmes only when they are given, or can carve out, opportunities to do so. Once again, in the entrepreneurial context, the implications are clear: entrepreneurs will not act unless they have available a structure of opportunities which, to their judgements, seem to provide a reasonable balance between prospects of return and the risk and effort involved in their exploitation. From our point of view motives can be regarded as the grounds for action; they are complexes of meaning which drive and direct action in cases where meaningful choice, and therefore a degree of voluntarism, is available to actors, i.e. in circumstances in which actors have the means and opportunities to act without being institutionally constrained. Institutional constraint refers to pressures emanating from the collectivities to which actors belong i.e. legal enactments, public opinion, competition, which externally constrain actors to keep their conduct in line with certain standards, regardless of their personal inclinations and motives to do so.

In this scheme means and opportunities refer to relatively objective factors, to those factors which are beyond the subjective influence or control of individuals and which thus function as barriers which prevent them from making history 'just as they please' - shortages of capital, lack of appropriate resources and entry barriers to markets are all examples of what we mean here. Motives clearly refer to subjective factors, to internally located stimuli which govern the nature, extent and intensity of purposeful human action, and it is in this and in the institutional arena that culture can possibly play an important role. Any account of entrepreneurial activity which aspires to comprehensiveness must, it seems to us, try to take account of all of the factors mentioned, and we shall try to do so in the analysis that follows. In constructing our analysis, therefore, we shall adopt a posture of analytical agnosticism towards the question of culture and its putative impact on economic conduct, and check, as carefully as we can, to see if Irish entrepreneurial conduct cannot be explained otherwise than by reference to culture. This we shall now proceed to do.

Irish entrepreneurial conduct: non-cultural explanations

We are going to argue eventually that the economic traditionalism of the Irish results from patterns of economic motivation which are coloured by the cultural values to which they relate their economic activities. Those who want to deny this have the possibility of developing an argument along the following line: In terms of their economic motivations the Irish are no different from any other people; their material interests are their most important interests. The behaviour, and failure to develop, which you seek to explain by reference to cultural influences on motivation is not, therefore, a matter of motivation at all, rather it is a result of the means and opportunities which are available to Irish economic actors. Granted that Irish entrepreneurs do appear to be traditionalistic when compared to entrepreneurs in other countries we could mention. This, however, has nothing to do with motives or culture, but is rather the result of the fact that they lack the means and opportunities to be other than traditionalistic. Give Irish entrepreneurs the means and opportunities that are available to entrepreneurs in other countries, say the UK, US and Germany, and they would behave in the same way as their British, American and German counterparts.

Arguments of this kind could be elaborated from within the traditions of political economy, Marxism, world systems-dependency theory and, indeed, Irish nationalisms that owe no particular allegiance to any of the traditions mentioned. Two sets of conditions, either singly or in combination, could be deployed to provide the ground on which the arguments could be made to stand. The first of these would have to do with the fact that Irish history was conditioned by a long colonial relationship with Britain: Ireland was, after all, Britain's oldest colony and was an integral part of the United Kingdom between 1801 and 1921. The second would advert to the fact that Ireland lacked the natural resources of coal and iron on which the industrial revolution in Great Britain was said to be founded. Ireland's subjection to the superior economic and political power of Britain could thus be said to have distorted her development; lacking coal and iron she could not hope to industrialise, and any industries which she did manage to develop could not compete with the products of more advanced British industry which poured into the Irish market, which could not, of course, be protected because Ireland was part of the United Kingdom. As a result Ireland was forced into relations of dependent exchange with Britain; she could only export primary products to Britain in return for manufactured goods supplied by advanced British industry. The means-opportunity structure confronting Irish entrepreneurs was accordingly limited; they had few export related manufacturing opportunities available to them; they were confined to exporting primary products and to manufacturing on a limited scale for small local markets in the non-traded sectors. Their so called traditionalism, therefore, has nothing to do with motivation and cultural values; they behave as they do simply because they lack the means and opportunities to behave in any other way; the nature and direction of the effort and commitment is proportionate to the means and opportunities available to them.

Arguments of this kind are not without a certain plausibility. However, on closer examination much of the plausibility dissolves like a Celtic mist on a sunny morning. To begin with the unfavourable circumstances adverted to above did not prevent the industrialisation of North-east Ireland - that part of the country which remained within the United Kingdom as Northern Ireland; it also lacked coal and iron and stood in the same relationship to Great Britain as the rest of Ireland, yet it developed world-class shipbuilding, engineering and textile industries. If nothing else this demonstrates conclusively that the conditions confronting Ireland were not absolute barriers to industrial development where appropriate entrepreneurial ability and willingness existed, especially since, as we saw in Chapter 1, the country was not short of capital and had an experienced and economically prosperous Roman Catholic commercial middle class who might have turned their attention to industrial development. The situation, therefore, may not have been as clear cut as it might have seemed. As Cullen (1969, p. 123) frankly observes, there is 'no easy explanation' for the the nineteenth century failure to develop:

> Lack of capital was not the cause.... The lack of adequate native coal supplies contributed, but only to a limited extent. Coal was as cheap as in many parts of England outside the mining areas, and in Belfast it was little cheaper than elsewhere. Poor entrepreneurship may have been at fault, and the success of individual business and the industrialisation of the north-east may confirm this.

Cullen, to be sure, uses the conditional 'may' here, suggesting possibility rather then certainty. The evidence, however, suggests that the possibility is a strong one.

We can see this if we examine the issue of how well the Irish performed in those areas of economic activity in which they had advantages. The truth seems to be that they did not perform very well. An Irish economic historian is quite frank about this:

> The real failure of nineteenth-century Ireland, it seems to me, was not with wool or cotton or glass, but in leather, meat-packing, fish-curing, cheese, farm machinery (Green, 1969, p. 99).

This statement must be read with some salient facts in mind. Throughout the nineteenth century Ireland was an integral part of the United Kingdom of Britain and Ireland; the United Kingdom was Ireland's home market. Ireland could thus be seen to be in a very fortunate position; she was part of a dynamic, thrusting, expanding market, the industrial districts of which needed food products which she had the raw materials to supply; she had, as we have seen the best pasture in Europe; she had the cattle; she had the fish. Irish cattle were, however, sent to Britain 'on the hoof'; the value was added in British-based plants; Irish butter was 'Heavily salted, often dirty and relatively unstandardised' (Cullen, 1987, p. 154), and so suffered heavy and effective competition when a better organised Danish industry sent better quality butter into the United Kingdom, taking in the process a large share of Ireland's home market away from Irish producers; nothing much was done about fish-curing, notwithstanding abundant supplies of fish living undisturbed in Irish waters.

We can only speculate whether Cullen's (1987) description of Irish butter as 'Heavily salted, often dirty and relatively unstandardised' led him to revise his earlier (1969) judgment to the effect that 'Poor entrepreneurship may have been at fault'; he has not, so far as we know, addressed the question subsequently. It is very difficult to see, however, why the supply of heavily salted, dirty butter of unstandardised quality to a market that was likely to respond warmly to a better product should not be counted as an example of poor entrepreneurship; the truth seems to be that the Irish enjoyed what Lee (1989, p. 622) describes as 'a cosy position on the English butter market' and simply took the market for granted, never considering the possibility that it might take receptively to a better product. And that, of course, is just what the market did; it responded very warmly to the superior Danish product to the extent that Danish butter exports to the United Kingdom - Ireland's home market to remember - grew remarkably in comparison to Ireland's; between 1870 and 1904 Irish sales to the remainder of the UK increased from 600,000 cwts to just over 800,000 cwts per annum; over the same period Denmark's exports to the UK rose from 150,000 cwts per annum to 1,500,000 (Lee, 1989, p. 663).

Figures like these speak for themselves; opportunities for greatly expanded sales existed if only Ireland could have produced the product of the right quality in greater quantities. Danish progress was based on a dynamic peasant cooperative movement which was stimulated by Neilsen's invention of the continuous cream separator in 1878 (Rush, 1970, p. 15; Milward and Saul, 1973, p. 506). Neilsen's device provided the peasants with a cheap, labour saving method of making butter to the high quality standards that were previously only possible on the well capitalised farms of the nobility, and thus with an opportunity of transforming their economic conditions through the exploitation of the opportunities available in the British market. Cooperation was essential; the separators could only be operated economically with a continuous supply of milk that was beyond the capacity of the individual holdings to supply. And so the Danes adopted cooperation; the first cooperative dairy was founded in 1882 and thereafter cooperatives spread rapidly, rising, as a contemporary account had it, 'like the waves of the North Sea'; eighty-four more were founded in the three years following 1892, and over 1500 had been established by 1914 (Rush, 1970, p. 16; Milward and Saul, 1973, p. 507). And cooperation was not restricted to dairying; in 1887 the first cooperative bacon factory was established - a larger and more complex undertaking than any dairy - and the movement spread, again, with great success. That success is reflected in the figures for Danish bacon exports to the UK; they grew from 18,000 tons in 1886 - the year before the first cooperative bacon factory was founded - to 87,000 in 1900 (Rush, 1970, p. 16). Producer cooperation quickly spread to the purchase of fertilisers and equipment, to export marketing and, as Rush (1970, p. 16) puts it, 'to virtually everything'.

The foundations for a cost-effective system of butter and bacon production were thus very quickly put in place in Denmark, and these, when combined with the consistently high quality standards which the Danes were able to maintain, made for products which were extremely competitive in terms of both their price and quality. The success of Danish butter and bacon on the UK market adverted to above bears adequate testimony to these points.

Danish industrialisation was strongly linked to its agricultural success; agriculture generated demands for machinery, not least for separators and refrigeration equipment, and rising farm incomes increased the demand for consumption goods (Milward and Saul, 1973, p. 512). Much of the new industry, to be sure, oriented to the home market. Nevertheless, industrial exports were developed in dairying equipment, machine tools and in related electrical fields (Johansen, 1987, p. 3; Milward and Saul, 1973, pp. 512-14). All these opportunities, and the possibilities that followed from them in terms of industrial development, were as open to Ireland as they were to Denmark.

Producer cooperation and creamery production were by no means confined to Denmark; the Irish took them up, for example, and by 1902 there were 236 cooperative dairy societies at work in Ireland (Cullen, 1987, p. 155). While these developments undoubtedly helped to improve the quality of Irish produce, they came, as it were, too little and too late; the cheap competition from Denmark and New Zealand moderated price rises on the British market and was reflected in a declining Irish share of that market (Cullen, 1987, p. 155). Many of the gains made were, in any case, subsequently thrown away. An Irish economic historian, James Meenan (1970, pp. 302-3), describes what happened:

> The ten years that followed 1914 brought much prosperity to Irish farmers and did a great deal to destroy their chances of maintaining it. In 1914 Ireland was a highly important supplier to the British market, not only of cattle, which had always been the case, but also of butter, bacon, eggs and poultry. The outbreak of the war gave the Irish producer very nearly a monopoly of the market in a period of rapidly rising prices. The opportunity was seized, and abused. A great deal of the advance towards standardization of quality and regularity of supply was lost: the variability of quality even within a single consignment became a by-word. When the war ended, and continental and overseas producers returned to the British market,

the Irish farmers had made a great deal of money and lost a great deal more of goodwill. In the process, they had also lost a great deal of what they had learned about the principles of cooperation. These principles had been all very well in earlier years when adherence to them would obviously bring better prices: once still better prices were to be got for the asking, they were thrown overboard.

As Meenan tells us elsewhere (1970, p. 92) the consequences were dramatic:

> During the war Irish agricultural products had been given the windfall of a near-monopoly of the British market, but this magnificent opportunity to acquire lasting good-will was thrown away. When the war was over and supplies from Denmark and overseas were again available, the British consumer had only too clear a memory of bad eggs and worse butter from Ireland. To restore the good name of Irish produce was obviously the first move towards recovery; it was not one that could have immediate results.

By the time recovery had gotten into its stride, the situation confronting Irish opportunity-takers had changed considerably; in 1921 Ireland gained its independence from Britain - though it remained within the Commonwealth until 1949; the great depression in the thirties, and, from 1931, moves by the UK government to foster British agriculture through restrictions on imports and a marketing board system which, while offering good prices to British farmers, kept consumer prices at low and competitively demanding levels for those who wanted to export into the market. Other factors of importance are, of course, changing patterns of consumer taste, and, last but not least, the vicissitudes that beset all primary producers stemming from variations in the terms of trade between primary and other products. Obviously these developments had adverse consequences for the Irish. However they also affected the Danes; if the opportunities open to the Danes were equally open to the Irish, the truth is that any disadvantages faced by the Irish were disadvantages which the Danes also had to confront.

While difficulties with markets and variations in the terms of trade pose difficulties and short term fluctuations, they do not, as the Irish historian Joseph Lee points, out, explain 'longer term levels of income or trajectories of growth'; the longer term consequences are due more to the adequacy of the responses which the problems provoke (Lee, 1989, p. 524). The same historian clearly found a comparison between Danish and Irish responses most stimulating.

As Lee reminds us, the fifties were difficult times for Denmark; she experienced the same balance of payments constraints as Ireland; her terms of trade deteriorated by some thirty per cent between 1949 and 1953, more than double the deterioration which Ireland experienced between 1953 and 1957; she experienced similar problems to Ireland as far as exporting into the British market was concerned (Lee, 1989, p. 525). These difficulties did not prevent the Danes from further developing their butter and bacon production and marketing; the fifties saw the introduction of foil-wrapped butter and vacuum-packed bacon for direct sale to consumers - the celebrated *Lurpak* and *Danepak* brands (Rush, 1970, pp. 38, 53); the period also saw the development of canned-meat production to compensate for the limited prospects for bacon sales in the UK. The results of the latter development were spectacular; while Irish pig numbers increased only modestly between 1949 and 1959 - from 675,000 to 852,000 - the Danish pig population exploded, increasing from 2.1 million to 6.7 million over the same period (Johansen, 1987, p. 115; Lee, 1989, p. 525). In the twenty years after 1950 exports of Danish canned meat increased tenfold; in 1968 over 150,000 tons were exported to the value of nearly £58 million, amounting to almost one-third of all Denmark's export earnings from pigs (Rush, 1970. p. 63). No similar development can be reported from Ireland, either in the fifties or subsequently.

Although they faced similar constraints to the Irish, therefore, the truth seems to be that the Danes succeeded in doing what the Irish failed to do: namely, to set their food processing industries on a continuous development curve by moving from raw commodities to the high value-added processing of an increasingly diverse range of products. The Irish failure here is marked by the fact that even in the nineteen-sixties, half of the cattle produced in the country were exported live. It is true that Irish-based processing has increased in the interim. However, the development has been extremely sluggish and remains limited in terms of the amount of value-added. Beef processing can be carried on to different extents, resulting in different amounts of value-added to the raw product. Carcase beef represents the most basic level of processing; here beef is chilled or frozen and sold bone-in to intermediate processors who de-bone it and sell it on to wholesale or retail outlets - forty-five per cent of Irish processed exports, in volume terms, are in this form. Frozen boneless represents a further stage of processing; here beef is de-boned and sold in bulk as a commodity product - some thirty-seven per cent of Irish exports, in volume terms, take this form. Chilled boneless beef is a still further processed product; here individual cuts of beef are vacuum-wrapped and packed in boxes for sale to supermarkets to be cut and prepared for retail sale. This is a trade rather than a consumer product and accounts for about sixteen per cent of Irish exports by volume. The manufacture of processed foods, of course, represents the most advanced level of processing; this involves the manufacture of consumer products in finished form. At present Irish exports of beef in canned or other processed forms is minimal; it 'is not yet large enough to be significant in the overall context', and accounts for no more than two per cent of total carcase utilisation (Roche, 1989, pp. 56, 58).

While the processing situation just described shows evidence of development, it also indicates that the Irish industry still has a long way to go; more than eighty per cent of Irish beef exports leave the country in either bone-in or frozen boneless form, i.e. as low value-added products. And markets certainly exist. The UK market consumes over one million tons of beef, ten per cent of which is accounted for by imports from Ireland. However only about twenty per cent of Irish exports are supplied in vacuum packed form, direct to supermarkets, so, even though the market for beef is declining, there is still tremendous potential for value-added exporting. Important markets also exist in France, Germany and Italy. At present Ireland has about two per cent of the French market, but only twenty-five per cent of the exports are in vacuum-packed form direct to supermarkets. The Irish presence in the other markets is less significant, athough Italy is the largest beef importer in Europe (Roche, 1989, pp. 61-2). Ireland also has access to markets in third world countries, principally in the Middle-east and North Africa. While these markets have proved to be lucrative - taking about thirty-five per cent of Irish production - they are not, as the evidence in Chapter 4 demonstrates, a secure basis for future development; they require only low value-added products - either carcase or frozen bone-in; contracts have to be won each year against fierce international competition, and depend entirely on EC export refunds to keep them competitive with South American exports; oil price weakness restricts potential customers' purchasing power and/or ability to pay for beef bought, and thus makes for volume variability and bad debts, as evidence in Chapter 4 again demonstrates; trade is conducted in dollars and can thus be hampered by exchange rate problems.

If the Irish beef processing industry is to develop, therefore, it must move away from unstable commodity trading and face the challenge of selling more high value-added products into stable markets (Roche, 1989, p. 61). As we have shown such markets exist - and have existed for a long time - and are there to be exploited if the industry is prepared to develop the capacity to do so. Opportunities also exist for developing the 'fifth quarter', the by-products of processing which are not disposed of for human consumption. Petfood is an obvious example of what can be done here. Ireland produces over 100,000 tons of raw material a year most of which is exported to the UK; it has only one small producer of petfood. There is vast potential here; the UK market alone is worth more than £1,000 million per annum at retail prices - and the UK, of course, is by no means the only market.

Underlying the failure of the Irish to fully develop beef processing are deep-seated, and long-standing problems. These have to do with cyclicality and seasonality. Cyclicality derives primarily from the structure of the industry. There are some 90,000 farmers engaged in beef production in Ireland. About fifty per cent of these are small, part-time farmers who find beef-cattle production attractive for two reasons: firstly, because it is not labour intensive and can thus be combined with off-farm employment; and secondly, because it requires little in the way of long-term capital commitment, as cattle can be sold for cash at any stage in the production cycle (Roche, 1989, p. 52). Around eighty per cent of Irish beef cattle are sourced from the dairy herd. Typically, calves are bought by small farmers in the West and sold on, usually more than once, to more capital intensive farm operations which develop and finally finish them for slaughter. From this one thing is obvious: namely, that many Irish beef farmers are farmers in a highly-qualified sense; they produce cattle it is true, but many do not produce them in finished form for sale to processors on a contract basis in a regular market, rather they produce unfinished cattle for sale to other farmers in a disordered market which is subject to price fluctuations and thus 'wheel and deal' as much as they farm. Breeding cows are the beef farmer's capital. However, as Roche (1989, p. 52) points out, 'the normal distinction between capital equipment and goods produced is not clear cut' in the beef industry because capital - the cattle - can be sold and turned into cash at any stage in the production cycle. When farmer confidence in the future of the industry is low, therefore, farmers sell-off breeding cows; this increases the number going for slaughter in the immediate-term but reduces supplies in the longer-term. Conversely, when farmer confidence in the future is high, breeding-cattle are retained, depressing supplies in the short-term but increasing potential supplies in the future. Producers can switch from an output-orientation to an investment-orientation quickly in response to changing market conditions, thus rendering cyclicality endemic in the industry. As a result meat processors are unable to rely on consistent patterns of supply and so cannot generate consistent profit patterns (Roche, 1989, p. 52).

Seasonality follows from the fact that beef cattle production is based on grazing; calves are born in the spring, over-wintered for one or two years, finished on the summer grass and disposed of to the processors in the autumn. In consequence Irish processors receive the bulk of their supplies in the latter-half of the year; sixty-six per cent of their supplies are taken in the July-December period, and forty-two per cent of their annual throughput is produced in the three months between July and September (Roche, 1989, p. 54). Seasonality poses serious obstacles to the development of beef processing in Ireland: In the first place it results in the under-utilisation of plant in the off-season - many plants have to close down altogether. Secondly, it makes it difficult for Irish processors to secure long-term contracts with foreign-based supermarkets; these require a continuous year round supply, a condition which, due to seasonality, Irish processors cannot always meet.

The problem of seasonality, however, is not confined to the beef industry; it is also endemic in dairying - which, like beef production - is grazing-based - where the Irish peak-trough ratio of 8.2 to 1 compares very unfavourably to the continental average of 1.5 to 1 (Roche, 1989, p. 24). Seasonality has severely limited the capacity of the Irish dairy processing industry to develop: In the first place it results in plant under-utilisation in the trough period - as with the beef sector many plants have to shut down during the winter months. Secondly, the lack of adequate year-round supplies places severe constraints on the range of products; it precludes many Irish processors from supplying high value-added, perishable consumer foods to supermarkets who want guaranteed year-round supplies, and encourages the manufacture of commodity products like butter and milk powder which can be stored for long periods. Thirdly, it affects the fat and protein content of the milk and results in variable product yields; it takes over 2,600 gallons of milk to produce a tonne of cheese in April, May and June, and only 2,400 gallons to produce the same quantity in July and August, when milk supplies are beginning to tail-off. Finally, it has an adverse impact on the consistency of milk quality because during the winter trough milk is stored on-farm for longer periods in order to economise on collection costs. Where adequate on-farm refrigeration facilities exist quality problems do not ensue. However, many Irish dairy farmers have no adequate provision for refrigeration, so bacterial multiplication takes place and milk quality is impaired. Quality can have significant implications for both product range and plant utilisation. High value-added products with short shelf-lives, for example soft cheeses and yoghurt, require high quality milk for their production; milk with a high bacterial count gives rise to the early onset of rancidity and thus reduces shelf-life. This has an obvious impact on plant utilisation; milk of differing quality has to be allocated to different processes and imbalances in quality and supply can force processors into situations in which they must constantly switch between processes and/or temporarily close down some lines, making production planning and cost control difficult.

Irish dairy processing is thus underdeveloped and reliant on a very limited range of commodity products. Historically its development was predicated on bulk commodity butter sales to the UK; individually-wrapped, branded consumer packs for direct sale to retailers came late - much later than in the Danish case - and was effectively confined to one product: butter. Export cheese production was, again, confined almost exclusively to one product, cheddar, which, with its long shelf-life fitted well into the dominant Irish pattern of commodity trading. Cheddar was sold in bulk to UK wholesalers for further processing, though more recently processors have sought to enhance value-added by supplying pre-packed, labelled cuts direct to the supermarket trade. This is a step in the right direction, involving as it does a move away from commodity markets and their highly volatile prices. As Roche (1989, p. 38) tells us, however, it still leaves the processors dependent on a single product and a single market. The contrast with Denmark could not be more marked; unlike the Irish, the Danes manage to produce and market an extensive range of soft, semi-hard and hard cheeses.

Ireland's accession to the EC has, if anything, intensified its dependence on a limited product range, especially butter. An Irish analyst expresses himself very candidly with reference to the impact of EC membership on the butter trade:

> Accession to the EEC gave a huge boost to Irish milk production and butter was seen as the most convenient outlet for this. With its low technology requirements, commodity sales without marketing effort and the safety net of intervention, processors found it difficult to resist the soft option (Roche, 1989, p. 35).

When the processors directed their increased milk supplies into butter manufacture they were left with large quantities of skim milk on their hands. Liquid skim is, of course, a normal by-product of butter manufacture, and was, in Ireland, usually sold-off for feeding to pigs. The EC, however, provided price support for drying skim milk into powder, turning it, in the process into a profitable enterprise. Irish processors took full advantage and built up a highly seasonal, highly intervention-dependent commodity trade in the product. For Roche (1989, p. 36):

The skim powder trade became a piece of textbook evidence of all that was wrong with the Irish dairy processing industry - lack of marketing effort, intervention dependence and consequent low margins.

From all that has been said here it will be obvious that the cyclicality and seasonality pose major problems for processors and farmers alike. For processors the problems have to do with plant utilisation, production planning and cost control and with limitations on product range which effectively restrict them to commodity trading, with its low margins and volatile prices, and preclude them from fully developing the processing industry through the cost effective, continuous use of their plants to produce high value-added consumer products which can be marketed direct to the retail trade. For the farmers, of course, similar problems arise; the low margins and unstable prices available to the processors are passed back to the farmers in terms of prices which are lower and less stable than they might otherwise be. The truth is, therefore, that the state of development of Irish food processing cannot be considered satisfactory from anyone's point of view; cyclicality and seasonality have acted as continuous brakes on its development.

Cyclicality and seasonality are deeply rooted, historical problems; they are not recent phenomena, but have been part and parcel of the low input-low output approach to farming in Ireland throughout the twentieth century, and indeed earlier. Given their generally refractory impact on development, it is clearly in everybody's interest that something is done about them. And this is the point: cyclicality and seasonality are not God-ordained, permanent features of the Irish agribusiness landscape; the former can be eliminated; the latter can be brought into line with peak-trough ratios prevailing in Northern Ireland (2 to 1) and/or Continental Europe (1.5 to 1), provided that is that processors and farmers are willing to coordinate the mobilisation of resources and undertake the investment in winter housing and feeding that is necessary to produce the required transformation. Yet very little has been done to alleviate the situation. And the failure cannot readily be explained by reference to the absence of opportunities and means. The markets exist - a cursory glance at the freezer compartments and at the processed and convenience foods sections of any supermarket will confirm this. And so do the means in terms of both a supply of raw materials and capital; Irish farmers are not short of capital and have access to credit - even in the depressed nineteen-thirties farmers were substantial creditors to the banking system, with the ratio of agricultural loans to deposits standing at thirty per cent, and some authorities have noted their failure to make effective use of credit in the financing of commercially viable projects (Department of Finance, 1958; Gilmore, 1959; Kennedy, Giblin and McHugh, 1988, p. 220); the processors have access to finance, including as we have seen, with reference to the Goodman and Ballybay cases, very generous state grants, loan arrangements and tax-breaks. It might, of course, be argued that the low prices and uncertain markets facing Irish farmers provided strong disincentives to investment, and so provided some rationale for the preservation of what is a patently unsatisfactory status quo. The validity of this argument is, however, more apparent than real because:

> the poor price environment faced by Irish farmers was partly due to inadequate attention to the marketing of Irish agricultural produce. Irish farmers were slower than their continental counterparts in combining together to market their output effectively and to secure satisfactory feedback from customers. No doubt the structure of Irish trade, with its emphasis on live animals and low industrial processing, militated against this. In any event, there was for long a failure to establish a clearly defined image for Irish agriculture products, and Irish farmers acquired the reputation of being erratic suppliers of goods that were sometimes inferior in quality, poorly graded or simply inappropriate to the market in which they were offered (Kennedy, Giblin and McHugh, 1988, p.215).

Again the contrast with the Danes has to be noted: The Danes did combine together to market their produce and to secure satisfactory feedback from customers; they gave their products a clearly defined Danish image; they made sure that Danish became a by-word for quality and reliability of supply. They reaped their rewards accordingly, where the Irish did not.

Kennedy, Giblin and McHugh's judgement against the farmers - and it is the judgement of Irish economists - points clearly to grossly inadequate entrepreneurship. By no stretch of the imagination or the limits of boundless charity, could entrepreneurs who inadequately market their products, who take no trouble to secure feedback from customers, who fail to establish a clearly defined image for their products, except perhaps an image that is associated with unevenness of quality and unreliability of supply, be regarded as adequate to the tasks of developing businesses in a competitive capitalist market in which significant others, i.e. their competitors, operate to higher standards. The following passage points even more clearly in the direction of the entrepreneurial problem, demonstrating, if nothing else, that there is no shortage of materials, investment funds and markets:

> 8 of the top 20 largest Irish indigenous manufacturing firms are dairy co-operatives engaged in relatively low value-added food-processing. Since 1960 this industry has changed radically. Total milk supply rose from 280 million gallons in 1960 to 920 million gallons in 1982. There was extensive rationalisation at the processing end, with the number of plants reduced from 160 in 1965 to less than 60 a decade later, and this was accompanied by a vast increase in investment in modern equipment. Despite the large growth in throughput, however, employment rose little, and has been falling since 1979, because the industry failed to upgrade significantly the product mix from the standard bulk commodities.... The high seasonality of primary production (with a peak/valley ratio of 14:1 compared with an EEC norm of 2:1) undoubtedly operated against high value-added products with short shelf lives. The vagaries of the CAP regulations have presented other inhibiting

factors, and in addition, the dairy co-operatives had little surplus funds for R & D and product innovation because of the determination of the farmers who controlled them to secure the highest possible current price for their milk. The industry is a sizeable one, however, and the difficulties mentioned are of a kind that might have been overcome by a greater organisational capacity and more willingness by the parties involved to work together for the long-term interests of the industry. Similar points could be made about meat-processing, where low value-added products also dominate. It may well be, therefore, that underlying the failure of indigenous manufacturing in Ireland to respond better to the outward-looking strategy lies a more general entrepreneurial deficiency affecting both the public and private sectors - namely, a lack of effectiveness in co-ordinating the resources and devising the instruments needed for the strategic management of large-scale manufacturing enterprise (Kennedy, Giblin and McHugh, 1988, p. 246-65).

In the light of the evidence presented here and elsewhere in the book, it is difficult to see how anyone could accuse Kennedy, Giblin and McHugh of overstating the case. If anything, in fact, their judgement seems to err on the side of moderation in limiting the problem to one of effectiveness in coordination. We say this because the fact that they themselves invoke 'willingness' alongside 'capacity' suggests that the problem may lie as much in a lack of interest in promoting change and growth as it does in a dearth of appropriate organisational effectiveness. If we read their statement against some of the evidence presented in Chapter 2 the conviction that a lack of interest is also a problem hardens. There, to remember, we saw evidence of an easy-going and unambitious approach to economic activity; many Irish entrepreneurs were, it seems, content to make 'a nice, neat little profit ... without much growth' (Irish entrepreneur quoted in Fogarty, 1973, p. 67); for too many, according to Brian Patterson, a home market no larger in size than Lancashire remained a sphere of operations that 'will do well enough' (quoted in O'Toole, 1987); a leading investment banker, Niall Carroll, reckons that many Irish companies are manifestly lacking in ambition and do not put enough effort into solving problems that cost them profitable opportunities for growth (Lattimore, 1989). In this connection we might also recall the remarks of the entrepreneur who was 'rather horrified', by the 'low moral values' he found to be prevalent in Ireland; by people 'making appointments which they do not keep'; by people making promises 'which they can't keep' (quoted in Fogarty, 1973, p. 97). And then, of course, there were those farmers who could not be persuaded that 'fifteen productive hours a week ... doesn't rate a forty hour salary' (Fogarty, 1973, p. 98), and who evidently wasted their land as well as their time:

It is depressing at times to see the vast amount of land that is wasted in Ireland. Rushes and bushes grow wild on fields, where, with a bit of care and attention, these are easily controlled. Often such owners are clamouring for more land. Applying fertilisers would improve the grass and provide not alone good grazing, but good quality food which would reduce greatly the cost of buying expensive feedstuffs in winter (Cullen, 1988).

The point, of course, must be that it does not require a vast amount of organisational ability to clear away rushes and bushes, nor indeed, one would imagine, to apply fertilisers in order to save on expensive winter feedstuffs - it does, however, require some interest and a little commitment. Likewise it requires little in the nature of organisational ability to avoid making appointments and promises which you know you cannot keep - it does, however, once again, require some little interest in and commitment towards the content of one's economic activity. Our point here is a simple one: namely, that evidence of the sort we have just presented speaks, not to a want of organisational capacities alone, but also to a limited interest and to the existence of a limited commitment and an absence of a sense of responsibility towards economic resources and opportunities.

Comments like those of the entrepreneur, Patterson and Carroll are also crucial. The entrepreneur - and, as we saw in Chapter 2, he was by no means alone - would hardly have commented as he did unless he saw that opportunities for growth were available to Irish entrepreneurs. Neither, we may presume, would Patterson and Carroll have complained about the lack of entrepreneurial ambition unless they saw that opportunities were available - if they did not believe that opportunities existed their comments would be devoid of sense. Patterson and Carroll can speak with authority here; Patterson is an erstwhile director of The Irish Management Institute, Carroll is a leading investment banker; both men know the Irish economy, and Irish business, and there is nothing in their records to suggest that they are naive optimists when it comes to their assessment of the possibilities that are available to entrepreneurs with ambition and drive. And the evidence presented in this chapter suggests that they are correct. The truth is that Irish entrepreneurs are not, and have not historically been, short of means and opportunities - that much is, by now, very clear. What is also, we hope, very clear is that Irish entrepreneurs have wasted many of the opportunities available to them; they have wasted them because they have lacked the interest and/or the wills and capacities to tackle the problems of cyclicality and seasonality with a view to deriving economies in production and improving their product range by moving away from low value-added commodity trading and into the manufacture of high value-added consumer products - they have retained the traditional 'soft option' of commodity trading underpinned, in more recent times, by intervention and export refunds from the EC; they have wasted them through lack of marketing effort and through a failure to attend to customer specifications and to create a positive image for Irish products in export markets; they have wasted them through engaging in customer-alienating 'sharp practices', through the sale of 'bad eggs and worse butter' and through a persistent failure to attend to problems associated with the quality and reliability of supplies. Again no moral judgement is intended here. The view we are expressing is a 'technical' one that is, we would submit, well justified by the evidence we have presented.

All things considered, therefore, the application of the term traditionalism as a summary characterisation of Irish entrepreneurial orientations seems to be justified; the bright new age anticipated by so many in the sixties does not seem to have been productive of a radical break with the past; continuity rather than change seems to be the order of the day. The traditional patterns of commodity production have not been 'traded-in' for a brand new approach to high value-added consumer products; the old problems of quality and lack of effectiveness in marketing have not been solved; traditional sharp practices remain evident, though they have become more sophisticated and moved beyond the supply of 'bad eggs and worse butter' to encompass, inter alia, some very sophisticated operations in construction, financial services and the like. If nothing else the sheer sophistication of some of the doubtful transactions which we have described proves that the problem does not lie in a lack of organisational capacities or in the absence of a taste for money-making; the Irish are as competent and as sophisticated as any when it comes to 'turning a buck'. Mention of the sophistication provokes us to a final thought, indeed, it gives rise to a hope, that this little book may perform one service at any rate: It may destroy, once and for all, the idiotic stereotype of 'the stupid Paddy'.

Conclusion

In this chapter we have tried to show that it is not possible to explain fully the traditionalism of Irish entrepreneurs, and their country's consequent failure to develop, by reference to objective factors having to do with shortages of means and opportunities which constrain actors to the point where a non-traditionalistic entrepreneurial orientation and the achievement of economic development are entirely precluded. We have tried to do this by the simple expedient of showing that Irish entrepreneurs have not been denied access to the means and opportunities necessary to an open, dynamic approach to economic life which would have been productive of a greater degree of economic development than the country has achieved, if entrepreneurs had chosen to become so engaged with their business activities. Irish entrepreneurs have not, therefore, been deprived of the possibility of making history, and, had they oriented to their economic lives differently, would have produced a different historical text. This is manifestly not to say that they could have written the text in any way they pleased; given the economies of scale and concentration enjoyed by many industries in countries which have undergone a process of heavy industrialisation it would clearly be unreasonable to expect to see Irish entrepreneurs advancing by industrialising along a wide front. As we saw an Irish economic historian (Green, 1969, p. 99) nobserve earlier in the chapter, however, the failure does not lie there, but rather in those sectors in which Ireland had the resources to build and expand: namely, the processing of the natural products of some of the best agricultural land to be found anywhere in the world. If Irish entrepreneurs had oriented differently here they could have written a different script. The fact that their orientation in 'failure' cannot be fully explained by reference to

131

objective factors (structural constraints) suggests, of course, that an examination of subjective factors is warranted. Here we return to the motivational and institutional factors referred to in the framework for analysis. More especially, of course, we turn to the question: if, and to what extent, entrepreneurial motivation is influenced by the cultural values to which entrepreneurs relate their economic activity? That, for us, is the key question. It is now time to see what we can do about providing an answer to it .

6 Culture and the entrepreneurial problem

Introduction

In the preceding chapter we tried to show that the traditionalism manifest in the behaviour of Irish entrepreneurs cannot be convincingly explained by reference to any objective shortages of means and opportunities; their behaviour is not determined by constraints lying in shortages of markets, capital and other relevant resources, and they do not act as they do because they have no realistic possibilities of behaving otherwise. Granted always, as we remarked in the conclusion to the preceding chapter, that it might be unreasonable to expect Irish entrepreneurs to advance along a broad front and establish, say motor and aircraft industries to rival the Fords and the Boeings of this world, there is no reason why they could not have developed industries directed to the processing of the natural products of their land to an extent that would have enabled them to rival the Danish and Dutch achievements in these sectors. When all the evidence is weighed, the truth seems to be that, in certain respects crucial to the prospect of development, the Irish are poor opportunity-takers; they have clearly not been willing to innovate and to solve problems on the organisational front; they have not been over-energetic in seeking out new markets, or, indeed, in servicing existing markets by reference to quality and reliability of supply; they have displayed a capacity for erratic and unscrupulous behaviour and have failed to internalise the virtues of honesty, integrity and hard and purposeful work. Now it might be thought possible to explain a lack of dedication to hard and purposeful work by reference to the structure of opportunities confronting entrepreneurs; why work hard if market conditions are limited and difficult to the extent that they yield what might be considered unsatisfactory rewards to effort expended? Maybe so, but it is difficult to see how such an explanation could be applied convincingly to account for the erratic unscrupulousness so clearly evident in much of the behaviour we have been examining. And this is, surely, the point: The absence of the virtues of honesty, integrity and hard and purposeful work cannot be explained by reference to hypotheses which have to do with shortages of means and opportunities precisely because such scarcities, if anything, put an added premium on the cultivation of the virtues mentioned; whatever chances entrepreneurs have of surviving and thriving in tough, competitive markets must depend on their willingness to attend to innovation, consistency, reliability and quality, and so, the tougher the market, the more certain are the consequences of an unwillingness to cultivate and maintain appropriate standards: namely, failure. Hypotheses about opportunities and means, therefore, cannot fully explain the conduct we are examining. If markets were easy and tolerant towards the 'failings' we have described, then the behaviour which exhibited those failings might be rendered intelligible by reference to such conditions. The fact that markets are neither so easy nor so tolerant renders that behaviour more, and not less incomprehensible, if we seek to explain it exclusively by reference to opportunities and means. The truth is, therefore, that while hypotheses which have to do with opportunities and means can do something to explain the inter-industry distribution of Irish enterprise, i.e. why Irish entrepreneurs might not be able to develop motor and aircraft industries to rival Ford and Boeing, they cannot tell us why it is that they have failed to develop those industries in which they had advantage and potential, and why it is that they have come to be driven by patterns of motivation which are associated with the failure to internalise the virtues of honesty, integrity and hard and purposeful work. If we want to explain the pattern of motivation and its characteristics we shall have to look elsewhere: namely, to the cultural values to which Irish economic actors relate their economic activity.

The case of culture: values and meanings

In Chapter 5 we used the term culture as a reference to the whole complex of ideafacts and artifacts produced by human groups in the course of their adaption to their natural and social environments. Concretely, to remember, a culture is a congeries of values, norms, beliefs, customs, technologies, practices and forms of artistic expression which reflect the thoughts, feelings and actions of a people, and which, since the ideafacts form inter-generationally transmitted world views and the artifacts conditioning environments, come, in turn, to structure the thoughts, feelings and actions of peoples through the shared cognitive, normative, aesthetic and technical standards which derive from them.

Cultural identities are formed out of the concrete contents of the components specified in this list; a human group may be said to share a cultural identity to the extent that its members orient to common beliefs, values, norms, technologies, practices and forms of artistic expression. Put another way, a cultural identity consists in the members of a given collectivity's sense of themselves; in a body of shared collective representations which express a shared understanding of their past, present and future, and which enable them to give common answers to questions like: who are we? what distinguishes us from others? what kind of life do we esteem? what kind of goals do we set for ourselves and mobilise our resources to achieve? The answers to these questions need not always remain the same; cultures are not immutable. Nevertheless, it is through their capacities to give common answers to these questions, and to others like them, that people come to develop and maintain that sense of belonging together as conscious sharers of a cultural identity.

It is, of course, from these bodies of shared representations as transmitted by families, schools, churches and other institutions of socialisation, that individuals come to develop their understanding of themselves as socialised beings - members of a particular society - and of the world that confronts them. It is through the bodies of shared representations that people come to give meaning to their life situations and activities and so learn to orient themselves, to take a stance towards, the complexes of objects, events, actions, and possibilities that make up that world. Values are particularly important in this context. Values are shared standards on which people in a collectivity base their moral and aesthetic judgements; they are shared conceptions of worth used to distinguish between right and wrong, good and bad, useful and useless, beautiful and ugly etc.. Peoples' thoughts, feelings and actions are, therefore, structured through their orientation to values, which orientation structures the answers to such questions as: what sorts of goals shall we seek to achieve? by what means? with what intensity? and, in what sort of relationships to other, and different, goals?

While all these questions are important, the fourth and final one is by far the most significant for our purposes. We say this because it calls attention to relationships of super and subordination between values and the activities they govern which are expressed through actors' prioritisation of the multiplicity of 'action-options' available to them. Economic activity is, of course, one of these 'action-options'. It is, however, only one among many and has to be prioritised in the range of 'action options' available to the actors. How then is it to be prioritised? Will actors see it as their most important 'action-option' to which all others will be subordinated? Or will they give it a lower priority and subordinate it to other 'action-options' having to do with leisure, meditation or whatever? Given that human beings are creatures of culture it seems reasonable to suggest that they will learn to ask and answer such questions meaningfully through the internalisation of the values of their society. It seems impossible to rule out *a priori* that different value systems may provide axiological recipes that move people to different patterns of prioritisation; some value systems may teach people that economic activity should be given number one priority; others, quite simply may teach people to give it a much lower salience, in subordination to other and more valued priorities.

Ireland provides striking evidence that value systems can work an impact on the priorities which people accord to their economic activity; the Irish themselves express an unambiguous awareness of a situation in which the priority they give to their economic activities is determined by some non-economic components of the value system to which they relate those activities. We saw this in Chapter 1 when we noted that:

> Managerial people [in Dublin] quite commonly acknowledge that their more relaxed attitude towards business activity stems from their religious outlook on life. In the words of one husband: 'I think we Irish are quite different from the English and Americans. The ones I've met seem to me to be wrapped up in the almighty pound and dollar. I've dealt with many Englishmen and my impression is that money and what it brings are their God. But we cannot get as concerned as they over business and material things. We are less active in these matters because always in the background of our minds we are concerned with a more fundamental philosophy' (Humphries, 1966, p. 219).

From this it is obvious - and the view, be it noted is a common view - that Irish business people see themselves as different from their English and American counterparts, being less active in the pursuit of business interests than their colleagues to the East and West of them. It is equally clear that, as the Irish see it, the reason for the difference does not lie in the fact that they are confronted with a less favourable structure of means and opportunities in their business lives, but rather in the fact that 'always in the background of our minds we are concerned with a more fundamental philosophy'. In the passage just quoted we are confronted by nothing less than the conscious expression of a cultural identity formed through the prioritisation of 'action-options'; the respondents' self-awareness of what differentiates them, as Irish, from the English and Americans lies in their sense that they give their business activities a lower priority because 'always in the background of [their] minds [they] are concerned with a more fundamental philosophy'. From this it is obvious that the process of enculturation into an Irish cultural identity is a process of learning to make economic activity meaningful in the context of relating it to 'a more fundamental philosophy' which dictates a comparatively limited and circumscribed commitment to the pursuit of business and material things. The Irish are thus 'less active' and 'more relaxed' in their pursuit of business objectives and material possessions.

Unless we are going to disregard completely the self-reporting of Humphries's respondents we had better set about the task of trying to find out what it is about that 'more fundamental philosophy' - and it is, of course, Roman Catholicism - that leads its adherents to take a 'less active' and 'more relaxed' approach to business activity and the pursuit of material gain. Before we do so, however, we need to note that the terms 'less active' and, especially 'more relaxed' are not without a certain ambiguity which is not explored by Humphries - and of which his respondents were clearly unaware - but which is clearly pointed up in the evidence presented in the earlier chapters of this book. It is thus possible for actors to take a more relaxed attitude to business through the agency of limiting the amount of time and effort that they are willing to commit to economic activity; they may not seek to maximise the inputs of time and effort with a view to maximising growth and earnings, but may be satisfied with little or no growth and lower profits in the interests of devoting time and effort to non-productive pursuits. Actors can, of course, take a more relaxed attitude to business in another sense entirely: namely, in the moral and/or prudential sense, by engaging in ethically questionable and unscrupulous conduct in the pursuit of gain. As Weber saw with reference to his 'economic traditionalists', and as the evidence presented here amply confirms, these two modes of 'relaxation' are by no means mutually exclusive; individuals who are relaxed in the first of our two senses of the term may still exhibit a greed for gain which will be serviced, not by consistent hard work, but by undisciplined outbursts of unscrupulous energy.

From this it follows that we need to extend our discussion and consider what might be involved in our use of the term 'activity'. Economic activity is, of course, goal-directed activity; economic actors set out to achieve something and deploy a battery of means in their efforts to attain their ends. Under the rubric of means we can include a variety of expedients, including, for example, hard and disciplined work, saving, investment, honesty and reliability, theft, force, fraud and fiddling of various kinds. In considering the impact of cultural values, therefore, we must examine their effects by reference to both means and ends and attend to what we shall call regulation as well as prioritisation. Prioritisation has to do with ends; in the present context it refers to the priority which a value system indicates that actors should give to economic goals, i.e. the pursuit of wealth, power, success or whatever, relative to the multiplicity of non-economic goals in which they may be interested. Regulation, on the other hand, speaks to the issue of means and has to do with the question of what a value system has to say about what means will be regarded as acceptable and legitimate for deployment by actors in the pursuit of their economic ends. Thus, at one extreme, a value system could indicate that actors should give economic goals a very high priority, but might provide for a strict regulation of means by indicating that economic ends should only be serviced by hard, disciplined work, saving for investment, competence and reliability in performance and honest dealing. At the other extreme a value system might suggest that actors should give the pursuit of economic goals a relatively low priority while being more permissive with regard to the regulation of means, showing greater toleration for incompetence, unreliability and, indeed, for theft, fraud and fiddling. Between these two poles lie other possibilities - high prioritisation with permissive regulation, and low prioritisation with restrictive regulation - but these need not concern us here. What is important, rather, is that the evidence we have suggests that, in Ireland, the behaviour of economic actors seems to orient in the direction of low prioritisation with permissive regulation.

Clearly the question which we have to answer here is: Why is it that the values to which Irish economic actors relate their economic interests and activities are such as to set, or suggest tolerance towards, standards which are low on prioritisation and high on permissiveness. Before we attempt to answer this question, however, there is a more fundamental question which needs to be addressed: namely, how is it that the standards of conduct derived from the value systems into which actors are socialised come to mould and shape their conduct in the first place? There seem to us to be three 'mechanisms' through which conformity to value-directed behavioural standards is secured in any given society: In the first place, it seems reasonable to suggest that, in the process of socialisation, individuals may come to feel a strong attachment to particular values and thus may seek to uphold them in their own, and in others', conduct because they believe them to be right and good, and because they, for whatever reason, wish to be right and good. In this case conformity springs from within the individuals' own moral sense and from a positive, willed commitment to what is seen, by him or by her, as the morally correct course of living. Where socialisation cannot inspire a sense of loyalty through commitment, it can inspire a sense of loyalty through fear or awe and thus socialise, not only values, but also sets of sanctions internal to individuals which coerce them into keeping their conduct up to the mark when they are tempted to do otherwise; individuals, therefore, may conform, not because they are enthusiastic about upholding standards, but because the contemplation and carrying out of deviant acts causes them feelings of guilt and unease - the pangs of conscience - with which they might find it difficult to live. And matters do not end here: Individuals who feel neither loyalty through commitment nor loyalty through fear may still keep their conduct in line with value-specified standards because they believe, rightly or wrongly, that those with whom they interact uphold those standards and will, accordingly, reward conforming behaviour and apply sanctions against deviant actors. In this case clearly the reference is external to actors; conformity is secured, not through internalised feelings of commitment or guilt, but by a desire either to retain the approval or avoid the disapproval - which may lead to sanctions being imposed - of others in the actors' milieu. Rewards and sanctions can, of course, take different forms and will vary in intensity depending on the salience accorded to the standards and the conduct they govern. Rewards accruing to conforming behaviour are many and varied; conformity may bring honour and esteem and will certainly enable those who exhibit it to secure all the advantages that flow to individuals who preserve their 'good names' among their circles of interactants. Sanctions too can take a variety of forms, ranging from mild expressions of disapproval through withdrawal from interaction to, the ultimate sanction perhaps, the imposition of legal penalties.

It is only through modes of orientation and action on the parts of human beings - and the three modes we have described are by no means mutually exclusive - that values have any life and 'force'; values may be proclaimed *ad nauseam* by politicians, priests, prophets, philosophers, patriots and by all the variegated hosts of moral entrepreneurs; they may be enacted in legal codes, enshrined in the constitutions of states, churches and secular institutions of many kinds, and will remain 'dead letters' unless their propagators can instil them into the minds and hearts of people who will carry and uphold them in their thoughts, feelings and actions. The fact that values may be proclaimed by moral entrepreneurs and enacted by legislators, therefore, provides no guarantee that they will become guiding forces in the practical lives of human beings; the fact that values often do provide such guidance does not mean that they cannot sometimes be rejected or evaded in cases where regulatory regimes operating through the informal forces of public opinion and/or those functionaries in institutions which are charged with upholding standards are permissive of deviance. This is a crucial point; the passage of a value from the moral entrepreneur's 'drawing board' to its practical application in everyday life and from the socialising agent to the socialised, can be a journey that is fraught with hazard for the meaning of the value; values that are proclaimed in one context can be taken up and deployed in other contexts in which they are interpreted selectively in applying them to people's actual life situations. What is all very well in theory, i.e. in the mind of the moral entrepreneur, may not be so good in practice, i.e. in the everyday lives of people who try to live by the moral entrepreneurial proclamations; the world has a nasty habit of transforming the products of its moral entrepreneurs in unexpected ways and in directions which they would not necessarily approve of. Such is life!

We make this point because there is an issue that we have to confront. Our issue arises from the contrast between Irish Roman Catholics as religious actors and Irish Roman Catholics as economic actors As religious actors Irish Roman Catholics have created and sustained a regime which is high on priority and restrictive on regulation; the Church, as we shall see, has succeeded in maintaining high levels of religious practice together with a regulatory regime which is restrictive enough to secure outward conformity even from those who have ceased to be believers. As economic actors, however, Irish Roman Catholics seem to have created and maintained a regime which is low on prioritisation and permissive on regulation because, in the words of the entrepreneurs quoted earlier in the book,

> what families, schools, the Church, the social system and the business system itself have failed to produce in Ireland is people with the basic virtues of honesty, integrity and hard and purposeful work (quoted in Fogarty, 1973, pp. 96-7).

There are two strong and obvious links between religion and the condition of economic life in Ireland as described by the entrepreneurs. The first of these has to do with the fact that honesty and integrity seem to be demanded by Christian ethics - 'Thou shalt love they neighbour as thyself'; 'Thou shalt not steal'; 'Thou shalt not bear false witness'. The second is connected to the fact that the Church, given its influence over the family and its all but complete control over the education system, moulds and shapes the young and prepares them for their occupational and business lives. Even in the context of business, therefore, the Church is the most important socialising agent; the legions of tax evaders, 'Phoenix syndrome' operators, fraudsters, smugglers and easy-going, ethically indifferent farmers and entrepreneurs, whose conduct has been described in these pages, together with those who are formally or informally in a position to regulate their activities, are, for the most part, products of the

Church, thanks, above all, to its domination of the education system. It is hard, therefore, to avoid at least the suggestion that there is a connection between the Irish economic regime and the Roman Catholic values which permeate so many departments of Irish life. Yet it is equally hard, indeed impossible, to take seriously the idea that Irish Roman Catholicism has formally abrogated the commandments concerning neighbourly love, stealing and bearing false witness. We have no doubt that the Church upholds these commandments. Yet the evidence we have suggests that many of its followers do not uphold them, at least in connection with their economic activities. The economic activities of the Irish seem, therefore, to have floated free from moral regulation with the results we have observed; namely, the combination of low prioritisation and weak regulation. How has this come about?

Economic traditionalism and the entrepreneurial problem

In the conclusion to Chapter 3 we borrowed the term economic traditionalism from Max Weber to use as a summary description of the orientations of Irish economic actors. Weber coined this term in order to characterise what he took to be a set of attitudes to economic life, analysis of which exhibited the meaning-frame through which actors made sense of their work and business lives in the context of their other life activities. One thing is clear about the Weberian traditionalist: If you ask him or her the question, 'what do work, doing business and making money mean to you?' you will probably get an answer that approximates to the following: 'I work, do business and make money in order to live, I do not live in order to work, do business and make money'. In essence what the traditionalist is saying here is that there is more to life than work, doing business and making money. If nothing else there are leisure, pleasure and festivities, family, friends, outlets for emotion and for the spontaneous enjoyment of life which come naturally to human beings and which the income generated by work, doing business and making money can be used to service. Why, therefore, should anyone become overly devoted to work, doing business and making money, when there is so much else in life that is worthwhile? Working and doing business are necessary activities, but they are necessary to be engaged in only to an extent sufficient to generate enough income to provide for a comfortable and balanced life which leaves plenty of room for leisure and enjoyment of the fruits of toil. Only fools, or those possessed of an immoral greed, would burden themselves with work and acquisition beyond these necessary levels: why work to pile up money for some ulterior purpose which, because of your engagement with work, you have neither the time nor the leisure to enjoy? Where is the sense in that?

To the economic traditionalist there is no sense in it, so he or she will not do it. Traditionalists, therefore, integrate work, doing business and making money into a balanced, 'civilised' round of activity which includes a high prioritisation of leisure and enjoyment. Work and doing business are, therefore, 'nothing special'; they are not objects of devotion, even less are they activities through which individuals prove their worth and standing either to themselves or to others in their communities. Accordingly peoples' commitment to work and business activity is limited; they will do enough to enable them to earn enough to enjoy the standards of living to which tradition has accustomed them, and so long as they can obtain this, by one means or another, they will rest content with a moderate engagement with work and business. It was not so much the case that traditionalists were incapable of forming capitalistic organisations. Far from it. According to Weber (1930b, p. 67):

> The form of business organisation was in every respect capitalistic; the entrepreneur's activity was of a purely business character; the use of capital turned over in the business was indispensable; and finally, the objective aspect of the economic process, the book keeping, was rational. But it was traditionalistic business, if one considers the spirit which animated the entrepreneur: the traditional manner of life, the traditional rate of profit, the traditional amount of work, the traditional manner of regulating relationships with labour, and the essentially traditional circle of customers and the manner of attracting new ones. All these dominated the conduct of the business, were at the basis, one may say, of the *ethos* of this group of business men.

As Weber depicts them to us, therefore, traditionalists are people who approach economic life with a 'do not disturb sign' firmly on display; they are a sleepy, complacent and undynamic lot who live off economic activity and not for it. The traditionalist, therefore, is not the rational income maximiser constantly trying to improve his position so beloved of the classical school; 'he' is not *homo economicus*, but rather *homo socialis*; 'he' is a social being whose interest lies, not in income maximisation for improvement, but in the income maintenance at a level that is sufficient to enable him to enjoy the leisured style of life to which tradition has accustomed 'him' and is thus satisfied with 'his' income so long as it is sufficient to enable 'him' to support that style.

Weber associates economic traditionalism with humanity in its state of nature. Human beings are not by nature given to a ruthlessly disciplined approach to life which places a high priority on disciplined devotion to work; they are easy-going creatures, given to spontaneity, irregularity and self-indulgence, not only in leisure and pleasure, but also in the exercise of that age-old human 'vice' the greed for gain. The fact that greed for gain will not move people to become more actively engaged with disciplined work, at a cost to leisure, does not mean that it will not move them to servicing their greed, as the opportunity arises, through unscrupulous dealings, often associated with erratic outbursts of energy, which enable them to make gains without requiring them to abandon their easy-going spontaneity in the interests of cultivating a self-disciplined devotion to work. It is for this reason that traditionalism is perfectly compatible with unscrupulousness in the pursuit of profit stemming from sheer unregulated greed; it could be traced in the activities of 'waiters, physicians, coachmen, artists, prostitutes, dishonest officials, soldiers, nobles, crusaders, gamblers and beggars' and other business operators who, in every age and clime, have been willing to push their greed beyond the limits dictated by ruling moralities (Weber, 1930a, p. 17; 1930b, pp. 56-58). Economic supermen have also existed in every age and clime; those who, like the Dutch Sea-captain referred to earlier in the piece, were captivated by the sheer excitement of money-making and who laughed at all ethical and conventional restraints in an approach which clearly regarded economic life as something of an adventure. If traditionalism involves low prioritisation of economic activity, therefore, it does so in association with weak patterns of regulation exhibited through unscrupulous outbursts of self-indulgent greed. According to Weber modern capitalism, that is bourgeois industrial capitalism, was not the product of unregulated self-indulgent greed, even less than it was a product of the traditionalists' lack of commitment and dynamism. It was created and sustained by entrepreneurs who were animated by a very different ethos, an ethos which brought greed under cover a strong pattern of ethical regulation and which thus transformed it into the spirit of capitalism.

This ethos, the spirit of capitalism, differed from traditionalism in two decisive respects: Firstly, it put an enhanced emphasis on business and economic activity, to an extent that amounted to a reversal of the traditionalistic view of business as an activity to be subordinated to other, more important, life interests; it made business activity the central life interest and subordinated all other life activities to the interest in business. Secondly, it put an enhanced emphasis on the self-disciplined regulation of human life and activity; it was, in short, ascetic. A new devotion to business was thus manifested under cover of an ascetic regimentation of life which killed-off the natural, easy-going spontaneous tendencies to self-indulgence in leisure and pleasure, and in ethically unregulated approaches to profit making. Business success became peoples' most prized goal; it became a means of proving their moral worth to others as well as to themselves. Thanks to the character of the ascetic regime, however, that success had to be achieved by endless, disciplined work, saving and investment, by the eschewal of all leisure and pleasure-seeking activities which wasted time and money that could be devoted to the business, and through the abandonment of ethically irregular sharp practices in commercial activity. A new gospel was thus proclaimed, the terms of which dictated high prioritisation and strong regulation: acquisition through industry and thrift; honesty is the best policy. *homo economicus* had arrived on the scene and pushed *homo socialis* into the background.

Somewhat controversially Weber located the origins of the new ethos in the teachings of ascetic Protestantism, principally in the development of the doctrine of the vocation. According to this doctrine all secular occupations, including that of the entrepreneur, were to be regarded as callings from God. God, it was held, had given believers time, talent, energy, capital and other resources and had called them to use all that He had given them to serve Him and to promote His glory. Occupational activity, including business activity, became the highest form of Godly services. Under this dispensation entrepreneurs could not retain their easy-going, ethically indifferent ways because their business activity

142

became, in effect, a form of religious service through which they proved the quality of their ethical and religious lives and thus developed their subjective conviction that God had called them to salvation. Puritan soteriologies underpinned this development; by insisting that salvation was a gift from God given directly to believers, either through predestination or a personal calling, they removed the Church and its traditional mediations and sacraments as mechanisms through which believers could obtain their assurance of salvation and thus left them with no alternative but to prove themselves through the iron consistency of their ethical conduct. Any anxiety which believers felt about their salvation could only be relieved by an assurance of salvation gained through ascetic business behaviour. An ascetic lifestyle thus emerged in which business activity was the central life interest to which all else was subordinated; disciplined, productive work, saving, investment, honest dealing and business expansion took precedence over relaxed self-indulgence in pleasure, consumption and unethical greed in the pursuit of gain.

In developing the doctrine of the vocation as it did, Puritan Christianity differed decisively from Roman Catholicism. Roman Catholicism did indeed have a doctrine of the vocation which promoted asceticism. However, it applied that doctrine only to a calling to the religious life, and did not extend it to secular occupations. The calling was thus confined to the clerical sector, and so asceticism remained in the monasteries; one was called to be a priest, a monk, a nun, but not to be a plumber or an entrepreneur. Consequently, Weber argues, lay Roman Catholics were not expected to prove their religious worth, and thus fit themselves for salvation, through the quality of their business lives; they proved their religious worth, and obtained their assurance of salvation, by establishing themselves as loyal sons and daughters of the Church; by submitting themselves to its authority; by relying on its mediation, on the prayers and intercessions of the saints and the religious, on indulgences and on the sacraments. Catholicism, therefore, was unable to consecrate economic life to a religious purpose and thus provide Catholic entrepreneurs with any reason to accord it a high priority or to develop a high sense of duty towards it and thus to subject it to a strong pattern of regulation; the Catholic's highest ideal, the assurance of his or her salvation, could be obtained without any reference to the quality of their business lives, i.e. by relying on the mediation of the Church, and so they had no need to abandon their easy-going, natural, self-indulgent traditionalism and transform themselves into ruthlessly self-denying ascetics precisely because the sacramental and other mediations of the Church provided them with the possibilities of obtaining pardon for their imperfections and compensation therefor through the merits of the saints which the Church claimed to be able to transfer to them through indulgences and other means. Catholics were thus enabled to live 'hand to mouth' ethical lives and did not need to cultivate the iron discipline of asceticism; thanks to confession and indulgences they were, as Weber (1930b, p. 118) puts it, able to live in 'the very human Catholic cycle of sin, repentance, atonement, release, followed by renewed sin'.

Vocational ethics, therefore, forced the Puritan to abandon traditionalism, where the Catholic did not have to. They also removed the traditional Christian suspicion of business and of profit-seeking - if business was a calling of God then how could profit-seeking and wealth be bad in themselves. Weber is, therefore, well able to claim that:

> This development of the concept of the calling quickly gave to the modern entrepreneur a fabulously clear conscience - and also industrious workers; he gave to his employees as the wages of their ascetic devotion to the calling and of co-operation in his ruthless exploitation of them through capitalism the prospect of eternal salvation, which in an age when ecclesiastical discipline took control of the whole of life to an extent inconceivable to us now, represented a reality quite different from any it has today. The Catholic and Lutheran churches also recognised and practiced ecclesiastical discipline. But in the Protestant ascetic communities admission to the Lord's Supper was conditioned on ethical fitness, which again was identified with business honour, while into the content of one's faith no one inquired. Such a powerful, unconsciously refined organised organisation for the production of capitalistic individuals has never existed in any other church or religion, and in comparison with it what the Renaissance did for capitalism shrinks into insignificance (Weber, 1950, pp, 36-8).

From what has been said so far it is evident that Puritanism was able to mobilise the sanctions described earlier in the chapter to support its cherished values; it was no doubt capable of generating commitment, but, if not, its adherents were kept up to the mark by internalised anxiety and/or the pressure of public opinion in their communities. As capitalism outgrew its religious roots and secularisation set in, of course, the focus of discipline moved away from the ascetic communities and located itself in the functioning of impersonal market forces; the fear of failure in the competitive jungle replaced the fear of the Lord as the point of pressure on individual conduct; a prudential sense of the need for survival - and the Saints had a sage awareness, for example, that honesty paid-off prudentially in that it helped them to attract and retain customers - replaced Divine edicts as the grounds on which devotion to business and the Gospel of diligence, thrift, honesty, integrity and hard and purposeful work rested. Capitalist-industrial society was thus bequeathed an ideal value system and a type of human character well suited to its needs.

Weber, of course. recognised that Puritanism had a strong appeal to the emerging capitalist middle-classes and went so far as to speak of the existence of an 'elective affinity' between Puritanism and the capitalism which those classes were bringing forward. Puritanism had little appeal to the aristocracy; in insisting that a person's worth derived from spiritual qualities proved in the quality of their ethical lives it was too democratic for those who wished to retain ascription as a basis for status and honour. Likewise it was too much based on scriptural exegesis to have much appeal to the aliterary masses. In any case it turned with contempt and disdain on both leisure classes: the idle rich and the idle poor; the debauched, spendthrift idle aristocracy and those who imitated them and the no less debauched, but obviously differently circumstanced, idle poor who shirked their duty to labour in God's vineyard. Puritan middle class character, therefore, turned harshly on idleness with ostentation and idleness with poverty; it attacked the former by undermining its monopolies on wealth and power and the latter by replacing traditional Christian charity with a harsh, impersonal code which insisted that relief had to be combined with the imposition of a Godly discipline: work. Clearly, therefore, Puritanism helped to provide the middle classes with legitimacy and reputability; it helped them to claim, and make good, 'their place in the sun'. Their place in society, such positions as they gained in terms of wealth and power, derived, not from birth, but from the sheer quality of their attention to their occupational and business lives - from industry, diligence and thrift and from the contribution which the exercise of those virtues enabled them to make to the service of their communities and societies: growth in business, growth in trade, growth in employment, growth in prosperity and the spread of what they, at least, took to be enlightenment, progress and civilisation. Their vision was, of course, contestable, and contested, but as they grew in power and influence, a power and influence which was legitimated and rendered reputable, by their industrial virtues and the supposedly progressive consequences of the exercise of those virtues, so they were able to establish their canons of reputability as the ruling values, the standards for distinguishing good from bad and right from wrong, of the societies which they came to dominate. The fixation on business and economic progress was thus consolidated in the culture complex of industrial society; the way to fame, esteem, reputability was to contribute to progress through the exercise of the industrial virtues. Even Marx - who might have suspected Weber's account of being overly idealistic in its temper - recognised the fusion of religion and asceticism with the economic interests of the middle class when he mockingly wrote about political economy:

This science of marvelous industry is simultaneously the science of *asceticism,* and its ideal is the *ascetic* but *extortionate* miser and the *ascetic* but *productive* slave .... Thus political economy ... is a true moral science, the most moral of all the sciences. Self-renunciation, the renunciation of life and of all human needs, is its principal thesis. The less you eat, drink and buy books; the less you go to the theatre, the dance hall, the public house; the less you think, love, theorise ... etc; the more you *save* - the *greater* your treasure which neither moths nor rust will devour - your *capital.* The less you *are* the less you express your own life, the more you *have,* i.e. the *greater* is your *alienated* life, the greater is the store of your estranged being ... all the things which you cannot do your money can do. It can eat and drink, go to the dance hall and the theatre; it can travel, it can appropriate art, the treasures of the past, political power - all this it *can* appropriate for you. Yet being all this it *wants* to do nothing but create itself, buy itself; for everything else is, after all, its servant .... All passions and all activity must therefore be submerged in *avarice* (Marx, 1963, pp. 111-12, emphasis in the original).

145

We cite this passage from Marx because it captures superbly the contemptuous incomprehension which the economistic asceticism of the self-denying bourgeois and his or her strange sense of duty to business and acquisition provokes in those who are deaf to the singular tones of its music. What a travesty it all seems to be. What a denial of all that is human and worthwhile is this seemingly mindless devotion to work and acquisition, this pointless self-denial that rests in the rejection of all those good things which make life worth living, this prostration of humanity on the altar of controlled avarice. While Marx admired the technical and productive achievements of industrial capitalism and regarded it as progressive, it is clear that he had nothing but contempt for the mind-set of those who were busily engaged in pushing its frontiers forwards. And he was not alone in this. Legions of conservatives and radicals alike bewailed the industrial capitalist order; it had destroyed community and had submerged all beauty and nobility in a sea of cunning and avarice; it had replaced personal human ties with the abstract connection of the cash nexus and contract and ushered in an age of calculation and cupidity in which human beings were reduced to the status of cogs in the wheels of industry; it developed a limited and debased vision of human character in which all virtues, save those of the industrial and avaricious kind, were excluded. For all that the votaries of the capitalist industrial order proclaimed it triumphs and celebrated its achievements, therefore, there were those who despised it and who rejected its ideals and achievements. As we shall see soon enough, the Irish were to be counted among the legions of its disparagers.

As we remarked above, Weber's thesis generated a good deal of controversy; it is not without its detractors and many have sought to qualify it in crucial respects, including one of the authors of the present work (Keating, 1985). It is no part of our business here to become embroiled in any controversy about the Weber thesis, of which, in any case, we are making only a limited use. In all we invoke Weber here for two reasons: Firstly, because some of what he says is borne out in the Irish experience and thus, as we shall see, helps to illuminate it. Secondly, because his ideal typical representations of traditionalism and the spirit of capitalism are useful heuristic devices; they represent an attempt to capture very different meaningful interpretations of economic life and thus offer suggestions which are helpful in elucidating the terms in which the Irish make their economic lives meaningful.

Meanings, motives and interpretations

In Chapter 1 we said that this book belonged to sociology, especially to that tradition in sociology which payed attention to the meanings and motives of human actors. We want now to develop this interest through the agency of asking the question: what motivates entrepreneurs? Now this is a question that might, in general terms, be answered by reference to the profit motive and economic interests: Entrepreneurs are motivated to service their economic interests through the generation of profits. Answers like this are quite plausible, especially when they are

146

underpinned by assumptions about *homo economicus*, the natural maximiser. Answers of the kind we are reviewing, however, are highly problematic because economic interests are not self-interpreting; human beings have to interpret them, they have to give them meaning and they learn to do this through the medium of the culture into which they were born and raised.

When we say that human beings endow their activities with meaning we are doing no more than suggesting that they have some understanding of the world they share with others and of their own and others' activities. To be sure that understanding may be less than complete, and what is possessed may not always lie at the level of actors' expressed consciousnesses, because actors are familiar enough with their social worlds and activities to be able to take meanings for granted and simply get on with life without too much pondering and reflection. None of this, however, detracts from the truth that if we ask people what they are doing, and why they are doing it, they will normally be able to give some account of themselves; they will be able to tell us something about what they understand by their activities, i.e. what their activities mean to them in terms of the purposes they serve and the part those activities play in the totality of the life situation of the actors concerned. In endowing their own and other people's activities with meaning actors are, of course, engaging in a process of interpretation; they are meaningfully interpreting actions and events using skills and a stock of intersubjectively available knowledge obtained through socialisation into the culture which they share with others in their milieu. Thanks to the skills and the knowledge base which actors possess they are able to make sense of their own and of others' activities; they are able to know, and to judge, what, when, where and how certain activities are appropriate or not appropriate; they are able to know and make judgements about what is important and significant, about accepted and acceptable priorities; they are able to know and make judgements about what is right and wrong, about what constitutes good living in the ethical and other senses of that term. It is only because they are able to know, and make judgements, about these and other matters that human beings can become effective actors in any social context; social life is a skilled performance in which social actors are constantly judging and being judged by others in the group to which they belong. If actors are to maintain face, to be thought well of, to be welcomed, to be praised as successful and worthy, and not to be cast out, devalued or deemed ineffective or unworthy they must understand and internalise the standards of the group, be it a club, an association, a community or a society, to which they belong. Culture is thus vital. It is through socialisation into a culture and its symbolic universe of meanings that the required understanding and internalisation can be achieved.

Thus briefly sketched is the context in which the motivational problem arises. As we defined them earlier motives are complexes of meaning in which the springs of action lie; they are, if it be liked, the grounds for the action concerned. For our purposes here meaningful reflection on the motivational problem has to do with the question: why is an action being performed? and with the complex of meanings associated with people's reflections on this question. Take, for example, the question: 'Why do

147

you work so hard Friend?' Friend could give a number of answers to that question, for example, 'I love my job, I derive great satisfaction from what I do, it's fun, it's fulfilling'. Alternatively Friend could reply: 'I want to prove myself, I want to get on, I have ambition, I want to rise in the world.' These answers, of course, demonstrate an old truth: namely, that action which, to outward appearances is the 'same' can spring from very different internal complexes of meaning. And the answers provided by no means exhaust the range of possibles; Friend, for example, might say, 'I work hard because the boss is a *** who will fire me if I don't, and I have to make a living; believe me if there was any alternative I wouldn't be here.'

What these answers, hopefully reveal, is something of the world of interpretation and meaning which lies behind human action; each of them reveals a meaningful interpretation of what is being done and of the overall context in which the act is taking place. In case one Friend has come to meaningfully understand hard work as a means to the end of fulfillment. In cases two and three Friend has come to see hard work as a means to the ends of achieving promotion (two) and avoiding dismissal (three), in which cases, of course, Friend has meaningfully interpreted not only Friend's own activities but the expected responses of others to them. It is through the interpretation of these means-ends complexes, and of their contexts, that Friend's motives become intelligible as grounds for Friend's actions: Very few people, we imagine, would cry foul if we said that Friend was motivated by the need for self-fulfillment (case one), by ambition (case two) and by the need to make a living (case three).

What Friend can achieve in terms of interpreting Friend's own actions, other actors can also achieve with reference to Friend - indeed in cases two and three Friend clearly hopes that they will interpret Friend's actions in the way Friend intends them to be understood, otherwise Friend may not be lucky in either obtaining promotion or avoiding dismissal. This reminds us that, as we noted above, actors routinely, and effectively, meaningfully interpret each others actions in the normal course of interacting and making their respective ways through their shared social world - how else could they make their way through it? In seeking a meaningful understanding of human action, therefore, sociologists are not doing anything particularly special; they are doing something that actors in the courses of their lives do routinely.

How can such interpretations be achieved? Here we must be careful; this is not a book about sociological methodology, let alone about sociological theory, and we do not want to let matters drift away from our primary purposes any more than is necessary. Our answer to this question will, therefore, be brief and will be directed to doing no more than outlining the procedures that we propose to employ.

Our procedure here derives from the view that a careful analysis of human conduct, and the contexts in which it takes place, can provide adequate insights into the motives of those who are undertaking it. The key lies in treating the conduct as a means and asking: to the achievement of what end is the conduct in question directed? Answering this question involves the construction of heuristic devices called ideal types. Ideal types are not ideal in any ethical sense. Their ideality is logical; they are, in fact, logical simplifications and accentuations of factors, which, as they show themselves in the real world, exist in complex conditions of variegation and admixture with other factors.

We can see what is involved here by using an example, which, in this case, can be the problem with which we are concerned: namely, Irish entrepreneurs and their motives. We have devoted three chapters of this book to describing the activities of Irish entrepreneurs, so we can now ask: to what end or ends could the conduct we have described serve to achieve through its deployment as a means? Could the end, for example, be the economic development of Ireland?

We can answer this question in the negative with some confidence precisely because after positing the economic development of Ireland as an end, we can work out, using our knowledge of Ireland's situation, the patterns of economic conduct which are required to achieve it. Working on the assumption that actors who are committed to achieving development will conduct their economic life along lines that are appropriate to the achievement of the end, we can begin to make progress. In working out the pattern, of course, we are making assumptions which do not hold in the complexity of social reality; we are assuming that all actors are equally and perfectly knowledgeable; that they are equally and perfectly competent; that they are undistracted in the pursuit of the end, and are not beset by conflicting interests lying in other economic or social ends that will tempt them to an attenuated commitment; that they have access to skills, capital, opportunities and so forth. These assumptions, of course, will not hold equally for each and every one of the tens of thousands of individual Irish entrepreneurs and that is why we cannot use our constructed pattern as a description of their conduct, but only as a heuristic device, as a standard against which we can measure and compare it. Nevertheless, the procedure does enable us to provide a clear exposition of the kind of conduct that is, in principle, required to achieve the end of economic development; that is all that is required of it and is quite sufficient for our purposes.

We have already gone a long way towards working out the patterns of conduct that will best serve the cause of economic development in Ireland. Clearly, Irish development requires that entrepreneurs break away from the traditional patterns of low value-added commodity trading and seek actively to expand existing productive capacities, and develop new capacities, with a view to creating new products, adding more value to traditional products and going for growth, growth and more growth, while at the same time avoiding the kind of unscrupulous activities which are damaging to development achievement because they alienate customers, damage other units in the economy and undermine state finances. If on reviewing Irish entrepreneurial conduct in the light of these specifications, we observe large numbers of entrepreneurs behaving in ways that more or less correspond to them, then we have rational grounds for concluding that their conduct is being driven by motives that are appropriate to the achievement of Irish economic development. Notice that we say 'motives' rather than 'motive' here. We do this because, as we noted above, patterns of action which are outwardly the same could spring from a variety of meanings, each of which might provide actors with different

149

grounds for their action. It is perfectly conceivable that development-appropriate entrepreneurial action might be grounded in a complex of meaning that related to patriotism; on interrogation a highly committed entrepreneur might say: 'I am Irish. I wish to contribute to the development of my country through my hard work and committed business activity. I take my profits as a justified reward for the contribution I make, through the wealth and jobs I create'. It is equally possible, of course, to imagine other complexes of meaning that might provide grounds for the appropriate patterns of conduct, meanings lying say, in a sense of obligation towards people, resources and ethical conduct derived from religious beliefs; meanings having to do with personal needs for achievement set within an ethical framework; meanings connected with a business-centered view of life, and many others besides. Ultimately it does not matter, at least for our purposes, what complexes of meaning provide the grounds for action, so long as the action is appropriate, that is, so long as it exhibits high levels of ethically regulated commitment to growth.

The 'trouble' is, of course, that when we use the ideal typical construction of development-appropriate conduct as a standard for comparing and measuring the reality of Irish entrepreneurial doings, we discover, not conformity, but deviations; in short, the use of the type indicates that Irish entrepreneurs are not behaving in ways that are appropriate to development achievement. How then can these deviations be explained? It could be, and this has to be said, that some of the conditionals which were built into the ideal type do not hold in the situations concerned; entrepreneurs may be short of commercial skills; they may lack capital; they may not have access to markets, and so their deviations may be conditioned by factors lying outside of their immediate control. As the evidence we have presented shows, however, the deviations cannot be explained convincingly by reference to the absence of the conditionals mentioned; as the 'stunts' described in earlier chapters show, the Irish are not short of commercials skills, and the country has not been starved of capital and markets to an extent sufficient to account for its present state of underdevelopment. If we want to explain the deviations, therefore, we have to look elsewhere.

We can do this, once again, by asking the question: to the achievement of what ends could the patterns of economic activity exhibited by Irish entrepreneurs doing for themselves serve as suitable means? To what end, for example, are the legions of tax evaders, smugglers and their customers, 'Phoenix syndrome' operators and the like seeking to achieve through their activities? In what complex of meanings can the grounds for their activities possibly lie? We would certainly not be able to take seriously the idea that their activities were grounded in any meanings having to do with patriotism; in our cultures patriotism has to do with serving, and not undermining, the nation. Nor, indeed, would we accept the view that their activities are associated with any meanings having to do with a sense of religious, moral or social obligation; in our cultures stealing is regarded as immoral and antisocial. We would hazard the view that people in leading positions in Irish business, state or church, would not rise up and publicly declare the activities we are considering to be

150

moral and socially acceptable; whatever they might think, or do, in private, they are still too formally committed to values that castigate these activities as immoral and socially unacceptable to be able to defend them without appearing in a poor moral light. Yet this is the point. There is only one plausible explanation for these activities in terms of the meanings in which their springs lie: namely, an amoral and anti-social greed; a selfishly individualistic meaning-frame in which economic activity is interpreted as a means to the end of making money in a manner that is divorced from any culturally conventional sense of moral, social or economic responsibility.

In reaching this point we have not exhausted the range of conduct which we need to explain. We have, therefore, to ask some further questions. To the achievement of what end, for example, could the behaviour of those entrepreneurs who are happy to make a nice little profit on the home market without much growth, who are indifferent to quality and reliability, and who hold others up by spreading a five hour working day over seven or more hours, serve as suitable and effective means? Likewise, what objectives are the farmers who let rushes and bushes grow in their fields and starve their cooperatives of funds needed for development by extracting the highest possible price for that which they, evidently, put little energy into producing, seeking to achieve by their activities? We could certainly not take seriously the idea that the ends were located in complexes of meanings associated with a patriotic interest in promoting economic development; that, as we have seen, requires a break with tradition, and these people are all too evidently happy with the status quo and are thus unwilling to make the break. It is also very difficult to locate these orientations in complexes of meaning which drive these actors to ground their activities in a sense of responsibility towards the resources they command which calls for their effective use in terms of increase and expansion; if any such sense of obligation existed we would not find rushes and bushes growing in fields. What then can we say? There is, surely, only one meaningful interpretation of the conduct of these people that will stand up to examination: It must be the case that the complex of meanings in which the grounds for their conduct lie stem from an interpretation of economic life as simply a means to the end of making a comfortable living; work and business are 'nothing special'; they are just activities which have to be engaged in to make a living; they will attract no more time and effort than is necessary to make them yield what is regarded as enough to enable actors to enjoy a comfortable life, and no doubt, the kudos and community standing that is associated with the ownership of a business or a farm. We are here clearly entering a world of meanings in which comfort, leisure and other non-productive activities are valued above the expansion of production. We are, in fact, entering the world of Max Weber's traditionalists.

The development-inappropriate meaning complexes we have described here are not mutually exclusive. The cattle which the easy-going farmers send to graze among the rushes and bushes are, as we have seen, often shot through with illegal hormones and growth promoters; the same easy-going farmers have also connived with unscrupulous vets to sell on animals infected with TB, turning, in the process, a £1 billion TB

151

eradication scheme into a fiasco, and supplied goods of doubtful or inappropriate quality at the cost of alienating customers, as did their fathers and grandfathers who waxed fat on their sales of 'bad eggs and worse butter' into the British market. The farmers, needless to say, are in the forefront of the profitable 'business' of tax evasion, a preoccupation they share with the hosts of middle Irelanders, the 'respectable' classes of the self-employed professionals, traders and easy-going industrialists:

> 84 companies and individuals have been named as major tax defaulters in 1986. The names include those of a Catholic priest and two gardai, one of them retired, and are contained in the annual report of the Revenue Commissioners .... Biggest outstanding tax defaulter was a Co Clare draper ... who ended up settling his tax arrears bill for a total of £395,168 .... Fr Eamonn Dillane of The Presbytery, Raheen, Co. Limerick eventually paid £30,650, with more than £11,000 of this accruing in interest (*Cork Examiner*, 1988a).

Year after year the Revenue Commissioners' lists of defaulters - and the one's who are caught represent the 'tip of the ice-berg' - contain a representative cross section of middle class Ireland; drapers, chemists, hoteliers, guesthouse proprietors, builders, merchants, farmers, company directors, show business personalities, politicians, police officers, solicitors, barristers, bloodstock breeders, not excluding, as we have seen, the odd priest. The truth, therefore, sems to hold, for Ireland at any rate, that an easy-going, liesure-oriented traditionalistic orientation towards work, production and resources is not incompatible with the presence of amoral, anti-social greed. The combination, the two modes of relaxation adverted to earlier in the chapter, certainly exists. When considered in the light of the country's prospects of achieving development the combination is, of course, a lethal one.

It will now, we hope, be obvious why it is that we are unprepared to take seriously the idea that material interests are self-interpreting for actors in the sense that their pursuit pushes actors to seek to maximise their incomes by reference to the most effective use of the time and resources they have available. We are quite happy to grant, as indeed Weber was, that human conduct is predominently driven by actors' material interests. Actors, however, interpret their material interests by relating them to different complexes of meanings, which direct their orientations towards those interests in ways that can work an impact on the nature and intensity of actors' commitments to them and thus on the nature and strength of their economic motivation. It is precisely because the complexes of meaning to which material interests are related and made meaningful can have a reference to values which originate in non-productive spheres that we need to concern ourselves with more general aspects of the culture in which economic actors work and do their business. To the extent that the cultural values to which economic actors relate their work and business activity can influence motivation, they are relevant in connection with the level of economic development that is achieved, or achievable, in a given society. This is the proposition that we shall now try to demonstrate with reference to Ireland.

The motivational problem: too many traditionalists

Weber's treatment of economic traditionalism is useful here because it helps us to interpret the behaviour of Irish entrepreneurs, and because it points to what Parsons (1960, p. 140) calls 'the core of the motivational problem'. Parsons held, and in this he is surely right, that for economic development to take place:

> 1) people must be motivated to serve the goals of *production* beyond the levels previously treated as normal, desirable or necessary in a society, and 2) they must perform those tasks to a far higher degree than before, in organisations specifically differentiated from nonproductive functional contexts (Parsons, 1960, p. 140, emphasis in the original).

To develop the argument from this point onwards we need to consider an example. Suppose, first, that actors give meaning to their economic interests by interpreting them as means to the end of obtaining a comfortable living, interpreted, in turn, in terms of a strong leisure preference, and, second, that they are satisfied with the standard of life made possible by a given level of engagement with economic life, say that which is considered as 'normal, desirable or necessary in a society', i.e. that which needs to be increased and expanded upon if economic development is to be achieved. Another question now arises: namely, what will induce these actors to increase their engagement with their economic activities? The answer is, of course, nothing; their economic interests are made meaningful through an axial principle in which they are construed as a means to the end of achieving a comfortable living; the actors concerned are happy with the standards of comfort being obtained, and so have no reason to disturb themselves further in the matter of their work and business activity. What we are saying here is that the complex of meanings in which the springs of their actions, i.e. their motives, lie with an objective which is extrinsic to the economic process as such, and so their commitment to the economic process is of a kind which is 'closed-ended' with reference to the external objective which stands at the centre of the meaning frame. Thus, in the example we have just provided, actors' commitments are 'closed-ended' by reference to the objective of comfort; so long as they are happy with the returns to comfort achieved by a given level of commitment to work and business they will see neither need nor sense in disturbing themselves further: to do so would, after all, involve a reduction in the comfort to which they aspire.

The 'closed-ended' commitment we have just described is, of course, the commitment of the traditionalist as Weber characterises that condition. And it must be patently obvious that economic development will not follow from it. The fact that economic development requires that the goal of production be served to a far higher degree than before will mean nothing to actors who meaningfully construe their productive activities as means to the end of securing a level of comfort with which they are content, for being content they will not be moved to a higher level of service. From this it must follow that economic development will be achieved only if actors develop commitment-patterns which are more 'open-ended', in the sense that they are not limited by reference to objectives which are external to the production process.

Arguably a translation from 'closed-ended' to' open-ended' patterns of motivation could come about in two ways: Firstly, it could come about as a result of disturbances in the milieu in which actors were operating - in which case we might say that actors were, more or less, forced into change. Secondly, it could come about voluntaristically; actors could learn to interpret their economic lives in new ways, ways that make enhanced levels of commitment seem right and good. An example of the first kind might be the arrival on the scene of ambitious and competitive individuals whose activities threatened, by competition, the economic interests of the comfort-seekers. If the activities of the arrivals created a situation which the comfort-seekers had to interpret meaningfully in terms like: 'these arrivals are producing a better and cheaper product than mine, so if I do not "buck my ideas up" and become more committed to my productive activity I will be forced out of business', then they would be likely to produce a transformation in the direction of a more 'open-ended' approach on the part of the comfort-seekers, always provided, that is, that they did not want to go out of business, and/or were not in a position to insulate themselves in some way against the pressures being generated by the arrivals. People could, however, conceivably make the translation voluntaristically by learning to relate their business activity to external ends that called them in the direction of 'open-endedness', or indeed by learning to treat business activity as an end in itself as in the development-appropriate patterns considered in the preceding section.

There is, however, one other aspect of the matter which we need to pursue before we can move on. The matter concerned is one that is easily, and very often overlooked, though not by Weber, who, after all, characterised the conduct of modern capitalist entrepreneurs as ascetic. Asceticism has a reference to self-denial, to sacrifice, and, therefore, to a species of idealism. Thinking of entrepreneurship in terms of self-denial and idealism seems strange; modern societies have come to see profits and wealth as desirable, and to take their pursuit as a natural and normal phenomenon which brings rich rewards which are sought self-interestedly by human beings. And so they are. Nevertheless, profit is not the only desirable end which human beings can pursue, and an open-ended commitment to its pursuit in a manner that is appropriate to the achievement of economic development in a country like Ireland can involve costs. To put matters crudely here: work takes up time which could be devoted to leisure; saving for investment requires a reduction in expenditure on consumption for leisure and for life's many pleasures and comforts. Here we arrive at the crux: the servicing of the end of production beyond the levels previously considered as normal and desirable will almost certainly call for a certain amount of self-denial on the parts of entrepreneurs who undertake it; insofar as they will have to work harder and invest more than previously, they will have to forego leisure and some consumption of life's many pleasures; to the extent that they will need to develop a more ethically-regulated approach to economic life, they will have to deny themselves access to easy profit opportunities that are available through unscrupulous, customer-alienating conduct. Given that human beings value leisure and consumption, often as much as, if not more than, work, it seems harsh not to credit those who are willing to forego some pleasures, work hard and behave with honesty and integrity with, at least, a measure of idealism. It also, of course, suggests that unless people are willing to be a little idealistic in these matters they may not be willing to make the efforts which the achievement of development requires.

The enduring appeal of traditionalism is that it rests in the integration of economic activity into a round of life that is facilitative of sociability and leisure as valued human objects; economic activity is not a particularly compelling life interest. And business is not a particularly compelling life interest for many people in contemporary Ireland, especially for the comfortably-off professionals, traders, non-trading industrialists and farmers. Business tends to be an easy-going round; it is small town, small city business, carried on by cosy circles of eligibles, orienting to local circles of customers in a situation in which business relations are impregnated with relations of kinship and long-standing friendship, which, when combined with the localised nature of the activities, do much to secure the community against the over-zealous application of cold, impersonal market criteria. *Homo socialis* keeps *homo economicus* at bay. A Contemporary Irish historian (Lee, 1989, pp. 392-3) goes some way towards capturing this traditionalistic ethos when he writes about the development of twentieth century Ireland and its industry:

> Not industry, but trade and the professions, dominated the non-agricultural sector. They developed protective devices to shield themselves from the impersonal insensitivity of market forces. Like the farmers they triumphantly maintained their claim to be considered more a way of life than an occupation .... Growth might depend to some extent on providing a superior service. Survival generally did not. Clienteles often consisted of a web of 'favours' rather than 'efficiency'. And even the industrial sector did not foster widely different mentalities. Family firms predominated. Some did achieve impressive records. But they were quite compatible with fairly comfortable stagnation. Inheritance within the family may have partly depended on the apparent performance potential of the children. Even here, the ablest son was often guided towards the professions, and the commercial inheritance left to less talented siblings. It was next to impossible for an outsider, irrespective of his ability, to break into the family circle, except through marriage. And marriage prospects were more likely to be determined by the family status of the suitor than by his performance potential. Not until the state-sponsored bodies began to develop did some openings arise for managers who had lacked the foresight to be born into the right families. As an eminent exponent of state enterprise observed 'The family-owned firm was dominant and the crown prince blocked promotion to the top posts'.

155

The same writer goes on the observe that the drive for industrialisation in the nineteen-thirties did not produce a new ethos: Once again continuity, not change, was to be the order of the day:

> Protection guaranteed possession of the market to the new firms within very relaxed performance criteria. The discipline of the market was generally kept at a very discreet distance. 'For more than thirty years our many state and private enterprises have produced managers by accident rather than managers by design' complained *Irish Management* in 1957, adding that it was futile to speak of scientific management 'if such factors as family ties, friendship, religion or national record are allowed to outweigh more significant qualifications' (Lee, 1989, p. 393).

And what did those 'very relaxed performance criteria' amount to? On this topic Lee (1989, p. 679) can quote a leading Irish businessman, Denis Brosnan, whom we also cited in Chapter 2. Brosnan is quite blunt in his estimation: 'Irishness I define as the capacity of the Irish to accept and/or deliver standards which appall many of us .... It is the antithesis of quality'. The fact that Brosnan made these remarks in 1986, together with the mass of evidence presented here, suggests that the modernisation drive from the nineteen-sixties was no more successful in producing a new ethos. Old ways, it seems, die hard, and so they live on; traditionalism is still very much the order of the day.

A tradition of traditionalism

Values, to remember, refer to complexes of ideas which function as standards against which members of a collectivity make judgements concerning what is good or bad, right or wrong, ugly or beautiful or whatever. As such values can arise, and derive force, from any number of sources; they can arise from the outpourings of religious or political 'prophets', moral entrepreneurs of various kinds and as reflections of the material and ideal interests of classes and status groups in any given situation or society, interests which, of course, may be influential in determining whether and to what extent the outpourings of prophets and other moral entrepreneurs find favour, and thus take root, in any given set of circumstances. Our interest here lies in the values to which the Irish came to relate their economic, especially their business, activities at a crucial stage of their historical development.

In Chapter 1 we noted that, under the whip of the eighteenth century anti-Catholic penal code, a powerful and prosperous Roman Catholic middle class emerged in Ireland. This class made its money from industry, trade and commerce, and its members evidently practiced industry and thrift to an extent that aroused the envy of the Protestant business community. As we also saw in Chapter 1, however, both the involvement in industry and commerce, and the ascetic lifestyle, were cultivated because the laws denied this group access to alternative economic pursuits, debarred them from land ownership and denied them access to occasions for lavish expenditure on non-productive activities. Their ascetic devotion to business was thus the result of external pressures and did not spring from any inner commitment either to business as a central life interest or to a thrifty, ascetic regulatory regime.

The truth of this assertion is not difficult to demonstrate. Speaking about the behaviour of wealthy Catholics after the restrictions of the penal code had been removed, Wall (1969, pp. 47-8), to remember, observed:

> Hitherto they had led lives in which ostentation could play little part and their opportunities for lavish expenditure were circumscribed. The desire, so long suppressed, to cut a figure in society, was now given opportunities for satisfaction, and Catholic merchants and manufacturers tended to divert more money than perhaps they should, from their commercial interests, while in many instances their sons entered the professions instead of entering the family business. It was unfortunate, perhaps, that in this way money and talent were withdrawn from commercial enterprise at the time of the union, when Ireland had, for the first time, met the great challenge of free trade.

One of the reasons why the Catholics were allowed to flourish in trade lay in the fact that the Anglican aristocratic establishment often held it in considerable contempt. Samuel Madden, one of the founders of the Dublin Society and a man with a strong interest in economic development, remarked, in 1738, how he wished the Irish would follow the example of those people who held trade in high esteem, and who thus 'never retire from business and buy lands and turn country gentlemen as we do' (quoted in Wall, 1958, p. 97). Arthur Young, who travelled extensively in Ireland, was struck by the same phenomenon some forty years later. Men of business, he notes, 'are quitting trade and manufacture when they have made from five to ten thousand pounds, *to become gentlemen*' (quoted in Wall, 1858, p. 97 emphasis in the original). This is a pity, Young observes, because it means that people are getting out of business at the point in their careers at which they are best able to command success. He, therefore, advises the Irish to stop imitating the follies of England and to imitate her virtues instead, especially 'her respect for commercial industry' (quoted in Wall, 1958, p. 97).

The Irish, with marked exceptions, did not heed Young's advice; in general they seem to have oriented positively to the canons of reputability enshrined in the aristocratic cult; they eschewed trade, as far as possible, in the interests of becoming gentlemen landowners, or failing that, joined the professions and thus engaged in activities deemed less disreputable by the votaries of the aristocratic cult. The wealthy Catholics referred to by Wall had clearly imbibed at the well of this cult. As she herself reports (1958, pp. 109-10) some of them began to put on airs by claiming that their ancestors had once been chieftains or princes of Milesian stock; their land purchases could, therefore, be seen, to some extent, as a return to the way of life of their ancestors, whose property was, of course, confiscated by the English.

The example set by the wealthy Catholics was followed by many of those who came after them in the nineteenth century. Writing about a century after Arthur Young made his observations, Thomas Keating, a Scottish businessman, noted that:

> a man accumulates in Ireland a few thousands, and if he keeps them he does not invest them; in England or Scotland his son would consider that just a good foundation for developing an industry or business .... In Ireland the sons want to be professional men ... the father dies and the business ceases. This is a very common thing in Ireland, because in the higher classes there is a vulgar contempt for work, and with those who aspire to mingle with them, the same contempt for work obtains. The first thing that an Irish man of the upper middle classes does is to get out of any connection with business the moment he can (quoted in Lee, 1969, p. 57).

Lee, to whom we are indebted for the reference to Keating, reckons that this charge is over-stated. Nevertheless, he recognises that many Irish business families regarded business as a halfway house to a better life among the professional or landed classes:

> There are many examples of brewers in the 1830's and 40's bleeding their businesses dry to purchase estates for £40,000, their businesses consequently declining for lack of working capital .... This strongly developed tendency to extract capital from industry helps to explain some of the more puzzling phenomena of nineteenth-century Ireland, such as the very rapid turnover of firms - only four of the thirty-eight coachmaking firms in Dublin survived among the twenty-five coachmakers of 1850 - the exceptionally large numbers of professional people, and the remarkable speed with which the encumbered estates [estates which became insolvent in the famine period] were gobbled up by middle class buyers once they came on the market. In a country allegedly short of capital, abundant capital was available to buy into landed society. Ironically families retired from business in Ireland not because they lacked capital, but because they had acquired capital (Lee, 1969, pp. 56-57).

The gentry who served as role models here were thoroughly traditionalistic in their economic outlook: Not only did they despise work, the made no stint in spending

> lavishly on everything that brought immediate pleasure at the cost of neglecting house and grounds ... There was no stint of servants, horses, cars, dogs, guns, fires, meat, wine and guests, yet English visitors noticed that rain trickled through ceilings, windows rattled and doors hung loose on their hinges (Maxwell, 1940, pp. 28-9)

Hutchinson (1970, p. 515) considers this an 'apt' characterisation of the gentry, and also of the middle classes, who 'aped the gentry'. As a result, he notes, the Irish people lacked 'an example of a bourgeois way of life which, if copied, might have led, as in Britain, to social and economic attitudes of mind appropriate to economic development' (1970, p. 515). It was not so much the case, as Lee (1973, p. 19) reminds us, that Ireland lacked a middle class, but rather the case that, again with exceptions we shall have to note, its middle class did not carry 'attitudes of mind appropriate to economic development'.

Ireland's failure to develop economically in the nineteenth century cannot, therefore, be ascribed to any shortage of capital. There is, however, evidence which suggests that it can be ascribed, in part, to Irish economic actors orienting to values which directed them away from work and business and towards the life of the gentleman, or failing that, the professions. The values in questions were, of course, values in social status, the pursuit of which is a regular and probably near universal human preoccupation. In Ireland, however, the highest status was accorded to those activities - and associated lifestyles - which were least productive of growth and development, so the pursuit of the value in status worked itself out to the detriment of development-achievement. Those who set the social tone in Ireland were not devoted to lives dominated by a business-centred, growth-oriented asceticism. Just the opposite was, in fact, the case. Those whose value in status drove them to emulation, therefore, had no business-centred asceticism available as an example to follow. Indeed the cultivation of any such lifestyle would have required them to endure low status, unless, that is, they were either willing to ignore the status order and/or to challenge and change it. For the most part they were either unwilling or unable to do any of these things.

Clearly a value in the cult of the gentleman presupposes a value in leisure and in the expenditure of time and money on leisure activities. As it happens orientation to value in leisure was widespread in Irish society; historically the Irish were renowned for their 'vivacity, wit, cheerfulness, friendliness and warmth, and for their love of conversation, music and dancing' (Hutchinson, 1970. p. 517. These attributes, as Hutchinson (1970, p. 517) observes:

> could be mainly cultivated only during hours of leisure. They are the products of leisure [just] as the dourness of the lowland Scot and the North-country Englishman is the product of Puritanism and the mystique that grew with the industrial revolution.

Hutchinson is, of course, referring here to the factors considered salient by Max Weber; an ascetic religion which accommodated itself to capitalist materialism and thus put value premia on the suppression of impulse and spontaneity in the interests of establishing a vocational commitment to innovative dynamism in economic life and the support it received from the structural pressures associated with the consolidation of the capitalist way of life. Visitors to Ireland who were devotees of this 'Protestant materialism' were often wont to regard the Irish as indolent and lazy; the peasants, and even the richer farmers appeared to be ill-organised and slovenly; they took little care of their implements and equipment; cultivated no gardens near their cabins, as the English did; and were easily diverted from their work by curiosity about strangers, idle gossip and, not least, by sport and festivities (Connell, 1950, pp. 78,187; Hutchinson, 1970, pp. 510-12; Mansergh, 1965, pp. 24, 356-7). These observers were, no doubt, being ethnocentric in characterising the Irish as they did. Yet we should not fall into the same trap in defending the Irish from 'charges' against which they may not have seen themselves as needing to be defended. As Hutchinson (1970, pp. 517-8) points out: The Puritan industrial 'virtues' were relevant, indeed essential, to industrial societies; they were the expression

> of values to which it was essential that all should adhere if society was to maintain itself and develop along lines that seemed desirable. They were irrelevant to societies, such as the Irish and many others, organised on the basis of quite different assumptions: and the use of such terms as "laziness" or "indolence" in discussing them [is] an unjustified extension to them of concepts developed in circumstances, and according to beliefs, that were entirely different. Such ethnocentricity has not yet disappeared from the arguments of all liberal historians, some of whom believed that the Irish were not "lazy" but worked very hard; or, if they were admittedly lazy, were justifiably so because of the economic and political situation in which they found themselves. The possibility that, for the Irish themselves, such categories had no meaning is not considered.

Hutchinson's point is, surely, well made and points to the key issue: namely, that the Irish, orienting to economic and social conditions and values which differed from those prevailing in industrial societies interpreted their economic lives differently; they did not see themselves as lazy or indolent and would not have understood those terms in the same way as those who observed their conduct, and applied those terms to it, did. Nevertheless, whatever subjective impressions underlie conduct and give it meaning for those who engage in it, the truth is that conduct has objective consequences, which were, in Ireland's case, social and economic decline. This decline was not, however, evenly spread throughout Irish society. If we measure it in terms of population we can see that one group suffered more than another; between 1861 and 1901 the Roman Catholic population of Ireland declined from 4,505,265 to 3,308,661, whereas the Protestant population decreased by only a little, from 1,243,299 in 1861 to 1,159,114 in 1091 (McCarthy, 1902, Appendix).

The question we must now face is the important one: Was religion significant in the evolution of the complex of cultural values to which people related their economic activities, and thus for the course of Irish economic development, especially when considered against the undoubted fact that the values in status shown to be influential so far were entirely secular in origin? Put another way this questions amount to: Can Weber's thinking about the relationship between ascetic Protestantism and economic life throw any light on the issues we are confronting here?

Although Weber said little about Ireland, he did think that the typical relationship between Puritanism and the development of capitalism held in

160

that country (1930b p. 198). On the face of things there is, it has to be said, some evidence to support his contention. The poet Keats, for example, hated Scottish Calvinism; it had deprived the people of their holidays and spread a dismal gloom over the land (1899, p. 310). Yet he recognised that the Scottish ministers had formed their people into 'regular phalanges of savers and gainers', into 'a thrifty army [that could not fail] to enrich their country and give it a greater appearance of comfort than that of their poor rash neighbourhood' (Keats, 1899, p. 310). The poor rash neighbourhood in question was Ireland.

Within that 'poor rash neighbourhood' Puritanism worked an impact as well. The orientation to the value in leisure to which we adverted above seems to have been widespread in Ireland, without distinction with respect to religion. According to an Irish historian, however,

> By the 1830s, it appears, Presbyterian and other Protestant churchmen in parts of Ulster has succeeded in suppressing or modifying the traditional amusements of their congregations, and thus in clearing the way for a new and more rigorous labour discipline. But if so, they had merely succeeded (in more favourable circumstances) in achieving something which their Catholic counterparts, both in Ulster and elsewhere, had also been attempting .... [I]t is also true [however] that their attempts to bring about a restructuring of popular attitudes and behaviour never achieved more than limited results. But this should not obscure the fact that they had shown themselves more than willing to make the attempt. If things had been otherwise - if their efforts had been reinforced by the sort of change that was taking place in contemporary England - then the Catholic church and its clergy might today be seen as having had a role in Ireland similar to that which historians of British development have assigned to Methodism or to the Association for the Suppression of Vice. It was not their fault that other actors were not so ready to play their parts, and that the whole project never got beyond the early stages of rehearsal (Connolly, 1983, pp. 243-4).

We shall leave aside for the moment the adequacy of Connolly's estimation of the nature and purpose of the Irish Roman Catholic project as it touched on moral reform - as we shall see both his estimate of the project's intentions, and the extent of its success, are questionable - and concentrate on his argument concerning what he takes to be its comparative failure. If we understand Connolly correctly, his reasoning is that the project failed because other actors failed to play their parts. From the tenor of his remarks we take it that he is referring to the failure of the Irish middle classes to create an industrial society in which the work disciplines imposed by the exigencies of industrial organisation would have reinforced the clerical preaching. As we know by now the Irish middle classes did nothing of the sort; they preferred to bleed their businesses for the funds to purchase land in pursuit of the gentleman's life. But activity of this kind was activity in pursuit of a secular value, devoid of religions significance, so, readers may ask, how could religion be relevant in explaining it?

Although he is unconvinced about the explanatory power of a Protestant ethic thesis with reference to Ireland, Joseph Lee unwittingly provides evidence that might indicate that such a thesis could help, at least partly, to illuminate the situation we are discussing. In considering the following which the aristocratic cult was attracting, Lee has to note that there were exceptions, 'notable exceptions', among whom he included 'the Quakers' and people in the Belfast area 'where the aristocratic cult never took as deep root as in the south' (Lee, 1969, p. 57).

The pity is that Lee does not, so far as we can discover, make any attempt to explain why the Quakers and many in the Belfast area refused to embrace the aristocratic life and quit business for the land. We say this is a pity because if Lee had looked to Weber he might have discovered an explanation which is as plausible as any other that might be put forward: namely, the contempt in which ascetic Protestantism held the idle, spendthrift aristocratic lifestyle. To the Puritan the gentlemanly ideal of a life of leisure and conspicuous consumption was the quintessence of ungodliness; it was not a pattern that received anything but reprobation in terms of the religious values to which he or she oriented. The truth is, therefore, that religion seems to have been a significant factor in determining orientations towards or away from the aristocratic cult; when Puritans related the possibility of cultivating the habits and 'occupation' of the gentleman to their religious values they found that avenue more or less blocked off, while the votaries of those tendencies in Christianity which lacked a tradition of this-worldly lay asceticism, i.e. Roman Catholicism and, to a lesser extent Anglicanism, had no such barriers to confront.

With respect to Connolly, therefore, the failure of those 'other actors' and thus the claimed failure of the Roman Catholic clerical reform project is a failing that is connected to the tenets of Roman Catholic religiosity. If the Roman Catholic church had promulgated doctrines which led to a work and business centred asceticism, it would have been much less easy for consistent Roman Catholics to identify with the aristocratic contempt for work and to become members of a class better known for its leisure and conspicuous consumption that for its devotion to thrift and toil. The fact is, as we shall see, that Irish Roman Catholicism lacked any notion of consecrating work and business to the service of any ideal, let alone a religious one, and so left its followers open to the attractions of the aristocratic cult in the interests of which, as we have seen, they quit business and so failed to play the part which Connolly thinks would have been helpful to the clerical reform project.

It is also arguable that Connolly both over-estimates the sweep of clerical reformist ambitions and under-estimates the success achieved by the clerically inspired and directed reform programme. As Inglis (1987) has shown the Church played a fundamentally important part in the Irish 'civilising process', and so helped to transform, in the course of the nineteenth century, a somewhat uncouth, 'ill-mannered' and often Rabelaisian people into a polite, civil, well-mannered and largely domesticated nation. The Church achieved this though reforming and controlling traditional festivities like wakes and patterns, through the imposition of a devotional revolution and the spread of Church discipline, adherence to which was secured through the spread of confraternities and other lay bodies, priestly discipline achieved through the agencies of the confessional, and, not least, the Irish mother who became, in effect, as the person responsible for the moral education and supervision of the family, the 'Church in the Irish home'. Thanks to this reform programme an ascetic frost did descend on Ireland, and, to the extent that it did, the reform programme was successful. It was, however, a sexual asceticism directed towards the control of sexual passions that was fashioned and maintained through the inculcation of feelings of shame and guilt about sex. Otherwise, as we shall see, the idea of duty enjoined by the rules and regulations of the Church took a rather formal and ritualistic turn, and was certainly not directed towards instilling a religiously inspired sense of duty that was connected to worldly work and to the use and deployment of economic resources. This, however, we shall see in the concluding chapter.

Conclusion

In this chapter we have tried to do a number of things: Firstly, we have attempted to define some key terms, not least the terms cultural identity and values, those standards by reference to which people enter their judgements concerning what it is they hold to be good or bad, ugly or beautiful and so forth. Secondly we have tried to expose the ethos of economic traditionalism and to exhibit something of the revulsion which the spirit of capitalism or industrialism inspired in many people who saw it as a force making for alienation and dehumanisation. Thirdly, we tried to show that the Irish entrepreneurial ethos was traditionalistic, before beginning the task of exploring the evolution of the complex of values to which the Irish related their economic activities. That, of course, was the fourth and final task undertaken in the chapter, and was designed to show how a value in status-seeking defined in terms of the cult of aristocracy, drew people away from business and towards occupations and lifestyles which were not fully appropriate to the achievement of economic growth and development. These values were, of course, secular. Nevertheless, we saw that religion was implicated in that the religious values of Puritan varieties of Protestantism made it difficult for those who oriented towards them consistently to embrace the life of leisure and consumption enshrined in the aristocratic cult; it was from the ranks of Puritans that the entrepreneurs in the Belfast region were drawn, and these, as we have seen, tended to stay with their businesses rather than to desert them as their counterparts in the South often did. We also saw evidence which suggested that Protestantism modified the behaviour of its adherents in reducing their leisure preferences in the interests of promoting a more disciplined approach towards economic life; as Black (1960, p. 157) puts it 'the people of the north did devote more time and energy to their work and less to fairs and race-meetings, patterns and wakes than did the people of the south'. The feeling that religion was implicated in the differential economic performances of the Protestant and Roman Catholic peoples is by no means confined to twentieth century historians like Black;

163

thoughtful Irish people, including Roman Catholics, were giving expression to this view at the turn of the nineteenth and twentieth centuries. Once of these was a Roman Catholic theologian called Mannix. At the dedication of a new church building in 1902 he spoke his mind in the following terms:

> Explain it as we may, it is the fact that Catholics often have much to learn from their non-Catholic neighbours in industry, in thrift, and energy and enterprise. There is something amiss when profitable, and honest, and honourable employments and departments of industry are left almost wholly in the hands of non-Catholics. There is something wrong with the education, and habits, and traditions of Irish Catholics when they can be beaten in their own ground, when they can be forced to emigrate, while non-Catholics can remain, and prosper, in the midst of Catholic communities (Quoted in McCarthy, 1902, p.16).

Clearly we had better start finding out if, then to what extent, and why, this came to be the case.

7 The Irish culture complex: Roman Catholicism and nationalism

Introduction

In Chapter 6 we began the task of exploring the relationship between economic action and cultural values in Ireland. We tried to show that the economic orientations of modern Irish entrepreneurs were coloured by traditionalistic meanings and traced something of the historical background in terms of the Irish tradition of traditionalism. With special reference to the nineteenth century we reported a body of evidence which suggested that, with exceptions, the Irish related their economic lives to secular values in status and leisure which directed them away from according a high priority to work and business activity. There also we reported evidence which suggested that religion was implicated in structuring the attitudes and preferences expressed in the behaviour of economic actors; Roman Catholics who oriented towards the aristocratic and peasant cults and their emphases on leisure met no resistance from the religious values to which they oriented their status aspirations. If nothing else this suggests that the religious values to which Irish Roman Catholics related their economic activities were influential in determining the nature and intensity of their engagement with those activities, and did so, moreover, in a way that was facilitative of the perpetuation of a traditionalistic ethos. It is true that the evidence presented so far suggests that religious values worked their impact only in a negative or permissive sense, i.e. orientation to them neither enjoined nor compelled traditionalism, just permitted it in the sense that they did nothing to disturb the consciences of those whose economic lives were directed in a manner that was traditionalistic. The testimony presented so far, however, by no means exhausts the supply of evidence that is available. As we shall show below the Church was more than simply a permissive influence because its views of economic life were openly traditionalistic in character. As such their influence went beyond being merely permissive of traditionalism; they actively fostered it as an ethos to be retained as desirable.

What we want to do in this chapter is to demonstrate the truth of this proposition by developing and deepening our exploration of the part which Roman Catholicism played in the formation of the modern Irish culture complex. As the supreme and, until very recently, unchallenged moral entrepreneur in Irish society the Church's role has been decisive. Nevertheless, it was not by any means the only decisive force with which we have to reckon if we are to achieve an understanding of the cultural base on which the preservation of Irish traditionalism rests. Irish nationalism also played a part; it also had its moral entrepreneurs whose formulated world view worked an impact on the nature and character of the emerging Irish identity. Its impact was not, to be sure, an independent one, as Catholicism and nationalism became fused together to provide a single, overarching and coherent body of ideafacts which provided the Irish with a distinct cultural identity and with a body of values for the ordering of their religious and secular lives. It is to an examination of the salient features of this identity and value complex, together with the bases of its power to move and determine conduct, that we now turn.

The Irish culture complex: Roman Catholicism

Raymond Crotty (1986, p. 49) tells us that the Roman Catholic Church was one of the four great success stories to emerge from nineteenth century Ireland - the other three, and they will not concern us here, were the banks, Guinness's Brewery in Dublin, and Harland and Wolf's shipyard in Belfast, Crotty is undoubtedly right about the success of the Roman Catholic Church; the nineteenth century saw a resurgence of Irish Catholicism that is easily measured in terms of the mobilisation of energy and capital devoted to the activities of the institutional church and to the consolidation of its power and influence over the mass of the Irish people.

The nineteenth century resurgence of Irish Catholicism must be seen against the background of the code of anti-Catholic penal laws which we described briefly in Chapter 1. While these laws were not always consistently and effectively enforced, they, nevertheless, put severe obstacles in the way of the effective functioning of the institutional church and deprived Roman Catholics of most of the civil rights exercised by members of the Protestant community. A Protestant establishment that was capable of passing such laws as these was clearly not an establishment that was wont to regard Catholics as its equals in any sense whatever; the Catholics were a vanquished race; they were held to be inferior to the Protestants in all points of civilisation touching the political, economic, moral, religious and civic senses of that term and the laws were designed to confirm that inferiority and to so demoralise the Catholic population as to render it incapable of any political, economic, religious, moral and civic self-assertion that might have threatened the domination of the Protestant establishment. As we also saw in Chapter 1, however, the laws, even when consistently enforced, were not successful; they did not 'persuade' Irish Roman Catholics to abjure their faith in order to become 'civilised' Protestants; they could not preclude Roman Catholics from engaging successfully in economic activity to the point at which a wealthy Catholic 'merchantocracy' could emerge; they did not so demoralise the lower orders of the Catholic population as to prevent them from seeking to redress their grievances through the unwelcome agencies of sedition, violence and rebellion against the established order. As a result of the failure of the penal laws, therefore, two very different groups became interested in consolidating the power and influence of the Irish Roman Catholic Church: Firstly, the political authorities representing the establishment needed to secure peace and public order and increasingly sought to deploy the Church as a means to that end. Secondly, the rising Catholic merchants and farmers needed to assert themselves and to demonstrate that they were as civil and as moral as the Protestants.

It was the Roman Catholic Church's consistent condemnation of violence and rebellion that persuaded, first, the government in London, and later the more enlightened members of the Irish Protestant establishment, that a changed attitude to Roman Catholicism was required. As the Irish historian Lecky (1916, p. 168) puts it:

> the higher Catholic clergy, if left in peace, were able and willing to render inestimable service to the Government in suppressing sedition and crime, and as it was quite evident that the bulk of the Irish Catholics would not become Protestants, they could not, in the mere interests of order, be left wholly without religious ministrations.

Thanks to the spread of such 'enlightened' government appreciation of the Church's potential utility, governments, both before and after the Union, came to look with increasing favour on the extension and consolidation of the Church's power and influence over the Irish. While nothing in the nature of a formal Church-State alliance emerged, the State, nevertheless, cleared away all the obstacles which the penal code had put in the way of Church functioning and allowed the Church to secure a dominating position in Irish society; the first of a series of Catholic Relief Acts was passed in 1762 and inaugurated a process that was to culminate in complete emancipation in 1829; state subsidies for the education of the priesthood were granted in 1795, though the possibility of wider subsidisation was rejected by Rome, by many of the clergy, and, not least, by the rising Irish middle classes who had no desire to see their Church become the subsidised agent of a state that might not always be supportive of the material and power interests of those middle classes. As a result the Church became an independent power bloc in Irish society, pursuing its own interests in developing and perfecting its institutional structures and consolidating its hold over the minds of the Irish people. In so far as it refused to countenance disorder and rebellion its activities were undoubtedly helpful to governments. Nevertheless, it was quite capable of confronting governments in its own interests, and in the interests of its lay supporters.

The extent of the Church's progress through the nineteenth century is not difficult to chart. In the matter of building, for example, it was most impressive. Thus, between 1800 and 1863 the building programme completed 1,805 churches at a total cost of £3,061,087; 217 convents costing in all £1,058,415; 40 colleges and seminaries involving a total expenditure of £308,018; and 44 hospitals, asylums and orphanages, the construction of which cost £147,135. Impressive though these figures are - the total expenditure comes to £4,575,995 - they rather understate the full extent of ecclesiastical development; they cover only twenty-five of the twenty-eight dioceses into which the country was divided and they take no cognizance of the church's school building programme. Between 1800 and 1863 the Church is estimated to have constructed some 2,290 national schools, and to have done so without any government aid whatsoever, in addition to the schools constructed by the Christian Brothers and by various orders of nuns, which have been estimated at sixty-eight and over 200 respectively (O'Reilly, 1865, p. 25).

If the figures just quoted tell us something about the scale of Church activity in terms of building and construction, they also tell us something else: namely, they are informative about the widening scope of Church influence over Irish life. The Church was active in education, not only building its own schools, but effectively denominationalising, under clerical management and control, the national schools provided by the state, to the point at which it had, by the late nineteenth century, an effective monopoly over the primary and secondary education of the Roman Catholic laity - a position which it largely retains to this day. It also moved into health and social services provision - as the reference to hospitals, asylums and orphanages shows - thus ensuring that 'the health and care of the Irish people was to become a thoroughly demoninational practice' (Inglis, 1987, p. 127). In addition the Roman Catholic clergy also took leadership positions in a wide range of organisations and activities; they were, as we shall see, often active in positions of political leadership; they played leading roles in cultural movements; they participated in the county committees of agriculture and in the agricultural cooperatives - in the first decade of the twentieth century about half of the cooperatives established in Ireland had a cleric as its chairman (Kennedy, 1978, p. 54).

The rash of building activity just described must be seen against the background of the impact of the penal laws, thanks to which Roman Catholics were forced to worship in less than satisfactory conditions - often in the open air or in back street chapels. Nevertheless, the building programme demonstrated high levels of commitment on the parts of both clergy and laity to establishing the Roman Catholic Church and endowing it with a prestige that was equal, if not superior to, the prestige attaching to the churches of the Protestant establishment. Church buildings were thus large, ostentatious and costly; monuments to the respectability of the wealthier Catholic merchants, traders and farmers who subscribed eagerly to their construction (Inglis, 1987, p. 120). If the Catholic laity were willing to contribute to the endowment of churches and convents, they were, it seems, no less willing to subscribe to the business of providing their clergy with a comfortable standard of living; the resurgent Catholics wanted their priest to enjoy 'a social position and residence that would compare favourably with that of his Protestant counterpart' (Murphy, 1965, p. 104). And, by all accounts, he (the priest) often did, cultivating, among other things, a taste for fine wine - an evidently astonished foreign observer noted in the eighteen-eighties: 'they each have their favourite claret: one likes Leoville, another Chateaux Margaux' (Connell, 1968, p. 154). By the closing years of the nineteenth century, therefore, the priests were well established and dominant figures in Irish society:

In new parochial houses and dressed now invariably in a recognizable clerical uniform they could exercise their functions not only within a world rendered less spiritually ambiguous than before but from citadels which spiritually and metaphorically proclaimed their distinctiveness and power. And in their mission of moral purification and influence they were also, as time went on, increasingly assisted by rising cohorts of regulars (members of religious orders) and above all of nuns - from about 120 in 1800 and 1500 in 1850 the number of nuns in Ireland rose to no less than 8,000 as the century came to a close. Whereas before the famine financial exigencies had limited the recruitment of priests, thereafter Ireland was able to export large numbers of surplus clergy to minister to emigrant communities in Britain and North America and later to those yet lesser breeds without the law in tropical and eastern lands. Here, indeed, was a Hibernian spiritual empire to surpass Britain's money-grubbing imperialism (Hoppen, 1898, p. 145).

Thus described is the church triumphant; the supreme moral entrepreneur; the undisputed guardian of the faith, morals and minds of its flock, over the members of which is exercised an unceasing and ever-vigilant supervision of care and control. Even so its triumph was achieved within the political limits of a United Kingdom with an overwhelming Protestant, and increasingly secular, Great Britain, the source of many malign influences from which the Irish had to be protected. The establishment of the Irish Free State in 1921 put a clear political boundary between Roman Catholic Ireland and the outside world and all but eliminated the awkward squad of Protestants and secularists; the population of the new state was over ninety per cent Roman Catholic; its administrations were staffed almost exclusively by Roman Catholics who were more than willing to confirm the church as the supreme moral entrepreneur and to defer to it when legislating on matters which touched upon its moral teachings. All this ensured that the church was able to play a leading role in the evolution of the Free State - later the Republic of Ireland - and to maintain itself as a dominating influence in Irish life well into the period about which we are writing.

The impressive progress of the Roman Catholic religious establishment has to be seen against the background of economic stagnation and decay that was the lot of Roman Catholic Ireland. Population figures tell the story of this decay well enough; between 1861 and 1901 the Roman Catholic population of Ireland declined from 4,505,265 to 3,308,661, whereas the Protestant population decreased by only a little, from 1,243, 299 in 1861 to 1,159,114 in 1901 (McCarthy, 1902, Appendix). It was this situation that provoked the thoughtful reflections of the likes of Dr Mannix, whom we quoted in the conclusion to Chapter 7. Mannix, to remember, was a Roman Catholic theologian who felt that his lay co-religionists had 'much to learn from their non-Catholic neighbours in industry, in thrift, and energy and enterprise', and who arrived at the conclusion that there was 'something amiss when profitable, and honest, and honourable employments and departments of industry are left almost wholly in the hands of non-Catholics'. In all his reflections forced him to conclude that something must be wrong

> with the education, and habits, and traditions of Irish Catholics when they can be beaten in their own ground, when they can be forced to emigrate, while non-Catholics can remain, and prosper, in the midst of Catholic communities (Quoted in McCarthy, 1902, p.16).

From this frank admission we learn that when it comes to the matter of economic activity the Protestants in Ireland are more industrious, thrifty, energetic and enterprising than their Roman Catholic neighbours, a condition of affairs which, together with the stagnation, hopelessness and decay which had settled on Roman Catholic Ireland as a result, the good doctor was happy to attribute to 'centuries of misgovernment and enslavement' (McCarthy, 1902, p. 16). Mannix is no doubt referring here to the economic, social, civic and political inferiority which was imputed to, and imposed upon, Roman Catholics by the penal laws to which we have adverted previously, and he is doing it, no doubt, with some justification. Nevertheless, his explanation has to be read against a certain background which tends to deprive it of much of its force. In the first place, he overlooks the fact that the penal laws did not prevent the rise of a significant and prosperous Catholic middle class in fact, if anything, they 'stimulated' its rise. Secondly, the disadvantages that had been imposed on Roman Catholics in the legal code had, by 1902, long been removed; the legal restrictions on Catholic economic, civic and political activities had been swept away when Catholic emancipation was achieved in 1829.. Thirdly, the Roman Catholic community was not short of capital - as McCarthy (1902, p. 17) pointed out, '£60,000 can be readily subscribed for a new church anywhere in Ireland'. Fourthly, as the Danish experience outlined in chapter 5 demonstrates, Irish Roman Catholics were not exactly short of economic opportunities. Finally, by 1902 the Roman Catholic Church had become the moral entrepreneurial power in the land; the education of Roman Catholics was in its hands, and the habits and traditions of the community were developing under firm sacerdotal influence. McCarthy's claim that Ireland was not short of capital was, as we have seen, well justified, generally and in the particular context of the laity's willingness to subscribe to the construction and maintenance of the 'sacerdotal infrastructure'. And this is quite a significant point. The point is not, and this needs to be made clear, that capital was abstracted for use in church building that might have been used in industry; Ireland was not so short of capital for this to be the issue, and, indeed, the construction and maintenance of the 'sacerdotal infrastructure' arguably provided employment that would probably not otherwise have been provided. No, the crux of the matter lies elsewhere: namely, in the fact that contributing to the construction and maintenance of the 'sacerdotal infrastructure' came to constitute a duty for lay Catholics, the performance of which became another canon of reputability. So far, therefore, we have been able to identify two canons of reputability in emerging Irish 'modernity': namely, 'aping the gentry' and contributing to the Church. Building a business does not figure.

Needless to say, the decline of the Irish economy and society provoked some debate and contention, not least with reference to the question of whether and to what extent the rise of the Roman Catholic Church might have been responsible for it. Critics emerged and argued strongly that the Church was damaging Irish society. More importantly the Church found a champion who 'gave as good as he got'. On the whole the controversy is instructive, and will repay the attention which we are about to give it. As we shall see the defences erected by the Church's champion are, in many ways, far more enlightening than the broadsides of its critics.

The Church on trial: a 'debate' about Catholicism and economic progress

The controversy we are about to review can be traced to 1902 and to the publication of a book called *Priests and People in Ireland*. Written by a Roman Catholic barrister called Michael McCarthy, the book contains a strong critique of the Roman Catholic sacerdotal establishment, at the door of which the author lays the blame for all Ireland's ills. McCarthy's point of departure is the economic and social decline of Roman Catholic Ireland, or, rather lay Roman Catholic Ireland, for, as he sees it, the decline of the laity stands in sharp contrast to the expansion of the sacerdotal forces of the Roman Catholic Church. McCarthy is undoubtedly justified in calling attention to the contrasting fortunes of the two groups; while the Roman Catholic population of Ireland declined from 4,505,265 to 3,308,661 between 1861 and 1901, the numbers of priests, monks and nuns serving in the country actually increased from 5,595 to 14,145 over the same period (McCarthy, 1902, Appendix). This proved altogether too much for the anticlerical McCarthy to endure. And so, practicing Roman Catholic though he was, he tried to demonstrate that the increasing domination of the priest and his allies was the chief cause of the laity's decay and lack of progress.

McCarthy saw the Roman Catholic clerical establishment as a vast, solidary network of material and power interests; to his view the priest had long outstepped the rightful bounds of his position and duties on the altar and in the pulpit, and, together with his helpmate the nun, had insinuated himself into education, the hospitals, the workhouses, the industrial schools, the technical instruction committees and into other walks of life, controlling and dominating areas of activity which were properly fields belonging to the laity. As McCarthy saw it this sacerdotal domination had two broad consequences for Ireland and her people: The first was material; the clerical establishment flourished at some financial and opportunity costs to the laity. The second was moral; sacerdotal domination was having a debilitating effect on the character of the Irish people.

In 1901 there were, as we have seen, 14,145 members of the Roman Catholic clerical establishment, giving, when the numbers of lay Roman Catholics is taken into account, a clerical-lay ratio of 1 to 233. The Protestants, by comparison had a clerical-lay ratio of 1 to 422, making their religion the more 'economical' to maintain (McCarthy, 1902, Appendix). The maintenance of this numerous sacerdotal establishment was a burden to the laity in two senses: Firstly, its expenses had to be defrayed out of lay pockets. Secondly, and perhaps more importantly, celibate orders of monks and nuns were appropriating large numbers of teaching, nursing and other jobs that would otherwise have been available to lay Roman Catholics who, if they but had these opportunities, would have been able to work and raise families in Ireland. In appropriating these economic opportunities for its celibate religious communities, therefore, the sacerdotal establishment was contributing directly to the economic, social and demographic decline of Ireland.

It was with the moral implications of sacerdotal domination, however, that McCarthy was most concerned. As he saw it the sacerdotal establishment was using its power and influence - not least its control over education - to mould and shape the character of lay Roman Catholics in ways that were thoroughly debilitating. What the Roman Catholic clerical establishment wanted, and was creating, was a body of meek and subservient lay Roman Catholics who could be relied upon to support the material and power interests of that establishment. Roman Catholicism, therefore, was not training its laity in ways that encouraged them towards independence of thought, action and initiative. Fearing no doubt that a strong, independently-minded laity might develop their own opinions and material and power interests in ways that might not be congruent with the opinions and material and power interests of the sacerdotalists, the ecclesiastical establishment used its influence to establish the strongest possible degree of identification between clerical and lay interests, an identification in which the latter were definitely subordinate to the former. The result was a warping of the lay mind and a weakening of lay character; the laity had no freedom of thought; they were a controlled and subordinate body whose members, thanks to sacerdotal domination, were becoming increasingly incapable of independent, self-helpful action. Being thus enervated they were incapable of meeting the challenges posed in their economic and social lives and of developing their economy and society. As a result lay Roman Catholic Ireland was stagnating while the sacerdotal establishment was flourishing.

To McCarthy's view the enervation process was accentuated by the nature and character of the religion purveyed by the priests; it was a formal, quasi-magical affair that did little to edify or elevate the people for whom it was provided. Something of what he takes to be the empty

172

formalism of Catholicism can be gleaned from his description of the priest at Mass:

The physical labour of saying a mass is, as we know, a mere formal recitation by rote of Latin prayers, the Latin responses to which are uttered by altar-boys who do not understand a word of Latin. But, what is more deplorable still, the congregations who attend those masses not only do not know what the priest is saying, but they do not understand the object or foundations of a single one of his many motions, genuflections, and Latin prayers. The priest is supposed to be in mysterious conversation with God; and if, as may be the case, he is saying the mass for several people's intentions, each of whom has paid him a fee, then his communing with God has special reference to his clients, but of this the congregation knows nothing ... If the priests preached sermons at these masses there would be something to be said in their behalf .... But the method of saying mass in Dublin is deliberately intended to kill-out the sermon. At five-sixths of the masses celebrated in the city on Sunday there are no sermons preached .... Then whenever it happens that a sermon is preached in a Dublin church, I am not going beyond the mark when I say that in nine out of ten cases it is an insult to the intelligence of any rational person to be asked to sit it out. The result of such sermons is palpable, for the most popular masses in Dublin - the masses at which the priests receive the most door money, and at which the chapels are crowded to overflowing, are those masses at which no sermon is ever preached. It can be truly said that the Sabbath sermon, as a means of edification and instruction, is well-nigh dead in Catholic Dublin. Archbishop Walsh himself sets the example of never preaching a sermon; and, of course, the illustrious precedent is not lost upon the priests of the city, who take advantage of it to relieve themselves of the worry of delivering sermons. And it is not much loss to the laity, for the sermons of the priests, instead of teaching children and adults not to tell lies, to be conscientious, industrious and sober, are mostly, if not altogether, reflections upon our fellow citizens [critical attacks on Protestants] or laudations of our Holy Mother the Church, and our Holy Father the Pope. One never hears a sermon in praise of duty. Indeed, the priests have perverted the meaning of that noble and important word; for when they mention "duty" it means going to confession and communion during Lent. The phrase, "did you do your duty?" means, Have you gone to confession and communion? formal acts which no man ought to consider as equivalent to the fulfilment of his duty (McCarthy, 1902, pp. 317-9).

If one leaves aside the moralising in the last sentence of the passage, McCarthy has a serious point to make: namely, that in confining duty to a limited range of formal religious observances, Roman Catholicism was treating lay social and economic activity as 'a thing indifferent', and was not making that activity a field in which lay people could prove their religious worth, and obtain the benefits of salvation, through virtuous

173

economic and social conduct independently of the sacerdotal establishment. If duty is confined to formal religious observances, the clergy has no need to exercise itself in making efforts to promote consistent ethical conduct in the economic and social realms. Indeed the laity do not need to concern themselves about ethical consistency in these, or in any other realms, because their duty consists in formal observances as required by the laws of the Church. The Roman Catholic mind is, therefore, turned away from the possibility of consecrating business, occupational and other this-worldly activity as Godly service; that mind is not brought to see any special virtue in these activities, or to see them as occasions for the exercise of any religiously relevant virtue. Roman Catholic character is thus weakened through slavish subservience to the priestly order, the religion of which occasions further enervation by making the Catholic indifferent towards the things of the world, towards its challenges, opportunities and possibilities. What Ireland needs to survive and thrive in the modern world are men and women of character, discipline and integrity. What is sacerdotalism giving them? Consider, for example, the crozier beads in which Irish Catholics were showing some interest in the early years of the present century:

The advantage of having these "crozier beads" seems to be that you can get the indulgences attached to saying the rosary without saying the rosary at all. They are, therefore, but one additional incentive to Irish Catholics to shirk duty and to scamp work; and these new-fangled beads will do their share in worm-eating our integrity and corrupting our national character (McCarthy, 1902, p. 202).

The point is very clear: a religion like this can provide its people with no incentive to become disciplined, ethically consistent people of integrity or to reform character which is weak and undisciplined in the direction of a disciplined consistency of conduct; if believers can gain the advantages which result from the exercise of disciplined effort - i.e. saying the rosary - without actually making the disciplined effort involved in saying that cycle of prayers, why should they bother disturbing themselves? Catholicism makes it possible for them to avoid disturbing themselves, and thus facilitates an easy-going, inconsistent, undisciplined and ethically lax approach to the business of living.

In making these points McCarthy is, of course, taking up a position regarding the relationship between Roman Catholicism and economic activity which is very close to the position that Weber was to take in his *The Protestant Ethic and the Spirit of Capitalism*, which was published two years after the first appearance of *Priests and People in Ireland*. Like Weber he is saying the following: Firstly, that Roman Catholicism does not make business and occupational activity fields in which lay believers can prove their religious worth through disciplined, ethically consistent conduct. Secondly, that Roman Catholicism facilitates undisciplined, ethically inconsistent conduct by providing believers with mechanisms through which they can obtain spiritual benefits while remaining ethically inconsistent. In a world which requires people to address their economic concerns with high levels of commitment, ethical discipline and the courage to take risks the Irish are bound to lose out; their religion has diverted them away from an active interest in the world; it has facilitated ethical laxity and indiscipline; and, in making them subservient to a sacerdotal order it has weakened their capacities for independent thought and action, their courage and their hope.

Needless to say *Priests and People* provoked a storm of protest; Catholic Ireland was neither amused nor flattered and reacted with a violence that precluded reasoned assessment. McCarthy was too easily dismissed as a bigot, a 'turncoat', that most execrable of beings a disloyal Catholic who did not need to be answered, just cast into exterior darkness. Nevertheless, similar ideas found more temperate expression in the writings of Horace Plunkett, a liberal Protestant Unionist who was passionately committed to the economic and social development of Ireland, and who devoted considerable time and energy to the development of agricultural cooperation and technical instruction. Like McCarthy, Plunkett was impressed by the industrial and economic achievements of the Protestants of North-east Ulster:

> In city life their thrift, industry and enterprise, unsurpassed in the United Kingdom, have built up a world-wide commerce. In rural life they have drawn the largest yield from relatively infertile soil. Such, in brief, is the achievement of Ulster Protestantism in the realm of industry. It is a story of which, when a united Ireland becomes more than a dream, all Irishmen will be proud (Plunkett, 1904, p. 98).

Plunkett's chief concern, however, lay with the impact of Roman Catholicism:

> Roman Catholicism strikes an outsider as being in some of its tendencies non-economic, if not actually anti-economic. These tendencies have, of course, much fuller play when they act on a people whose education has (through no fault of their own) been retarded or stunted. The fact is not in dispute, but the difficulty arises when we come to apportion the blame between ignorance on the part of the people and a somewhat one-sided religious zeal on the part of large numbers of their clergy. I do not seek to do so with precision here. I am simply adverting to what has appeared to me, in the course of my experience of Ireland, to be a defect in the industrial character of Roman Catholics which, however caused, seems to me to have been intensified by their religion. The reliance of that religion on authority, its repression of individuality, and its complete shifting of what I may call the moral centre of gravity to a future existence - not to mention other characteristics - appears to me calculated, unless supplemented by other influences, to check the growth of the qualities of initiative and self-reliance, especially amongst a people whose lack of education fits them for resisting the influence of what may present itself to such minds as a kind of fatalism with resignation as its paramount virtue (Plunkett, 1904, pp. 101-2).

From these passages it is clear that Plunkett shares McCarthy's view that sacerdotal domination is not conducive to the production of an 'industrial character'; that domination produces a mentality which is subservient to an authority which is too little interested in industrial and economic matters to stimulate the laity into being actively concerned with economic and social progress. As a result the Roman Catholic Irish exhibit 'a striking absence of self-reliance and moral courage'; they display 'a listlessness and apathy in regard to economic improvement which amounts to a form of fatalism' (Plunkett, 1904, p. 110).

Not surprisingly, perhaps, Plunkett's opinions gave offence to the Roman Catholic community in Ireland. What is more important, however, is the fact that they provoked a serious and thoughtful reply from a Roman Catholic clergyman (O'Riordan, 1906). O'Riordan's reply is interesting because it represents the voice of Catholic 'civilisation'; it articulates a world view which points up the limitations of 'industrialism', the 'civilisation' of which is represented as inhumane and inadequate. Accordingly O'Riordan sets out to provide Plunkett with what amounts to a lesson in civilisation.

From where O'Riordan stands the idea of character and the view of progress adopted by Plunkett are 'low and narrow'; you cannot ascribe character to people only on the basis of economic achievement; you cannot, likewise, reduce human progress to a state in which it is measured exclusively in economistic terms (1906, p. 123). If we define character in terms of consistent striving after a set purpose, O'Riordan contends, then we find human beings displaying character in all walks of life; the saints of the Church who dedicated themselves single-mindedly to the achievement of their salvation were persons of character; so were the legions of Irish men and women who endured persecution rather than abjure their faith. How then can character be imputed to a people on the basis of their economic achievements alone? It cannot:

> To identify with one thing a quality which many things have in common is a pitfall into which hobby-jockies invariably and unthinkingly tumble. Sir Horace is possessed of the industrial spirit, and he easily takes for granted that there is no such thing as character unless that spends itself in industry .... But a philosopher would open his eyes and look without prejudice before and around him over the whole field of human activity where every human energy is exercised and every human activity pursued. As a Catholic I must look at life in that way, and if I narrow my reason exclusively within a spiritual sphere, in so far do I turn off at a tangent from the Catholic ideal. The spirit of Catholicism is opposed ... to the spirit of industrialism. Industrialism and experimentalism are like a magpie's nest; everything on which their votaries can lay their minds or hands goes into it. Those who are led on by that spirit want to gather into their own narrow corner of interest every human activity, as if men were made to live either in a laboratory or a factory, or at least should have their highest interest there. Those who are possessed by the industrial spirit, and who call themselves "men of science" are ever boasting of their

breadth of view, whilst they are amongst the most narrow-minded of mankind. The consumptive talks of health, because he has it not, and the men of fallen fortune talk of wealth, for they feel the need of make-believe. So with many that affect enlightenment beyond their kind. They are the magpies and the bullies of the day; but a bully is soon beaten, and his rule is never long; and once he is beaten he soon shows himself for what he is. The naturalistic economist or the "man of science" is satisfied to think of men as only evolved animals - will quickly concede everyone to be an ass except himself - provided he reigns as silver-king, or as philosopher among the apes (O'Riordan, 1906, pp. 126-7).

We quote this passage at length because it shows that the Catholic ideal holds the industrial spirit in considerable contempt; the naturalistic economists and men of science who uphold it are mere 'hobby-jockies'; they are a narrow-minded crowd who go on the principle that men were made for nothing more than the factory or the laboratory. Human beings were, of course, made for better things; they have a supernatural as well as a host of natural purposes, spiritual, moral and material, each of which 'must have its proper place, working into one another in the machinery of human life' (O'Riordan, 1906. p 127). In making economic interests dominant, therefore, the naturalistic economists are degrading humankind; they are denying the salience of the spiritual realm; they are 'placing men and kangaroos on the same specific level'. They do not like to be reminded of this; they are 'frightened by the ghost which their own philosophy raises' and try to put it out of sight. Logic, however, will not let them:

> They like the reality, but they dislike the name; just as certain persons *will* be "fast" men and women, but they affect offence and show resentment when taken for such. The philosophy of naturalism is perfected before the looking-glass; it penetrates one's personality no deeper than one's achievements in the dining room (O'Riordan, 1906, pp. 123-4).

If the naturalists vision of human character is limited and degrading, so is their idea of progress. Granted that the people of North-east Ulster have made progress in terms of developing their industries. So what!

> they have the "civic virtues and efficiencies" and we are asked to take that as the test of civilisation, since it is the religious ideal of naturalism. Of literary life, there is a painful absence in wealthy Balfast; it has not produced even a respectable newspaper or magazine. Of art, they seem to have little conception. The practical life they live unfits them for the ideal. I suppose it is the sign of the "economic sense"; for Sir Horace Plunkett thinks we should put away the thought of art in our churches and wait for "the native artistic sense and the industrial spirit now beginning to seek creative expression". But if Belfast means to wait for its art till a Giotti or a Fra Angelico has arisen, it will have to wait a long time.

No national art has ever grown in that way. The artistic genius is created, or rather discovered in the process of growth. If the people of Perugia were like the people of Belfast, Perugia would probably have gone to his grave unhonoured and unknown. And the "industrial spirit seeking creative expression" has simply no meaning in aesthetics. The highest point in the way of art which the industrial spirit could reach is the photograph; but that is not art unless we impart elasticity to the word (O'Riordan, 1906, pp. 245-6).

Thus speaks the voice of Roman Catholic civilisation, and it speaks from a standpoint which regards those who have become infested with the spirit of industrialism as narrow-minded individuals who put people and kangaroos on a plane of equality, and as money-grubbing philistines whose highest point in art is evidently the photograph - if that can be called art. On this view clearly industrial civilisation is a very low kind of civilisation, the achievements of which no sensible people will try to emulate. By all means let us have material progress, there is nothing wrong with that. But, let us keep it in perspective. Above all let us not elevate it to the point where its achievement becomes a significant standard, if not the most significant standard, against which we measure our own or other people's worth. Human beings were not made for the factory or the laboratory; they were made for God; to save their souls; to enjoy beauty; to exercise creativity in all that life has to offer:

Money is only a means to an end. A wise man makes money for the sake of his own personal comfort; he is a fool who inverts the order of nature by sacrificing his comforts for the sake of making money (O'Riordan, 1906, p. 215).

In writing in these terms, of course, O'Riordan is reflecting the traditionalistic attitudes to economic life described so well by Max Weber; anyone who seeks to make money beyond the needs of personal comfort is evidently a fool who violates the natural order of things. It is easy to see that this reflects a 'low view' of economic activity; evidently the only natural purpose in money making is to serve one's personal comfort; anyone who sacrifices personal comfort for the sake of making money is engaging in an 'extreme of foolishness'. It does not seem to occur to the Reverend Author that people might be willing to sacrifice their personal comforts in order to make money for a variety of reasons; they may do so because they put a premium on making a business grow; because they want to create employment, spread prosperity; because they want to see their cities, towns and countries grow, prosper and advance, and because they want to contribute to that advance. There is evidently no room for self-denial or idealism in economic life which might be directed towards the attainment of some supraindividual, civic, national or communal end; there is certainly no room for the consecration to economic activity in the service of an ideal related to a religious purpose or purposes; the sole objective of money making is the achievement of personal comfort, and anyone who sacrifices that comfort in the interests of money making is a fool. On this view clearly, economic action is not regarded as a sphere of endeavour in which individuals can prove their civic or moral worth through levels of devotion or commitment which are higher than those which are necessary to procure their comforts; all that such devotion could possibly prove is that they are fools.

While the Roman Catholic priestly ideal of civilisation, as expounded by O'Riordan, is, therefore, a broad and lofty one, its vision of economic life is a low and narrow one. Perhaps this low and narrow view follows from its vision of the bourgeois as a naturalist Philistine, incapable of anything in the nature of high-minded idealism. Of course this latter view may be a caricature - indeed it most probably is. Nevertheless, caricatures can act as powerful negative models against which the commandment 'Thou shalt not emulate' can be formulated and powerfully embedded in people's consciousness. It was, after all - and this is the point - the O'Riordans of this world who had charge of the education of the Irish people; it was the priests and their helpmates in the schools who formed their consciousness of themselves; who established the value frame through which they made their judgements as to what was to count as good and bad, right and wrong, ugly and beautiful, and through which they prioritised the action-options available to them. In so far as it touched the middle classes education in this wise no doubt produced rounded 'ladies and gentlemen'; no doubt they appreciated art and beauty and were informed by a high sense of religious idealism. It is hard to see, however, how such education could do anything to imbue those whom it touched with any sense idealism that could produce a feeling of responsibility towards economic resources or a high level of commitment to economic activity; the only natural reason for making money is one's personal comfort, anyone who is so committed to business as to sacrifice personal comfort is unnatural and a fool. A limited, and somewhat inwardly-selfish and individualistic commitment is, therefore, the order of the day, one that leaves time for God and for enjoyment, for art, for travel. It is, after all, O'Riordan (1906, p. 246) who tells us that:

> Sir Horace's aesthetic philosophy reminds me of a paper I heard read [on the subject of art] a few years ago by one of his disciples; he impressed me on that occasion as one who had studied art in guide books, but never saw the master-pieces to which he alluded, and I have since learned that he had never been outside Ireland.

What is enshrined in the sentiments expressed in the Catholic ideal is traditionalism pure and simple. If one excludes the obvious religious reference, the parallels between the views of O'Riordan and the views of Marx which we quoted in the preceding chapter (see above, p. 146) are quite striking; it is clear that both men see bourgeois society and its preoccupation with economic activity as narrow and limiting; it does not embody a way of life that is truly human; its view of character is a travesty; it is the seed bed for a life-denying Philistinism which sacrifices all that is good, comfortable, beautiful, enjoyable, all that makes life worth living, in fact, on the altar of controlled avarice. It is a fools' paradise inhabited by deluded, degraded and disfigured monstrosities, whose delusions are the more reprehensible because they have somehow convinced themselves that they have scaled to the high point of civilisation when, in reality, they have plumbed the depths of its opposite.

From the allusion to the arts and foreign travel we may gather that O'Riordan was writing in the 'Romantic mode' and that he was addressing himself to better-off, middle class Roman Catholics. We should not, however, jump to the conclusion that the Church was lacking in solicitude towards its less well off members. It was, of course, well aware that many of its people 'enjoyed' standards of living that were too low to permit of foreign travel, or even a life of decent comfort when measured by middle class standards, or even by the standards of life enjoyed by increasing numbers of the working classes in England and Scotland. Would it not, therefore, be better for Ireland to become like England and Scotland? Would not the application of the industrial spirit move Ireland in these desirable directions and raise the standards of her people? Clearly McCarthy and Plunkett thought so. But did the Roman Catholic Church? Father Tom Burke, an Irish Dominican preacher speaking in 1872, provides an answer:

> But you may ask me: "Wouldn't it be better for Ireland to be as Scotland is - a prosperous and contented province - rather than a distressed and discontented nationality?" Which of these two would you have the old land to be, my Irish fellow countrymen? To which of these two would you prefer to belong? to Ireland as a prosperous and contented province, forgetful of her glorious national history, deprived of her religion, no light upon her altars, no God in the sanctuary, no sacramental hand to be lifted over the sinner's head - Ireland banishing the name of Mary - Ireland canny and cunning, fruitful and rich, but having forsaken her God - Ireland blaspheming Patrick's name, Patrick's religion - turning away from her graves and saying: "There is no hope any more - no hope, no prayer" but rich, canny, cunning and common-place ... Ireland a province! No; rather be a child of a nation, rather be the son of a nation, even though upon my mother's brows I see a crown of thorns and on her hands the time-worn chains of slavery. Yet upon that Mother's face I see the light of faith, of purity, and of God; and far dearer to me is my mother Ireland, a nation in her sorrow today, than if I beheld her rich, and commonplace and vulgar, and impure, and forgetful of herself and of God (quoted in O'Farrell, 1975, pp. 150-1).

From this it is obvious that Irish Catholicism's rejection of bourgeois society and its industrial spirit springs from more than a Romanticist aversion; the industrial spirit is English and Protestant, so nationalism and sectarianism are implicated as well. Industrialism may bring prosperity, but that is a snare; the poor have their consolations, and prosperity on the British model would involve altogether too much loss to be contemplated with equanimity; there would be neither God nor faith; there would be a turning away from hope and a sinking into vulgarity, impurity and the commonplace. Little wonder, therefore, that the priest-novelist, Canon Sheehan, put the following words into the mouth of one of his characters:

Father Martin. The good priest was replying to an Irishman who had spent some time in England and who had become so deluded as to think that England had a progressive, civilising mission. Father Martin does not agree:

> 'I never think of England but as in that dream of Piranesi - vast Gothic halls, machinery, pulleys, and all moving the mighty rolling mechanism that is crushing all the beauty and picturesqueness of the world ... England's mission is to destroy and corrupt everything she touches -' 'What you call congenital prejudice', said Father Martin gravely, 'I call faith. It is our faith that makes us hate and revolt from English methods. To the mind of every true Irishman England is simply a Frankenstein monster, that for over seven hundred years has been coveting our immortal soul. He has had his way everywhere but in Ireland; therefore he hates us' (Quoted in O'Farrell, 1975, p. 54).

If we think for a moment about the implications of the sentiments we have been examining, one point, surely, becomes obvious: namely, that the sentiments are expressive of a sense of cultural identity. As revealed thus far the identity has two elements: a negative element and a positive element. The former rests in a vision of industrial society as represented by England (more properly Britain) which is clearly abhorrent to the Irish Roman Catholic mind; it may represent prosperity, to be sure, but it represents godlessness, cupidity, cunning, the common-place, the immersion of all life and beauty in a sea of industrialism and materialistic, money-grubbing philistinism. That is what Ireland is not, must not, and will not be. Better the crown of thorns and the chains of bondage, if the faith and Irishness can be preserved thereby. *Pace* the naturalistic economists character can also be built and sustained through endurance; their view that character, as such, turns to industrial pursuits because it belongs to economic life is false and follows from the mistaken view that character 'is essentially meant to act rather than to suffer' (O'Riordan, 1906, p. 128). As to the positive element, O'Farrell (1975, p. 55) can quote the priestly author of a social science textbook published in Ireland in 1932 in point of the contrast it draws between the Irish and English peasants in the nineteenth century. The former was then 'probably the oppressed and impoverished human type in Europe', in contrast to the English who were, free, prosperous and the citizens of a great imperial nation:

> Yet in all the best things in life, domestic happiness, contentment, consciousness of his human dignity, moral and intellectual culture ... the Irish peasant enjoyed immeasurably the greater share of temporal happiness ... his advantage in that respect over his English neighbour was due almost entirely to his Catholic faith.

The Irish, therefore, to their view, had something worth protecting. And the bishops and priests who flocked to support the Irish language movement and constitutionalist nationalism from the closing years of the nineteenth century were very conscious of the need to protect it. 'If the Irish language were to become extinct', one of the bishops remarked,

> English modes of thought and English forms of expression, English fashions and tastes in politics, industrial life, and possibly after a time in religion would come into vogue (quoted in McCarthy, 1902, p. 154).

The inclusion of 'industrial life' in this list of sorrows seems to us to speak for itself.

Enter nationalism

The political and military struggles of Irish nationalism which we described briefly in Chapter 1 are not, of cardinal importance in the present connection. Our concern lies rather with the cultural identity which Irish nationalists sought to create and uphold in the face of what they took to be the growing Anglicisation of Irish society. Anglicisation here was measured by what was taken to be the diffusion of English culture into Ireland. As a result the Irish people were losing their language, their Gaelic civilisation and their distinctive national character. Political independence would not provide a remedy for this condition on its own; without a cultural revival, Ireland, whether politically independent or not, would remain a cultural province of England, without a true identity of its own. As one ardent nationalist put it:

> Unless we are a nation, we are nothing, and the growth of a civilisation springing from the roots of one of the oldest in Europe will alone make us a nation, give us scope to grow naturally, give us something to inspire what is best in us, cultivate our national pride and self-respect, and encourage our self-dependence (Moran, 1905, p. 114).

The same writer did not scruple to speak to the idea of 'the battle of two civilisations'. And neither did the poet W.B. Yeats:

> If you examine to the root a contest between two peoples, two nations, you will always find that it is really a war between two civilisations, two ideals of life (quoted in Lyons, 1979, p. 49).

The battle of the civilisations had to be fought, and won, because English culture was not only destroying Ireland's Gaelic civilisation but weakening the character and morality of her people as well. A Roman Catholic archbishop was in no doubt about this:

> if we continue ... effacing our national features as though we were ashamed of them, and putting on, with England's stuffs and broadcloths her masher habits, and other such effeminate follies as she may recommend, we had better at once, and publicly, abjure our

nationality (quoted in Lyons, 1979, p. 40).

The archbishop who expressed himself thus was Dr. Croke of Cashel, the first patron of the Gaelic Athletic Association. Founded in 1884 to promote the Irish games of hurling and Gaelic football, the association was an important landmark in the development of the revival movement; its promotional activities were successful in securing wide support for the games it organised and in helping to imbue the younger generation with a nationalist spirit. In its work of promoting things Irish the Association was ably assisted by organisations of later foundation, including the Gaelic League, the Celtic Literary Society and the Daughters of Erin. Concerned, as they were, for the artistic tastes of the Irish, the Daughters are an interesting case; they were determined, among other things,

> to discourage the reading and circulation of low English literature, the singing of English songs, the attending of vulgar English entertainments at the theatre and music-hall, and to combat in every way English influence, which is doing so much injury to the artistic taste and refinement of the Irish people (quoted in Foster, 1988, p. 450).

Evidently the battle of the civilisations had to be waged along the widest of fronts; masher habits, low literature and vulgar entertainments were quite incompatible with the Celtic ideal.

We have already seen something of the nature of the Irish ideal as exposed through the thoughts of Catholic apologists, and we shall soon have cause to see more it. It would, however, be a mistake to suggest that Roman Catholics monopolised the work involved in the attempt to foster the Gaelic identity. On the contrary, many of the scholars and antiquarians whose research contributed so much to the Gaelic revival were members of the Anglo-Irish, Protestant, landowning ascendancy. Uneasy at the rise of Irish nationalism, and at British governments' tendencies to make concessions to it, some members of this 'class' realised that the best way to retain their positions and properties was to forge stronger links with the generality of the Irish. One of their number, Sir Samuel Ferguson, put it in these terms:

> The Protestants of Ireland are wealthy and intelligent beyond most classes of their numbers in the world; but their wealth has hitherto been insecure, because their intelligence has not embraced a thorough knowledge of the genius and disposition of their Catholic fellow-citizens. The genius of a people at large is not to be learned by the notes of Sunday tourists. The history of centuries must be gathered, published and digested (quoted in Lyons, 1979, p. 30).

Ferguson contributed his mite to the revivalist enterprise; he translated some of the old, and all but forgotten, bardic poetry which recounted the sagas of Ireland's heroic pre-Christian period, especially the Red Branch or Ulster cycle, whose mythical fighting hero *Cuchulain* - no 'masher' he - was to become an inspiration to militant nationalists. Other members of the Protestant ascendancy who made notable contributions were Standish O'Grady and Douglas Hyde; O'Grady's *History of Ireland: The Heroic Period* did much to inspire the interest of others, including that of the poet W.B. Yeats and Lady Gregory - two further Anglo-Irish contributors; Hyde was a founder of the Gaelic League and as determined an exponent of de-Anglicisation as could be found. Unlike Hyde, who later became the first president of Ireland, neither Ferguson nor O'Grady were nationalists in the political sense; Ferguson was a staunch Tory, and O'Grady sought to uphold the aristocratic order in the face of democracy which he feared and detested. Nevertheless, their work, and the efforts of others like them, provided a foundation on which people of a very different temper could build.

Yeats stood at the centre of a coterie of Anglo-Irish writers who gave Ireland both a literature and a theatre of world renown. Although this literature and theatre was preoccupied with Irish themes taken from the far West of the country - the last stronghold of the Gael - it was written in English by authors, who, however sympathetic they may have been towards nationalism in broad terms, were cosmopolitan in outlook and unwilling to generate an art which subserved nationalism of a narrowly sectarian kind. Finding much that was inspirational, and thus worthy of preservation, in the culture, customs and lifeways of the Gael, they sought to build bridges between the two civilisations rather than to become protagonists in the battle between them. Cultural nationalists, however, could have no truck with bridges; they were working for an Irish civilisation that was to be quite distinct from that of England; their enterprise required both a language and a literature that was Irish.

Yeats and his coterie, however, contributed something that was essential to the formation of the Irish identity; they helped to develop and foster the myth of rural civilisation, a myth which, as Goldring (1982, p. 89) observes, came to dominate, not only in the literary renaissance, but in political and religious life as well. To Yeats's view the peasants were the custodians of all human culture; folk-art was the oldest of the aristocracies of thought, refusing all that urban culture was so evidently willing to embrace, namely, the clever, the vulgar and the insincere (Yeats, 1970a, p. 139). It was, therefore, only in the countryside that true art could flourish; it was there that the only true, living language could be discovered, the language of the peasant and the aristocrat, bonded indissolubly in the struggles against the corrupting influences of commercialism and materialism, preserving imagination and heroism, telling stories such as Homer might have told (Yeats, 1970b, p. 61: Robinson, 1951, pp. 32-3; Goldring, 1982, pp. 56-7). There is no room for the bourgeois and the town in this image; it is aristocratic and contemptuous of the vulgar culture of the modern industrial world. The cult of the aristocrat and the cult of the peasant were thus fused.

Yeats's aristocratic contempt for the modern urban industrial world - and he was a representative of the class which the Irish middle classes 'aped' - is, of course, a typically romantic reaction to modernity. Nevertheless, Protestant Anglo-Irish aristocrat that he was, his vision was shared, as we have seen, by Roman Catholic priests and prelates who were equally emphatic in their aversion to the corrupting materialism of modern industrial and commercial society. In so far as they were drawn into the revival movement, urban working class intellectuals came to share this repulsion. Thus the writer Sean O'Casey saw Ireland and England in radically discrepant terms: In his view Ireland was equated with language, literature, theatre, earth, tree and with happy people, while England was characterised by reference to textiles, glass, blast-furnaces, commercialism, industry, Mammon, old age pensions, social security, meals for needy people, and, we may presume, the presence of a great deal of human misery. It is for these reasons, no doubt, that he exults in the following terms:

> Ireland never was, never will be ... furnace-burned ....
> Commercialism is far from her shores ... she, in her language,
> national dramatic revival, has turned her back upon Mammon
> (quoted in Goldring, 1982, p. 55).

Emphatically though they may have rejected the English language products of the Anglo-Irish literati, the Gaelic revivalists shared in their myth of rural civilisation; they also made the peasant their cultural hero, if only because the peasant was the last bastion of an ideal of civilisation which they sought to uphold and restore. It was among the peasantry, more especially in the West, that the Irish language and way of life persisted uncontaminated by the clawing menace of Anglicisation and its cupidity, cunning, masher ways and low entertainments. There lay the true Ireland, Irish Ireland, the Ireland that needed to be cherished and restored. The restorationist vision is well expressed by the Irish revolutionary leader Michael Collins when writing about his experience in the West of Ireland:

> impoverished as the people are ... the outward aspect is a pageant.
> One may see processions of young women riding down on Island
> ponies to collect sand from the seashore or gathering turf, dressed in
> their shawls and in their brilliantly coloured skirts made of material
> spun, woven and dyed by themselves .... Their cottages also are
> little changed. They reman simple and picturesque. It is only in
> such places that one gets a glimpse of what Ireland may become
> again (quoted in Goldring, 1982, p. 59).

That Collins spoke for the generality of the Celtic revivalists is not to be doubted. To their views the peasants represented not only Celtic civilisation, but maintained, as O'Brien (1970, p. 21) puts it:

> the kind of dignity and the kind of health that the industrialised
> world, the modern world had lost; the Ireland [the revivalists] loved
> had an enormous West coast and no North-east corner.

Whatever else may have separated them, therefore, poets, priests, writers, revolutionaries and constitutional nationalists of every shade could unite:

> to celebrate a version of Irish pastoral, where rural life was a

185

condition of virtue inasmuch as it remained an expression of an ancient Irish civilisation uncontaminated by commercialism and progress. In doing so they helped to confirm Irish society in the belief that rural life constituted an essential element in an unchanging Irish identity (Brown, 1985, p. 84.).

Seeing the revivalist programme as a means to protecting its flock from the impact of English habits in religion, the Roman Catholic Church had little difficulty in adjusting itself to the demands of the times. And the revivalists were happy to reciprocate by moving towards the incorporation of Catholicism as an essential element in the true Irish identity. Eoin MacNeil, one of the founders of the Gaelic League, was in no doubt about the connection between religion and revival: 'When we learn to speak Irish', he observed, 'we soon find that it is what we may call essential Irish to acknowledge God, His presence, and His help, even in our most trivial conversations' (quoted in Lyons, 1982, p. 80). The Protestant Douglas Hyde concurred, though as Lyons (1982, p. 81) observes, he must have been disturbed to find that what he took to be an essential link between Gaelicism and Christianity was interpreted by others as a union between Gaelicism and Roman Catholicism. As a result revivalism took a sectarian and even a racist turn; a strong element within the Gaelic League came to see patriotism as Gaelic and spiritually Catholic (Foster, 1988, p. 453).
If the fusion between Irish Catholicism and Irish nationalism was not inevitable, it is certainly understandable. An Irish historian, Terence Brown (1985, pp 28-29) tells us why:

Crucial to the institutional and popular achievements of the Church in the period following the Famine until very recent times was the role played by Catholicism in confirming a sense of national identity. The Church ... offered to most Irishmen and women in the period a way to be Irish which set them apart from the rest of the inhabitants of the British Isles, meeting the needs thereby of a nascent Irish nationalism at a time when the Irish language and the Gaelic culture of the past were enduring a protracted decline. And the Catholic faith was particularly suited to play a role in that nationalist awakening. Bound up in the past with the traditional Gaelic way of life to which the famine had largely put paid, historically associated with the repression of the eighteenth century when the native priesthood had heroically resisted the proscription of their faith, permeated with that profound sense of the supernatural which had characterised the countryside for centuries, Catholicism was richly endowed with attributes appropriate to its modern role in the nation's life. Accordingly ... Irish Catholicism increasingly became a badge of national identity at a time when the Church felt able to propound doctrines that enshrined the rights of private property. In a nation where nationalist aspiration was so often rooted in the farmer's attachment to his land, all this was to help ensure the Church's continued role in Irish life....

In this passage Brown describes well the nexus of material and ideal interests which produced and supported the fusion between Roman Catholicism and nationalism. In doing so he reminds us that Roman Catholicism was not imposed on an unwilling people; the Irish took it to their hearts because it provided them with a centre of identity and a focus for loyalty which reflected their deepest aspirations. It did so, however, as Brown reminds us, in circumstances in which a sense of the material interests of the people was not entirely absent from either their own, or from the Church's consideration. If the people supported the Church, the Church was willing to reciprocate; it endorsed the expression of their economic and political interest, in proprietorship and national independence. Mention of proprietorship, of course, reminds us that Catholic-nationalist revivalism was qualified in a crucial sense; there was to be no revival of any Celtic communalism; bourgeois property rights were accepted without question; indeed they were loudly and trenchantly asserted by cleric and laic alike. Catholic-nationalist Ireland was thus made safe for persons of property.

Conclusion

We have used this chapter to try to exhibit the salient characteristics of the Catholic-nationalist culture complex. On examination the complex reveals itself as a Catholic-nationalist Arcadianism, upholding an ancient, spiritual, rural civilisation against the forces of modernity, secularism and Mammon. In presenting our account of the Arcadian complex we adverted to a controversy about the impact of Irish Roman Catholicism on the economic and social development of the country. If nothing else this controversy demonstrates that we are not the first people to reflect on the economic role of Roman Catholicism, though the debate is interesting for other reasons: namely, for the nature of the criticism that was directed at the Church and for a very able and clearly expressed reply on its behalf. Some of the criticism, as we saw, echoed points which Max Weber was to make in connection with Catholicism's impact on economic life, not least its 'failure' to provide a basis on which lay peoples' economic activity could be consecrated to a religious purpose, and its magical ministrations which, to remember, were said to facilitate ethical inconsistency. What was especially interesting, however, was the defence entered on behalf of the Church. This defence constituted an all out attack on industrialism and the industrial spirit. Enshrined in it was a vision of economic life which seemed to confirm the views of McCarthy and Weber; economic life was interpreted as a means to the end of securing comfort; this was seen to be the natural order of things and only a fool would violate nature by engaging in economic activity to an extent that required the sacrifice of comfort. From this it seems to follow that economic activity cannot be consecrated as a means to the end of any kind of idealism, religious or otherwise; it can certainly not be seen as a duty and thus as a field in which individuals can prove their moral worth through the ethical quality of their conduct. The defence has thus, to some extent, conceded the critics' case, though it has wrapped the concession up in a swingeing attack on what it takes to be the critics' diminished and dehumanised views of human character and civilisation. It is that concession and the view of civilisation associated with it that we must now examine in connection with Irish entrepreneurial and economic development. As we shall see, neither the concession nor its associated civilisational perspective, have been at all helpful in the development context.

8   Entrepreneurship and the Irish culture complex

Introduction

In introducing this book we set out to say what our problem was and what we intended to do about it. That problem, of course, arose from a research interest in the activities of Irish entrepreneurs and in the strongly related issue of the failure of the Irish to achieve economic and social development via the free market, free enterprise route. We began our address to the problem by invoking a comparison between Ireland's economic record and the records of twenty-two other European countries, a comparison which, to remember, showed the Irish performance in a very poor light. Thereafter we tried to provide a brief sketch of the historical background to our problem before moving, in Chapters 2,3 and 4, to the provision of an account of the activities in which Irish entrepreneurs engaged in the process of 'doing for themselves'. The material presented in these chapters pointed to the core of the problem which was shown to lie in the disposition of Irish entrepreneurs to accord a low priority to work and business, activity in which was, when evaluated against moral and prudential regulative criteria, also shown to be weakly regulated in these moral and prudential senses. This combination of low prioritisation and weak regulation was seen to accord closely with Max Weber's definition of his concept of economic traditionalism, so much so that we borrowed the concept to use as a summary characterisation of the orientations and activities of the Irish entrepreneurial community. Traditionalism, of course, also carries connotations connected with a reluctance to break with long established patterns, and this also we showed to be the case with reference to the Irish entrepreneurial scene. For all the hopes expressed in the nineteen-sixties no real change in entrepreneurial orientations could be demonstrated to have taken place; continuity with the past, rather than change, remained very much the order of the day. It was the seemingly unyielding preference for the old ways that militated against the possibility of Irish entrepreneurs making an effective contribution to Ireland's economic and social development. In the first place, their complacent satisfaction with the status quo meant that they were unwilling to drive the production threshold beyond traditionally prevailing levels. Secondly, their unscrupulous activities provided added hindrances to development-achievement by alienating customers, damaging other productive units in the economy, detracting from their country's commercial reputation, and weakening the State by depriving it of much need tax revenue.

All that we did in the first four chapters of the book was done against the background of an expressed conviction that the situation which we were describing could neither be understood nor explained without some reference to the cultural values to which Irish entrepreneurs related their economic activity. From Chapter 5 onwards we began the process of trying to redeem that claim. We did this, firstly, by trying to show that the behaviour of Irish entrepreneurs, and thus their country's existing state of underdevelopment, could not be explained fully by reference to objective factors lying in the absence of means and opportunities. As we saw the evidence suggests that Irish entrepreneurs were not unduly constrained by such objective factors; they were not trapped in their traditionalism by a lack of means and opportunities which could have been exploited and deployed to the achievement of a higher level of development, if the entrepreneurial will to do so existed. The fact that the problem could not be divided by objective factors without leaving a remainder points ineluctably to the salience of subjective factors, that is to entrepreneurial motives, those complexes of meaning in which the springs of human action are to be found; Irish entrepreneurs had choices open to them; they did not have to write the script that was written; their hands were not so tied as to preclude them from writing a different script, the final act of which would have been a celebration of a higher level of social and economic development for Ireland. To write a different script, of course, Irish entrepreneurs would have had to be motivated to do so. The problem lies in the evident fact that they were not, and still are not, in the context of development-achievement, appropriately motivated beings.

In Chapter 6 we tried to show how the motivational problem was linked to the cultural meanings through which entrepreneurs learned to understand and interpret their economic activity. Using interpretative procedures we tried to grasp the subjective complexes of meanings in which the springs of Irish entrepreneurial action, i.e. the motives that gave rise to it, were to be found. Analysis here suggested that Irish entrepreneurs meaningfully interpreted their economic activities as means to the end of achieving a comfortable living for themselves and their families, and did so, moreover, in a manner which suggested that they saw economic activity as a field that could be ploughed without too much need for moral scruples. The root of the problem was seen to lie in this pattern of interpretation; in the subjective understanding of Irish entrepreneurs, economic activity was given no meaningful relationship to any supraindividual purpose or ideal lying in national, religious, moral, business or other criteria which might have indicated the necessity or desirability of enhanced levels of commitment and responsibility towards the opportunities and resources available. Economic activity was thus seen to be the outcome of a 'closed-ended' pattern of motivation; one that indicated that work and business should be engaged with only, and not beyond, the levels that were needed to secure the standards of comfort to which tradition had accustomed the business classes, and which did so, moreover, in circumstances which, given the absence of a relation to a moral dimension, provided few obstacles to actors spontaneously self-indulging in outbursts of amoral and anti-social greed. Low prioritisation and weak regulation were thus placed in the context of meaning; they were shown to be the product of people who had somehow come to render their economic activities subjectively meaningful to themselves in a particular kind of way.

Ultimately the question we must face is: Why is it that Irish entrepreneurs have come to self-understand their economic activities in ways that indicate that patterns of activity exhibiting low prioritisation and weak regulation are appropriate to their needs and situations? In Chapter 6 we began to examine this question by providing a sketch of the Irish tradition of traditionalism, which, to remember, we traced to the cult of the gentleman and peasant spontaneity. In Chapter 6 also we noted that actors could be driven to break with traditionalism by pressures originating in two very different regions. The first of these had to do with disturbances in the traditionalists' milieu; the incursion of more dynamic and committed individuals might, we noted, provoke the traditionalists to 'shake up their ideas' through pressure of their competition, unless, that is, the traditionalists could find ways to protect themselves from intruders and the consequences of intrusion. The second was connected with a learning curve of a different kind: namely, with the possibility that the traditionalists might come to relate their activities to values which provided axial recipes which indicated a need for increased commitment. This, as we shall see, is a crucial point.

We say this because, as we saw in Chapter 6, Irish traditionalists were able to insulate themselves from pressures of the first kind; their cosy, small town, small city world was one in which impersonal market forces could be, and were, kept at bay. The milieu in which Irish traditionalists operated was not disturbed sufficiently to provoke a break with traditionalism; so long as entrepreneurs were satisfied with conditions of a comfortable stagnation, they could enjoy a relatively prosperous and comfortable life which called for a limited exertion in the interests of their work and business activity. It is here that the values to which they relate their economic activity become vital. Development-achievement requires, as we know, that entrepreneurs break with tradition and exert themselves more in the interests of production. If their economic milieu provides no pressure for them to do this, the value system must be considered. Briefly, if the value system through which entrepreneurs make their economic lives meaningful is one which suggests that traditionalistic satisfaction with the status quo is the morally correct or desirable course, then, in the absence of pressure from disturbances in their milieu, actors will be locked into the traditionalistic framework and no development will take place. It is precisely because the Irish insulated themselves from such pressures in the milieu that the question of values assumes importance and that is why we devoted Chapter 7 to the business of describing the salients of the Catholic-nationalist Arcadian culture complex. The values associated with that complex were thoroughly traditionalistic. Instead of orienting people away from traditionalism, they oriented them towards it. In doing so, given the absence of pressures from the milieu, they locked the Irish into a traditionalistic meaning frame and so confirmed orientations to work and business which were inappropriate to development-achievement.

Culture and the entrepreneurial problem

In Chapter 5 we used the term culture as a reference to the whole complex of ideafacts and artifacts produced by human groups in the course of their adaption to their natural and social environments. Concretely, to remember, a culture is a congeries of values, norms, beliefs, customs, technologies, practices and forms of artistic expression which reflect the thoughts, feelings and actions of a people, and which, since the ideafacts form inter-generationally transmitted world views and the artifacts conditioning environments, come, in turn, to structure the thoughts, feelings and actions of people through the shared cognitive, normative, aesthetic and technical standards which derive from them. In short, as we saw, a culture is a body of shared representations which, being distinctive to the members of a given collectivity, provides its members with a sense of themselves through the provision of a shared understanding of their past, present and future. It is through their engagement with these collective representations as transmitted by families, schools, churches and other institutions of socialisation, that individuals come to develop their understanding of themselves as socialised beings; they are the media through which people become enabled to give meaning to their lives and to take their stances towards the complexes of objects, events, actions and possibilities that make up the world. Values are particularly important in this context. Values are shared standards on which people in a collectivity base their moral and aesthetic judgements; they are shared conceptions of worth used to distinguish between right and wrong, good and bad, useful and useless, beautiful and ugly and so forth; they form the bases on which people make judgements about the moral worth of goals and actions, so that they can prioritise them, and make moral judgements about their own and others' standing in their communities. Peoples' thoughts, feelings and actions are, therefore, structured through their orientation to values, which orientation structures the answers to such questions as: what sorts of goals shall we seek to achieve? by what means? with what intensity? in what sort of relationships to other, and different, goals? What sort of life will we esteem? On what grounds will we accord people honour and respect? On what grounds will we deny them honour and respect, and deem them to be unworthy? On what grounds will we ourselves be able to command the honour and respect of others?

These are the kinds of questions that are most important in terms of the present study. We say this because the questions that have to do with what goals? with what intensity? by what means? and in what relationship to other and different goals? have a clear reference to what a value system has to say about the prioritisation and regulation of actors' activities, including, of course, their economic activities. Likewise the questions connected with what kind of life will be esteemed and so serve as a basis for honour and reputability are crucial also because, given that human beings wish to maintain themselves in good repute, they have a strong relationship with issues connected with the capacity of values to mould and direct human conduct. We noticed this in Chapter 6 when we discussed the question of how it is that values come to have the power to determine human conduct. While we were happy to admit that values can have the power to stimulate devotion and loyalty through inspiring a commitment to what is right and good for its own sake, or through internalised guilt, we noted also that a reference to an individual's public standing had to be considered. Unless a collectivity is very tolerant of deviance, individuals who want to maintain normal social relationships will have to behave in ways that are more or less approximate to the dictates of the community's values, or give that appearance, if they are to remain in good standing and avoid becoming the objects of disapproval, hostility or worse. The key question now becomes: What do the values in the Catholic-nationalist Arcadian culture complex have to say about the issues raised in the questions we are currently concerned with? More precisely, what sort of goals do they suggest individuals should seek to achieve? with what intensity? by what means? in what sort of association with other and different goals? what sort of life do they suggest individuals should esteem? on what sort of grounds do they suggest that honour and esteem should be bestowed on individuals, or withheld from them as the case may be?

It is very obvious that the ideafacts produced by the votaries of Catholic-nationalism were intended to articulate a cultural identity as we have defined the term in the present context; they were intended to delimit the boundaries of Irishness in ways that pointed clearly to what was distinctive about it in order to give the Irish a collective sense of self formed through a set of specifics which, at the same time, enabled them to distinguish themselves from others, most notably, as we have seen, from the English. What is most immediately striking about the project is its rather negative characterisation of modernity as represented by industrialism and the industrial spirit. Modernity is, of course, associated with England, and that, in itself, might have been enough to damn it; England is seen as an oppressor, as a dark power which covets Ireland's soul and hates Ireland because Ireland will not submit. There is, however, more to the matter because, as we have seen, industrialism and the industrial spirit are evaluated negatively for their own sakes as well, being associated with cunning, cupidity, vulgarity, with commercialism and Mammon, with an endless quest for material gain which is foolish and unnatural; with secularism and godlessness, with a degraded view of humanity - a naturalistic vision which puts human beings on the same level as kangaroos and which treats them as if they were born for the laboratory or the factory only; and with a diminished civilisation in which all that is holy, all that is beautiful, all that raises human beings above the level of the brute beast is given up and sacrificed to the great Mammon upon the altar of controlled avarice. The modern world is, therefore, devoid of sanctity, beauty, culture and intelligence all of which it has perverted in the interests of its Mammonistic quest; everything is tainted and corrupted by the need to make it subserve Mammon; sanctity and beauty give way to science and vulgarity; nature is despoiled; the natural spontaneity and spirituality of human beings is strangled by a dehumanising straitjacket in which virtue and character are identified only with work and economic acquisition.

Modernity is rejected here on very clear grounds; there is nothing that is at all obscurantist in the Catholic-nationalist Arcadian attitude. The Irish, quite simply, have a better civilisation and want to defend it. That they have a better civilisation is due in large measure to their Catholic faith and to their simpler and healthier rural lives. Thanks to this happy combination they have a higher culture, a broader and loftier view of humanity and its destiny that is rooted, ultimately, in a knowledge of God and of humanity's spiritual destiny; they know that human beings were not made for the laboratory or the factory, but for God, for the enjoyment of His world, for sanctity, beauty, culture, for those things which make life worth living, and which the industrial spirit with its Mammonistic devotion to work and accumulation is drowning in a sea of slavery, cunning, cupidity and vulgarity. Modern industrial life is, therefore, at base a materialistic pig trough. The Irish, however, are not pigs; they are human and civilised and have a proper sense of what a civilised life is about. Above all they know about money:

> Money is only a means to an end. A wise man makes money for the sake of his own personal comfort; he is a fool who inverts the order of nature by sacrificing his comforts for the sake of making money (O'Riordan, 1906, p. 215).

As we noted in Chapter 6, therefore, the Irish were to be counted among the disparagers of industrial society and its associated spirit, and their thunderbolts against both are directed from what they take to be the civilisational high ground. For all that, however, the view of economic life expressed by O'Riordan is, as we noted earlier, arguably a low and narrow one. We say this because it does not allow for any self-denying idealism in association with economic endeavour; in holding anyone who sacrifices personal comfort for the sake of making money to be a fool he is clearly ruling out self-denial in the interests of growing a business for its own sake, or for the sake of some value that is rooted in patriotism, civic pride, religious duty or any other. On O'Riordan's view one thing is certain: devotion to business is in no sense a religious duty; it cannot be a field in which an individual can through self-denying zeal and devotion prove his or her moral worth in a religious or any other sense; all that self-denying zeal in connection with business can prove is that the individual who engages in it is a 'fool who inverts the order of nature'.

O'Riordan's views are thus thoroughly traditionalistic in the Weberian sense of that term. And he was a Roman Catholic priest, whose work was very much the approved Irish Roman Catholic response to the attacks of the wicked modernists, those benighted upholders of the industrial spirit.

We are now in a position to see what answers Catholic-nationalist Arcadian values offer to the questions we were asking above. Individuals who learn from those values will learn that the answers to the questions which have to do with goals, means, intensities and prioritised relations between goals will be pretty definite in their relation to their work and business activities. Orientation to these values will indicate that work and business are but means to the end of securing a comfortable life; that they are not a matter that has anything to do with patriotic, religious, moral or other idealism; that there is no duty, as such, attaching to them, and that it is foolish and unnatural to exert one's self in them at the expense of one's comforts - to do so is to become involved with cunning, cupidity, vulgarity, with Mammon, that great and dangerous anti-God, involvement with whom endangers, not only individuals' comforts, but their immortal souls, by calling them to a godless materialism. Devotion to work and to business expansion are not, therefore, means through which individuals can establish their moral worth and good standing in their communities. If anything, in fact, the opposite is the case; given the negative association with Mammon - as if that god had no following in Ireland - godlessness, cunning, cupidity and vulgarity, a life of too much devotion to business is likely to be interpreted as morally dubious. As we shall see later this interpretation is reinforced because Irish society has developed what amounts to an anti-success ethic. This, however, is a point to which we shall return.

The bases of the attitudes of the Dublin managers which Humphries reported from the nineteen-seventies will now, we hope, be clear. Humphries - and we apologise for repeating the quotation, but is does help to establish the point - reported that:

> Managerial people [in Dublin] quite commonly acknowledge that their more relaxed attitude towards business activity stems from their religious outlook on life. In the words of one husband: 'I think we Irish are quite different from the English and Americans. The ones I've met seem to me to be wrapped up in the almighty pound and dollar. I've dealt with many Englishmen and my impression is that money and what it brings are their God. But we cannot get as concerned as they over business and material things. We are less active in these matters because always in the background of our minds we are concerned with a more fundamental philosophy' (Humphries, 1966, p. 219).

From this it is obvious - and the view, be it noted is a common view - that Irish business people see themselves as different from their English and American counterparts, being less active in the pursuit of business interests than their colleagues to the East and West of them. It is equally clear that, as the Irish see it, the reason for the difference does not lie in the fact that they are confronted with a less favourable structure of means and opportunities in their business, but rather in the fact that 'always in the background of our minds we are concerned with a more fundamental philosophy'. We have now seen something of what is involved in that fundamental philosophy and of the impact which it worked. And this is the point: There is nothing in Irish law, nothing in the Irish economic environment that would prevent these managers from becoming like their UK and US counterparts, and, no doubt, if they related their business activities to the sort of Mammonistic values which they see as obtaining in those countries, they would have done so. The point is they do not wish to do so; their more relaxed attitude is, to their view, the proper and morally correct one and is so, on their own self-understanding, because they have learned to read the text of their economic lives through relating them to a value complex - the more fundamental philosophy - which has indicated that this should be so.

It will now, we hope, be obvious why it is that we are unprepared to go along with the view that economic motivation can be regarded as a universal constant that comes to us from the womb, and why it is that, while being sceptical about placing a naive overemphasis on the impact of culture, we are also unwilling to countenance explanations of economic activity and its consequences which are so structurally and economically deterministic as to rule out culture as a possible independent variable. The fact that entrepreneurial conduct is structured by the means and opportunities available to actors makes that activity no less meaningful to those who perform it. Economic activity is rooted in actors' senses of purpose, which are, in turn, governed by their self-understanding of what it is they do, why and how they do it, and, not least, how they relate it to the 'thousand-and-one' other purposeful activities that make up the rounds of their everyday lives. However important their economic activities may be, business people are more than just business people; they are actually or potentially also praying people, playing people, family people, friendship people, sporting people, artistic people, political people, patriotic people, and heaven knows what sort of other people besides. Relating their economic activities to the values of the Catholic-nationalist Arcadian culture complex has clearly taught these actors that the values which praying, playing, sporting, the family and friendship serve are too important to be trampled under the feet of a rushing gang of Mammonistic devotees to the false gospel of work and accumulation; the praying, after all, represents the spiritual interests which must not be sacrificed to Mammon; the balance of the list represents the comforts which it is foolish and unnatural to sacrifice in the interests of work and accumulation.

We have now, hopefully, demonstrated the impact of Irish cultural values in terms of the more relaxed attitude to business which the Irish themselves see as part of their world outlook. As we noted in Chapter 6, however, there are two senses in which we have to examine relaxation: namely, in terms of a low prioritisation on work and business activity, and by reference to relaxation in the moral sense, i.e. the weak patterns of ethical and prudential regulation of business conduct. So far we have addressed the question of relaxation which has to do with prioritisation.

We must now bring the question of regulatory relaxation to the fore. Doing so requires a closer examination of the canon of Irishness embodied in the Catholic-nationalist Arcadian culture complex. The question we must ask is, of course, how is it that the upholders of the canon are so tolerant of moral laxity in economic life?

The canon of Irishness and economic life

The Catholic-nationalist Arcadian identity is important here because, insofar as it made a virtue of a lifestyle that was 'uncontaminated by commercialism and progress' and confirmed Irish society in its belief that such a life, most especially in its rural manifestations, was an 'essential element in an unchanging Irish identity' (Brown, 1985, p. 84) it provided Irish society with an operative canon of Irishness. What we mean by this is that it provided a value-standard by which Irish men and women could judge, and be judged, as to their moral worth as measured in the quality of their Irishness. Put another way what the canon did was to provide a moral heuristic which enabled the Irish to make judgements between what counted as a 'good' Irish person and a 'bad' Irish person and it thus provided standards, the upholding of which became the basis for the maintenance of individuals' self-esteem and, needless to say, their good standing within the community and society to which they belonged. Orientation to the canon, therefore, became a means by which individuals could prove their moral worth to themselves and to others in their milieu. It was in terms of this canon, and the judgements and prioritisations which were derived from it, that the values of Catholic-nationalist Arcadianism worked their impact. So, how did it come to turn out that they worked an impact of the kind that provided so much toleration of ethical laxity?

We can best answer the question we have just asked respecting the canon by addressing ourselves to a further question: namely, what did the canon require of those who sought to establish their moral credentials in the eyes of their fellow citizens, and so secure the social honour and esteem which was accorded to those who were counted among the ranks of the good and worthy? Allegiance to the Nation was certainly important. This involved support for the struggle to achieve independence, and, after independence had been achieved, for the restoration of national unity through the integration of the partitioned area of the Six Counties into a United Irish Republic. It also involved support for Irish culture; for Irish music and dancing, for Irish games and pastimes, and for the restoration of the Irish language. Adherence to Catholicism - and Catholicism was the religion of the overwhelming majority - was also a part of the canon; to be a loyal son or daughter of the Church, to uphold its teachings and its place in society, became important, if not indeed, essential to the maintenance of the individual's moral standing. In elaborating these standards we are not suggesting that the Irish were a violent and intolerant people; the desire for national unity did not imply a support for violence as a means to the end of achieving it; the standard in allegiance to Catholicism did not imply a lack of respect for Protestants or a desire to discriminate against or interfere with them.

This is not to say that Ireland lacked a violent and intolerant minority - what society does not? - and it certainly contained zealous enthusiasts who equated Irishness with Catholicism to the point at which they wished to convert those errant and deluded souls who embraced the 'other creed' to the true path. For the most part, however, the minority was allowed to set its own standards; the canon was not ruthlessly imposed on those who could plausibly claim exclusion from its terms, and, as we shall see, some established groups achieved some partial exemptions from its coverage. For the Catholic-nationalist majority, however, it existed and functioned.

What we need to do now is to take some notice of the scope of the value-standards enshrined in the canon. In short these turn out to be political, cultural (in the narrower non-anthropological sense of the term) and religious. One can thus prove one's Irishness - and, therefore, one's 'value' or 'worth' as an individual - by supporting the nationalist political platform, by upholding the Irish language and culture, and by being a loyal Roman Catholic. What the canon says little about, however, is the sphere of the economic; it does not contain specifications which enable one to prove the quality of one's Irishness - and, therefore, one's 'value' or 'worth' as an individual in and through the quality of one' economic performance. In so far as the canon orients towards economic life, as we have seen, it does so in terms that are not calculated to inspire devotion to it; economic life is just a means to the end of obtaining life's comforts; that is its natural purpose and anyone who cultivates economic pursuits at the expense of comfort violates nature and is a fool. Clearly, therefore, economic activity cannot be consecrated to any ideal, national, religious or whatever; it is nothing special, just something human beings have to do in order to live, but need not, and should not, engage at levels which are above and beyond those necessary to secure their comforts. Politics, culture and religion are consecrated with idealism, but not economics; one can demonstrate one's moral qualities, and therefore one's good standing in the community, through one's devotion to national and Catholic political, cultural or religious objectives, but not through one's devotion to work and business expansion. Where devotion is called for, even if it be of a formalistic and lip-serving kind, people will tend to react adversely to those whose lives and activities show indifference or hostility towards those objectives to which devotion is required, and so those who exhibit indifference or hostility will lose their good standing and may even find themselves subject to the attentions of either informal or formal regulatory regimes, i.e. the sanctions of public opinion or the law. Where no devotion is called for, however, or in circumstances where devotion is disfavoured, as with economic activity, people are far less likely to react adversely to expressions of indifference or hostility and to bring those who exhibit themselves through such negative orientations under the power of informal or formal regulative review. It is very much the case here of 'blessed are they from whom nothing is expected, for people will not worry when they fail to deliver, or try to regulate them in order to make them deliver when they fail, and cursed are they from whom much is expected, for their failures to deliver will be noted and they will be regulated'. Thanks to their canon the Irish expect something from themselves as national and religious beings and are thus prone to regulate behaviour in spheres which are deemed important in the light of their national and religious aspirations. They expect much less from themselves as economic actors and so tend to be rather less critical of themselves and others and thus less prone to regulate and move against failures to deliver. The truth is, therefore, that the values which indicate that actors should accord work and business activity a low priority also tell us why it is subjected to so little ethical regulation. After all if economic life is to be accorded a low priority, and is not regarded as a field in which one demonstrates one's ethical standing, why subject it to regulation? In strictly ethical terms, so long as one does not break the bounds of tradition, economic life is a thing indifferent to ethics as such. Paradoxical as it must seem, therefore, the anti-Mammonistic values in the Irish canon clear the way for an ethically unregulated devotion to the very anti-god they disdain. In denouncing Mammon the Irish have liberated Mammon. In berating cunning and cupidity they have liberated these 'vices'. They have done these things because, in regarding economic activity as simply a means to the end of achieving comfort, they have robbed it of positive ethical significance and of any association with what might be regarded as a high priority duty for individuals. The higher the priority a people attaches to a duty the more they will regulate activity associated with it. Where a low priority duty, or no duty at all, is involved the regulation will either be much less severe or non existent.

The paradox of Irish economic traditionalism can now be resolved at the level of values; the strange combination of an easy-going and relaxed attitude to work and business activity, which lends itself so readily to the kind of anti-materialist interpretation imposed on it by the Dublin managers, and the erratic unscrupulosity, the magnificent displays of unethical cunning and cupidity we have reviewed in these page, stem from the same source, i.e. a complex of values through which people render their economic lives meaningful to themselves. These values teach people that economic life is a thing of little significance. If people come to interpret something as being of little significance, we can hardly be surprised if they come to interpret the sins associated with it as being of little significance also. Sins they may be, to be sure, but they are not big sins, not life killing sins that whirl one's soul to damnation, sins that need to disturb the conscience too much. Entrepreneurs who relate their economic activities to such values will, therefore, learn the appropriateness of low prioritisation and weak regulation and will not experience too many pangs of conscience when they take a relaxed attitude to work and resources and when they indulge themselves in a little money-making by unscrupulous means; there is no internal regulation through conscience. The public who relate economic life to the same values will see no need to become critical of those who engage in either or in both modes of relaxation; they may become excited over some particular scandal, if it gets publicity, but it will be a 'nine day wonder', and so, by and large, the legions of tax evaders, 'Phoenix syndrome' operators, smugglers and the rest can go their happy ways without too much obloquy being heaped upon them; there is no regulation through the force of public opinion. And so it is with those whose business it is to formally regulate economic and social life, a responsibility which lies, ultimately, with the politicians who run the soft Irish state. They also relate economic life to the value complex and this, coupled with the fact that public opinion makes few demands for regulation, facilitates their somewhat lax approach to the business of regulation. As we have seen they do not give the appearance of being over-zealous in this department, and, indeed, sometimes seem concerned to protect those who behave in ethically dubious ways. In all they seem to regard the sins of the boardroom, the office, the shop and the abattoir as being of a somewhat venial character. To put the matter somewhat crudely, but essentially correctly, they, like the Church to which they belong, are far more concerned with the sins of the bedroom. This, however, we shall see,

People who are not familiar with Ireland, and indeed those who know and like the country, may find this explanation hard to accept, and may even recoil from it because they find it offensive. Any readers who are so tempted, however, must read the evidence and tell us how the situation which that evidence describes can otherwise be explained. As it happens there is more evidence to be presented in connection with the questions of prioritisation and relaxation, and for this reason we can ask any doubters to suspend judgement for the time being. Before we present that evidence we need to revisit the Irish tradition of traditionalism.

The tradition of traditionalism revisited

Irish economic traditionalism was not, in any sense, the product of Catholic-nationalist Arcadianism; as we saw in Chapter 6 it had a long history and did not need the new nationalism to bring it into being. Catholic-nationalist Arcadianism came into its own after Irish independence in 1921. The Catholic-nationalist Ireland which began to chart its own destinies in that year had for long been experiencing economic and social decline; its population, as we have seen, had fallen dramatically since the tragic years of the famine; it had practically no heavy industry, and the record of agriculture and food processing industries was, when compared with those of the Danes, a poor one. Decline took place in a society which had a middle class that was by no means lacking in either capital or business talent. Members of that middle class, however, often deserted business for the land as soon as they had acquired enough capital to do so; they were clearly captivated by an aristocratic cult, the gentlemanly life and its associated contempt for work and industry. The aristocratic cult was not, however, the only source of a non-work ethic in Irish society; peasant spontaneity provided an alternative leisure ethic which was no less effective because it was more attainable to the large majority of the poorer members of the community. In pondering on the accusations of laziness that were levelled against the Irish, Hutchinson (1970, p. 516) observes that the charges were,

> in their essence, no more than a tacit recognition that the Irish people very generally organised their lives on the basis of values that were not those of their observers. It is likely that among these values, as among the values of many other communities, was one

that accorded to leisure a position surpassing that given to work. To the degree that subsistence agriculture was predominant, and production patently for a living, not for commerce ... the pursuit of work beyond the minimum necessary to satisfy these conditions had little function. Were leisure essential for proper attention to be paid to other important features of community life, the burden of work would not have been increased unnecessarily. We do not refer only to other forms of economic production, hunting, fishing and domestic manufacture. We mean also those features of social life - as, for example, conversation, dancing, festivities and celebrations - which, regarded by industrial society, somewhat as time-wasting inessentials, in simpler communities are an integral part of the system of social relationships .... The insistent demands of industrial society created the belief amongst its members that a man not working was doing nothing; or at any rate was doing nothing of importance. That this view was the reverse of that held by the majority of the world's pre-industrial populations seemed only to confirm its validity.

Hutchinson's description of pre-commercial Irish society is useful here because it enables us to suggest that, if the Catholic-nationalist Arcadian culture complex arose as a reflection of material interests, the material interests which it reflected were those of a pre-commercial age; its insistence that the pursuit of money-making should not be carried on at the expense of comfort becomes intelligible against this background; so does its anti-Mammonism, its anti-commercial triumphalism and its rejection of industrialism and its spirit on the grounds that they had ruined civilisation precisely because they regarded as time wasting inessentials all those features of life, which, to the pre-commercial world view, made it worth living. Catholic-nationalist Arcadianism can, therefore, be put into a context in which we can best appreciate it for what it was: namely, a pre-commercial world view upholding pre-commercial values. By the time Catholic-nationalist Arcadianism came into its own, however, Ireland had entered the commercial age. Those who elaborated its canon were, however, remote from this commercial world, and detested it, and provided the Irish with a complex of pre-commercial values through which to interpret their material interests. As a result when other peoples - peoples against whom the Irish were competing - had either learned or were learning to relate their material interests to values that were more appropriate to success in commercial rivalry, the Irish learning curve was blocked off by the adoption of the pre-commercial canon, in which the kind of devotion to economic life which brought success in the competitive struggle was denigrated through the use of terms like Mammon, cunning, cupidity, vulgarity, which, of course, denoted vices. If the Irish had been able to persuade other peoples to accept their interpretation all might have been well. The trouble is that other peoples had translated the vices into terms like growth, expansion, and progress and so had enabled themselves to extol and honour the kind of conduct which the Irish had little time for, precisely because they saw it as conducing to success. Through their adoption of their canon the Irish were thus disabled from honouring commercially appropriate conduct, and, indeed, as we shall soon see, from honouring success itself. As a result they were disabled in the competitive race for success.

Theorists of the superstructure would no doubt wish to interject at this point and suggest that Ireland's entry into commercialism would generate values that were appropriate reflections of actors' material interests in the changed situation; commercial pressure, i.e. competition would put a premium on work, effort, success, money making, expansion etc and so lead to the emergence of a value system which reflected these necessities by investing them with moral salience - what else could we expect given that theorists of this kind regard values as superstructural reflections of material interests, which are, of course, the ultimate determinants of conduct? Whatever plausibility an argument like this might have in theory dissolves on application to the practicalities of the Irish case. The commercialisation of Irish society did not necessitate any new, and different, orientations on the parts of actors toward work and commercial criteria. Irish agriculture commercialised against the background of a move to extensive grass-based beef and dairy production. These are not activities that require large inputs of labour and human effort. Increased effort and greater attention to resources can bring increased rewards through better prices, and an increased volume of sales, for increased supplies of higher quality products, but the older ways are not inconsistent with survival and with a comfortable prosperity. There was no real pressure from the milieu. The opportunities to make the break were available, but the Irish chose not to take them. The Catholic-nationalist Arcadian values confirmed the choice and provided a relentless canonisation of the traditional orientations.

That the traditional ways persisted is obvious from evidence from the nineteen-eighties as much as its persistence is demonstrated through evidence available from the earlier years of commercial involvement. The German economist Moritz Bonn, who visited Ireland in order to 'study backward economic life in the one western country where it had been preserved', speaks eloquently to the point when he informs us that:

> Irish grass farming mainly consists in this, that Heaven causes the sun to shine and the rain to fall, and that Man sends the cattle to the pasture and gives himself no further trouble about them (Bonn, 1906, 38).

From this, and from the evidence presented in Chapter 2, it is manifestly the case that the commercialisation of Irish rural life did not provide grounds for the emergence of a value system which made virtues out of work and business activity. Nor, indeed, the commercialisation of urban Ireland. With few exceptions, Irish industry was carried on by family businesses which were able to insulate themselves from the full impact of competition because they oriented to local markets for non-traded products. Otherwise urban Ireland was the Ireland of the professionals and traders, the Ireland of the small town and small city of the cosy circle of eligibles described in Chapter 6. Here again the dark forces of competition could be kept at bay and a comfortable prosperity maintained in conditions of stagnation. Commercialisation dictated no new orientation.

The comfortable stagnation on the farm and in the town was facilitated by the Irish tradition of emigration; all those who were surplus to requirements, and whose continued presence in the country as poor, under or unemployed individuals might have been a focus for pressure for change, voted with their feet and got out. The army of children who did not inherit 'down on the farm', and who could not be deployed as relatives assisting, got out; those who could not find work in the urban areas did likewise and so reduced the burdens and charges on the comfortable prosperity of many of those who remained. The commercialisation of the Irish economy, therefore, provided few grounds on which a new and more commercially appropriate value system was necessitated. So long as people equated their material interests with comfortable stagnation, as opposed to growth and increased prosperity, there was no compelling reason for change in activity patterns or in values that reflected them.

The main lines of the entrepreneurial conduct-patterns described in Chapter 2,3 and 4 were, therefore, well and truly laid and ballasted before the Catholic-nationalist Arcadian canon of Irishness came into its own in the newly independent Ireland of 1921. The easy-going complacency was evident in rural and urban life. And so were those spontaneous outbursts of unscrupulous greed by which people enriched themselves in the short-term at the expense of long term damage to their interests, as the farmers who abused their monopoly of the British market during the Great War by supplying it with 'bad eggs and worse butter' shows well enough. As we saw in Chapter 6 the abuses of the farmers here did damage to their longer-term prospects; their unethical behaviour lost them good will and customers. Yet the evidence presented in Chapter 2 suggests that they have not learned the lesson that ethical conduct in business is often prudent in that it attracts rather than repels customers. The lessons were there to be learned from the material conditions in which the Irish operated, but the Irish were not, it seems, apt pupils. The pressure from material conditions, therefore, was not strong enough to force a break from traditionalism.

If the pressure from the material base was not strong enough to force a break with traditionalism, the value system in the ideal superstructure could not do so either. Just the opposite was, in fact, the case; the value system reinforced traditionalism by hallowing and sanctifying the status quo and the traditional outlook by representing both as quintessentially Irish. As a result people who render their economic lives meaningful by relating them to the values in the canon find, if they are ever tempted to disturb the comfortable status quo by striving for improvement, the temptation related to a battery of negative evaluations having to do with Mammon, materialism, cupidity and cunning and unnatural foolishness, and is, if he or she decides to give into the temptation, open to the adverse judgements of those who still uphold the canon and its plethora of anti-Mammonistic negativities.

The result is the 'sheer torpor' that characterises Irish society. And a society that is characterised by a sheer torpor is unlikely to develop a 'success ethic' which can celebrate a triumph over a traditionalistic 'remain satisfied with the status quo ethic'. In fact, if anything, there is a tendency for a society thus circumstanced to develop an 'inactivity', or even an 'anti-success ethic'. A leading Irish entrepreneur, Fergal Quinn, has some sense of this:

> Anyone with drive cannot fail to be depressed by ... the low value we put on action .... Anyone with drive, with a truly innovative or entrepreneurial spirit cannot fail to be dragged down by the sheer torpor that characterises our society (quoted in Kerr, 1986).

What disturbed Quinn even more than the torpor, however, was his observation that those who do break the mould are 'torn to shreds' by others in their milieu (Kerr, 1986). In so expressing himself Quinn was merely echoing the sentiments of the Irish author Brendan Behan who, noting the same tendency in his people, remarked savagely: 'If there is one vice the Irish really abhor, it is that of success' (quoted in Hutchinson, 1970, p. 522). Comments like these indicate well enough that breaking the mould of economic traditionalism is not the way to gain esteem in Irish society. Traditionalism in Ireland has resulted in economic stagnation, and its survival is predicated on the traditionalists capacities to insulate themselves against the intrusions of those whose dynamism might upset the status quo and thus deprive them of their cosy prosperity and their accustomed place in the traditionalistic status order. As Lee (1989, p. 646) puts it:

> It was not only John Healy's mother in Mayo who was making 'an almost culturally programmed response' when holding that 'her village was the best village, her family the best family, and you did honour to it by denigrating the families from villages which threatened both'. Threats to the family could also come from within one's own village. The success of a neighbour's child in the United States was acceptable. That did not disturb the local pecking order. It could be glossed over as a tribute to the village as a whole. The success of the same neighbour's child at home would upset assumptions about the natural order of things. The reactions were correspondingly more resentful in the steeper valleys of the squinting windows when the rare individual dared to rise above his allotted place. Envy of the thrusting neighbour frequently lurked below the cloak of ridicule, 'a method of cutting others down to size, especially those who tried to shake off the local apathy and get ahead'.

Traditional Ireland was thus 'consumed with envy' (Lee, 1989, p. 647), an envy which, if Quinn and Behan are correct, is still alive, well and vital enough to have spread into urban Ireland. The existence of such envy clearly must reinforce the traditionalism carried in the value complex; if nothing else it makes the way of the anti-traditionalist a hard and thorny way.

Myth, reality and reinforcement: elective affinities and institutional power

There is a truth that has to be told about the Catholic-nationalist Gaelic Arcadia: namely, that it was, in important respects, a myth. Yet, as we have seen, it was a myth that took root in Irish society and provided it with a collective representation of itself which was not lacking in the capacity to attract allegiance and to motivate people to mobilise in accordance with its sacred values. Myth, of course, can be serviceable to a society, or to sectional interests within a society, so we should not be surprised that Gaelic Arcadia became operative and influential. This, however, hardly absolves us from asking how and why this came about. As we shall see it is an instructive question to ask and to answer.

The reality differed from the myth in a number of crucial respects. In the first place the Arcadia was no Arcadia; the West of Ireland, that last bastion of the Gael, was no idyllic haven of a lost civilisation, but a neglected, backward poverty-stricken area, many of whose inhabitants showed what they thought of it by leaving in large numbers for the lands of cunning, cupidity and vulgarity - these provided what the Arcadia could not provide: a decent standard of life. Secondly, the vision of Ireland as a land that was free from the materialism, cupidity and cunning was hardly tenable; as these pages have shown time and time again, cunning, cupidity and a materialistic interest in money-making are far from absent in Ireland. The somewhat lofty and superior self-image enshrined in the canon was always, therefore, a questionable one, as the Irish writer Frank O'Connor saw well enough:

> After the revolution .... Irish society began to revert to type. All the forces that had made for national dignity ... began to disintegrate rapidly, and Ireland became more than ever sectarian, utilitarian, the two nearly always go together, vulgar and provincial .... Every year that has passed ... has strengthened the grip of the gombeen man, of the religious secret societies ... of the illiterate censorships .... The significant fact about it is that there is no idealistic opposition which would enable us to measure the extent of the damage (quoted in Brown, 1985, pp. 154-5).

O'Connor's point is well taken; the serviceability of the canon rested substantially in the fact that it obscured reality by lending it a dignity which, in a more open and critical society, might, and probably would, have been contested.

The myth, of course, had no service to offer those who were forced to leave the Arcadia in order to earn a living. For those who remained behind, especially the relatively prosperous middle Ireland and later the parvenus climbing the social ladder, it had indeed functions to perform. Middle Ireland arguably took it to heart because it recognised that an elective affinity existed between its verities and their material and ideal interests. The better-off farmers, their friends and relations among the shopkeeping and trading fraternity and in the professions and the Roman Catholic priesthood, formed the backbone of middle Ireland. All these had struggled together to make good their claims to 'a place in the sun'; the farmers for their rights to proprietorship in the land, made good through agitation which, by the first decade of the twentieth century, resulted in the enactment of legislation which enabled them to transform themselves from tenants to proprietors on relatively easy terms; the shopkeepers and traders against the cooperative movement extending to the wholesale and retail sectors; the professionals against the Protestant domination in the professions; the priests for the rights and prerogatives of their Church and people. Middle Ireland thus developed a criss-cross pattern of interests, reinforced in a small society by ties of kinship and friendship, which were able to function in alliance and to find a unified focus in the national struggle and in the Catholic-nationalist identity; the farmers, shopkeepers, traders and professionals contributed to the support of their pastors; their pastors reciprocated by supporting the farmers in their struggles for proprietorship, by refusing to support the development of cooperation in directions that adversely affected the interests of the traders, by securing a Catholic University for the education of the professional classes, by providing them with employment opportunities through the establishment of Catholic hospitals and through their support for nationalist politics. This last, of course, was essential; with nationalist control of local and central governments, came control over policies and appointments and the sweeping away of Protestant and alien control over the opportunity structures available to the professionals and allied groups in middle Ireland. To say that the Catholic-nationalist canon was also essential is not, of necessity, to accuse middle Ireland of hypocrisy; middle Ireland saw itself as oppressed, not only in terms of its material interests, but in terms of religious and ideal interests also; it saw itself as deprived of its dignity and reputability as well as its prosperity. To recover both it had to assert both and so the advancement of its material interests went hand-in-hand with the assertion of its religious and national distinctiveness. The fact that middle Ireland's allegiance to the canon may not have been materially disinterested does not, therefore, enable us to conclude that it was entirely cynical.

Nor does it enable us to conclude that those who elaborated the canon were doing no more than providing a convenient superstructural reflection of the material interests of middle Ireland. Many of the poets and revolutionaries who contributed to the formation of the canon would, in fact, have despised middle Ireland. The aristocratic contempt which Yeats harboured towards them is superbly captured in the following lines:

> What need you, being come to sense
> But fumble in a greasy till
> And add the halfpence to the pence,
> And prayer to shivering prayer, until
> You have dried the marrow from the bone;
> For men were born to pray and save
> Romantic Ireland's dead and gone,
> Its with O'Leary in the grave.

The title of the poem from which these lines are taken, *September 1913*, is a reference to a prolonged and bitter labour dispute that took place in Dublin in that year. Mention of this brings us to a further point at which the reality of Ireland differed from the Arcadian myth: Dublin, the city in which a combination of sweating employers, rack-renting slum landlords, shopkeepers, publicans and corrupt politicians preyed on the degraded working class denizens of its teeming tenements, slums which, for overcrowding, filth, squalor and general uninhabitability, were unequalled in Europe, and probably anywhere else outside of the proverbial Calcutta. If nothing else this shows that if middle Ireland felt oppressed, there were those in Ireland who felt middle Ireland bearing down on them as an oppressor. It also demonstrates that some nationalists, in supporting workers' claims to social justice, had a social vision that extended in range beyond that of middle Ireland.

Nevertheless, the passage of an ideal from the theoretician's drawing board to its practical application in the workaday world is, as we noted earlier, a journey that is fraught with hazard; ideals have an unfortunate habit of being modified in their application, of finding use in contexts and circumstances other than those to which the theoretician would wish to see them applied. If by nothing else this is almost guaranteed by the fact that all great movements for social and political change attract a variegated host of 'followers', ranging from disinterested idealists to those opportunistic characters who go along for the ride and with an eye to the main chance. No doubt middle Ireland contained its Gaelic enthusiasts; those who cultivated the language and Gaelic culture with love and enthusiasm were by no means absent phenomena. They were not, however, by any means the only 'type' to be found in middle Ireland; the idealists had to rub shoulders with those whose public proclamations of political and religious correctness were accompanied by a more restrained enthusiasm for things Gaelic. There were groups in middle Ireland - prosperous professionals and so forth - who had attained to a certain Englishness in their tastes and sociability patterns, and which, being economically influential, were able to secure certain concessions; these acquired a few words of Irish, no doubt, and made sure that their children obtained an adequate grasp of the language, since it was compulsory in the schools and essential to securing preferment in the state-controlled sectors of Ireland's economy and society, but did little more. Even fiercely nationalist Roman Catholic religious orders like the Christian Brothers ensured that those of their secondary schools which were designed to cater for the better-off middle Irelanders played rugby football and cricket, games that, as English games, were frowned on by nationalists, and games that were certainly not offered in those schools run by the orders for Irish children of the more plebeian sort - these were required to play the Irish games of hurling and Gaelic football. From this we may gather that some 'things English' had a certain 'snob appeal' to some elements in middle Ireland. And so they had, for middle Ireland, despite its veneer of nationalism, was, in many ways, quintessentially an English - albeit a provincial English - sort of place; the cosy, comfortable world of the well-off professionals, traders and farmers was often the world of the golf club, the tennis club, and, where appropriate, the yacht club; it was a world which combined easily with the more Irish world of the cosy circle of clients and customers; the small town and small city world where business and commercial relationships were impregnated with ties of friendship and kinship of long standing; an undemanding and comfortable world of the family firm and family farm, inhabited by a circle of eligibles whose ties of friendship and kinship enabled them, together, to cultivate business relations from which the cold, impersonal, demanding criteria of the competitive market could be safely excluded - it was, in short, the economic traditionalism so brilliantly characterised by Max Weber.

It is true, of course, that the middle-Irelanders were not the cultural heroes of many of those who elaborated the Arcadian identity; the Church tended to favour them - not surprisingly, perhaps, given that many of the priests came from middle Ireland families - but for the more literary types that mantle fell on the Western peasant. That the Western peasant represented traditional Ireland was a myth; glorified though 'he' may have been, 'he' was, in reality, a poor deprived, marginalised, peripheral character without power or influence. Whether the Arcadians knew or cared for the fact mattered not, middle Ireland was part of traditional Ireland, far more part of its reality than the Arcadians' cultural hero, the Western Gael; middle Irelanders were not poor, deprived, marginalised and peripheral, they owned wealth, had education, controlled resources and gathered much of the power and influence available in society into their hands. The ideology which hallows and sanctifies the myth, however, can also be made to hallow and sanctify the reality which differs from the myth. Any ideology that hallowed and sanctified the mythical traditional Ireland, therefore, hallowed and sanctified the real traditional Ireland, that is middle Ireland, also. In hallowing and sanctifying middle Ireland it hallowed and sanctified its cosy traditionalism. Orientation to the values of Catholic-nationalism, therefore, confirmed middle Ireland in its traditional ways; it enabled middle Irelanders to cover their easy-going, undemanding approach to economic activity with a veneer of Catholic and nationalist piety, adherence to the tenets of which guaranteed their respectability and thus the continuation of their status and influence, be they ever so irresponsible and relaxed in their approach to business activity and resources. After all the canon preached respect for property rights, and thus bourgeois property was guaranteed - the ethic of possession was in place. In indicating a low prioritisation and sanctioning weak regulation, however, the canon did nothing to instill in middle Ireland a sense of duty or responsibility towards their economic activities and the resources they commanded, and so an ethic of responsibility towards work and resources was lacking. Middle Ireland's possession and comfortable prosperity was thus confirmed in circumstances in which middle Irelanders were under no pressure from their consciences, public opinion or the regulatory authorities to do much by way of exertion in the deployment and expansion of the resources on which their comfortable prosperity was based; they could enjoy their dignified lives of comfortable prosperity without feeling, or being made to feel, that it had to be paid for by exertion, commitment, a sense of responsibility to growth and development and a pattern of living that was characterised by an exhibition of the 'virtues' of 'honesty, integrity and hard and purposeful work'.

Nationalist middle Ireland was conservative; the revolution which it supported and sustained was a political revolution and not a social revolution; it was content with political independence and so a marked concern for social justice and social reform was not to be allowed to obtrude on its sensibilities. The political party that represented its interests, *Cumann na nGaedheal* formed the government in the early years of the Free State, and made sure that nothing was done to disturb the comfortable status quo ante. National revival was, therefore, accompanied by fiscal rectitude and support for the farmers and for private enterprise; the comfortable nature of life in middle Ireland was sustained through low taxes, facilitated by cuts in the pensions and welfare benefits 'enjoyed' by the less well-off members of Irish society. Those who were not of middle Ireland had, as a result, good reasons for being other than best pleased.

The reaction of the other Irelanders, the workers, the unemployed, the smaller farmers - those who did not emigrate - and the parvenus, was adverse, but not with reference to the Catholic-nationalist ideal. However much the Irish Labour Party may have opposed the government on social issues, it expressly eschewed anything in the nature of radical socialist, let alone class war, politics in the interests of upholding the Catholic-nationalist ideal; Irish Roman Catholicism would have no truck with godless communism, so Ireland was not the place in which men and women of the left could hope to make much of an impression. The radical populism of the *Fianna Fail* party, which attracted the support of the parvenus, the small farmers and many of the workers and the unemployed was no barrier to its staunch support for all that was Catholic and nationalist. What divisions existed in Irish politics were, therefore, easily subsumed under the compelling rubric of the Catholic-nationalist identity; whatever Irish men and women argued about, the identity stood almost as the great unquestionable. Standing at the centre of Irish life, and striving with all its might to ensure that the status quo remained intact, was the towering 'edifice', resplendent in its might, majesty, dominion and power: the Irish branch of the Roman Catholic Church.

The pivotal role of Roman Catholicism

If the canon of Irishness took root because elective affinities existed between its salients and the material and ideal interests of the middle and other Irelanders, it took root also, it has to be said, thanks to the institutionalised power of the Roman Catholic Church. As the supreme moral entrepreneur in Ireland the Church can be deemed to have been the custodian of the canon. Its influence is all pervading, thanks to its extensive organisation, and, not least, its almost total control over education. It was thus able to exert a very strong impact on the formation of Irish character; it had a strong input into primary socialisation; almost total control over secondary socialisation and a tremendous capacity to maintain surveillance over its people at all stages of their social, economic and religious lives.

The ability of the Roman Catholic Church to spread and maintain its influence rests substantially in its organisational effectiveness. Organisationally speaking the Church is a hierarchical bureaucracy; authority rests ultimately at the centre - in Rome - and is exercised locally by diocesan bishops, appointed by and reporting to Rome, who in turn appoint and supervise the work of the parish and other clergy. It is the parish clergy, of course, who are in the closest day-to-day contact with their flocks, preaching, catechising, administering the sacraments and exercising routine functions of moral supervision and control.

Numerous though the diocesan clergy are, they account for fewer than one in seven of the Church's personnel (Inglis, 1987, p. 45). The balance of the clerical forces available to the Church - and the numbers make it the largest organisation in Irish society - are accounted for by regular priests, brothers and nuns belonging to religious orders. Traditionally these have engaged in teaching, medical and welfare work. Nuns have played an especially crucial role in the maintenance of Church influence, not least through their educational, medical and welfare activities. Inglis (1987, p. 46) describes their role in the following terms:

> It is the nuns who have disciplined, trained and educated almost every Irish girl who progressed beyond primary school. They refined and polished these girls into paragons of modern Irish virtue .... It was the nuns who virtually took over the management of the Irish hospital system in the nineteenth century, and since then have run many of the hospitals, nursing homes, remedial homes, orphanages and other charitable institutions in the country.

The regular orders of priests and brothers also engaged in teaching activities, and, according to Inglis (1987, p. 48) 'have educated and trained every male who has attained a high position in Irish society'. As vocations to the religious have declined in recent times, priests, brothers and nuns have had to abandon many of their teaching and medical roles. Nevertheless they retain control of their schools, hospitals and other institutions, filling the most senior positions and employing lay staff whose salaries are paid by the state (Inglis, 1987, p. 46).

In 1982, 491 of the 572 secondary schools in the Irish Republic were Catholic, the great majority of which were managed by the regular orders of priests, brothers and nuns. The primary sector was, if anything, even more firmly under Church control; 3,400 of the 3,500 national (primary) schools are under Catholic management, though the state pays the costs associated with the construction and maintenance of the buildings and the salaries of those who teach in them (Inglis, 1987, pp. 55-8)). It is within these schools that the principles of Catholicism are imparted to Irish children; they are taught the catechism, prepared for their first confession and communion and generally educated in an atmosphere in which religion dominates. The rules by which the national schools are organised and operated are quite definite about the part which religion is to play: 'Of all the parts of a school curriculum, religious instruction is by far the most important' (quoted in Murphy, 1980, p. 155).

The control which the Church exercises over education would be impossible without state support; its maintenance requires, as Clarke

(1984, p. 202) asserts, that the state accepts the Catholic principles that, firstly, children have a right to a Christian education, secondly, that parents have a right to educate their children in line with the dictates of their consciences, and finally, that parents have an obligation to educate their children in Catholic schools. On the whole Irish governments have had no difficulty whatever in accepting these principles, as the words of an Irish minister for education serving in the nineteen-fifties make very clear:

> The State approach to education in the Irish Republic is one which overwhelmingly accepts the supernatural conception of man's nature and destiny. It accepts that the proper subject for education is man whole and entire, soul united to body in unity of nature, with all his faculties natural and supernatural, such as right reason and revelation show him to be. It accepts that the foundation and crown of youths entire training is religion. It is its desire that its teachers, syllabuses and text books in every branch be informed by the spirit underlying this concept of education, and it is determined to see that such facilities as ecclesiastical authorities consider proper shall be provided in the school for the carrying on of the work of religious education (quoted in Whyte, 1984, p. 20).

The Church's influence in education is by no means confined to the primary and secondary sectors. Throughout the nineteenth century the Church fought a campaign to effectively denominationalise university education in Ireland; it refused to allow Roman Catholics to attend the University of Dublin, a Protestant foundation, and did everything in its power to prevent them from attending the non-denominational Queen's Colleges which were established in Belfast, Cork and Galway in 1845. The Church's campaign ultimately bore fruit; in 1908 the Government established the National University of Ireland, establishing a college in Dublin and incorporating the former Queen's Colleges in Cork and Galway. Although formally undenominational, the National University was so constituted as to allow the Roman Catholic hierarchy to exercise considerable influence on its governing bodies, and thus over its appointments and curriculum (Inglis, 1987, p. 58; Whyte, 1984, p. 18).

If control of education has helped the Roman Catholic Church to maintain its power in Ireland, so, undoubtedly, has the fact that it maintains extensive control over the health and social welfare services provided for the Irish people. Quoting an authority on the subject, Inglis (1987, p. 85) informs us that:

> by the beginning of the 1970s: "Religious personnel either owned or had charge of 46 private hospitals, 25 nursing and convalescent homes, 32 geriatric homes, 35 homes for the mentally handicapped, 11 homes for the physically handicapped, 31 orphanages, 29 industrial schools and reformatories, 15 welfare hostels, and 20 student or business hostels".

Much of the ground gained in these areas was won in the nineteenth century when the Church, driven by the view that Roman Catholic people should be treated by Roman Catholic doctors and Roman Catholic nurses, either established or gained control of welfare institutions in order to keep its people out of the hands of the state (Protestant) system. As a result the Church has a major role in the education and training of doctors, nurses and allied personnel; the medical departments in the universities are dominated by Roman Catholic medical ethics; religious and medical discourse is firmly interlinked and medical personnel are formally subject to the Roman Catholic regime in Church controlled hospitals, and informally subject to it in those controlled by the state.

Thanks to the scope and effectiveness of its organisation, and the support of the Irish state, the Roman Catholic Church is the supreme moral entrepreneur in Irish society. Its control over the education system enables it to shape and mould the consciousness of the Irish people. Broadly the Church has used its control over education with three ends in view: Firstly, to secure recruits for the ranks of the religious. Secondly, to establish and maintain its influence over the ruling elite, as a Jesuit priest put it:

> a suitable and thorough education for this body manifestly lies at the very bedrock of Ireland's moral, intellectual and material well-being. If they are sound, the country is safe (quoted in Titley, 1983, p. 153).

The third objective had, of course, to do with ensuring that the broad masses of the Irish people remained loyal sons and daughters of the Church, through what one recent Irish writer has described as 'indoctrination' (Clarke, 1984, p. 281). Inglis, however, maintains that discussion about the impact of education must be seen in a wider context:

> With control of the schools this indoctrination is easily sustained since a lack of genuine alternatives leads each new generation of indoctrinated and unquestioning Catholic parents to go along with the existing system. The schoolchildren reintroduce institutional adherence among the parents who may wish to avoid difficulties by not contradicting what is taught in school. While this argument has validity it does not take into account the crucial role, especially mothers, played in passing on the faith and in creating vocations. Nor does it take into account the importance which a control of Irish health and welfare has had in maintaining an adherence to Church rules and regulations once education has been completed (Inglis, 1987, p. 58).

Control over education, health and social welfare, however, by no means exhausts the range of expedients available to the Church; it has other ways of keeping its people in line; it has, in addition, a powerful parochial organisation centred on the parish priest. The priest in Ireland is a ubiquitous and powerful figure. According to Inglis (1997, pp. 42-3) he is a spiritual and moral adviser who is consulted on a wide range of social, political and economic issues. His formal status derives not just from being head of the parish, but also from being the manager of the local school, and traditionally one of the more refined and educated members of the community. Informally he is often the most respected member of the community. Any outsider or group which becomes involved in the parish, whether at a social, political, or economic level, will usually make contact with the parish priest. There is rarely any local committee or social occasion of importance which he is not asked to attend. It is as the guardian of virtue and morality that he can have most influence. He is the one who supervises access to social and moral respectability.

In 1981 there were 3,653 diocesan clergy in Ireland, giving Ireland a ratio of one priest for every 978 of its Roman Catholic inhabitants - this is one of the best priest-people ratios in the world and compares very favourably to ratios prevailing in other Roman Catholic countries, i.e. Italy one to 1398, France one to 1445, Poland one to 2,200 and Portugal one to 2,460 (Inglis, 1987, p. 41). These are the front-line troops of the Church, charged with responsibility for maintaining the faith and morals of the people. Ultimately their power rests in knowledge of their parishioners and in the sanctions which they have at their disposal. Knowledge is acquired through the supervisory agencies of the confessional, visitations and the parish grapevine. Confession clearly gives the priest the opportunity to interrogate his people closely, in secret and against the background of a very severe sanction: the denial of absolution, which, for the penitent, means that the sins confessed will remain unforgiven and thus render him or her ineligible for salvation. Home visitations, however informal and friendly they may be, have a definite supervisory and investigative purpose designed to reveal whether and to what extent the members of that household are adhering to the rules and regulations of the Church. Thus, according to one priest,

> At some stage or stages in the informal chat there must be spiritual welfare business and investigation, e.g. "I suppose you have the family rosary" or "I'm sure have all made the Easter duty." The question about the rosary should be asked only to keep them at it (quoted in Abbot, 1961, p. 10).

The parish grapevine is another valuable source of information about peoples' behaviour. Given the priest's high social standing lay people in the parish derive social prestige from being on close terms with him, and will usually tell him about those who are behaving in morally suspicious ways, becoming, in effect, a sort of auxiliary force to the priest (Inglis, 1987, p. 44). According to Abbot (1961, p. 9),

> People will certainly from time to time drop useful hints or volunteer information about neighbours. If they do so, the priest need not block his ears. After a short time he should resume the conversation ignoring the hints and the information. These hints,

however, may furnish reasons for vigilance and direct enquiries.

If Irish priests are usually able to keep themselves informed about the doings of their flocks, they are also in a position to apply powerful sanctions to those who fail to cultivate the good life as the Church ordains. The priest's power here rests in the fact that he is the mediator between God and the people, who require his mediations, not least through the sacraments of confession, communion and the last rites, in order to be saved. The denial of absolution in confession, or worse excommunication, are thus no small matters to believing Roman Catholics. And nor indeed are the possibilities of open censure and public denunciation by the clergy; it is still, especially in rural Ireland, difficult, if not impossible, to retain one's social prestige if one is publicly denounced by a priest - and, in any case, many Irish employers have traditionally asked job applicants to provide a reference from their parish priest (Inglis, 1987, p. 42).

In addition to the above it must be remembered that the Roman Catholic Church in Ireland has enormous powers of patronage which it can, and does, use for purposes of social control. In 1982 the Church in Ireland owned or operated 2,639 churches, 219 religious houses of priests, 213 religious houses of brothers, 859 convents, 591 charitable institutions, 3,844 primary schools and 900 secondary schools. The Church, therefore, controls the appointments, and career prospects, of large numbers of teachers, doctors, nurses and welfare personnel. Loyalty to Church teachings is thus a criterion governing appointment and advancement in these employments, so it will not profit a Catholic working in the health and education fields to openly dissent from his or her Church. As Inglis (1987, p. 71) points out:

> Religion and morality are public matters in Ireland. Teachers, nurses and doctors can be under an obligation to behave in a manner deemed moral by the Church. If they do not they may be regarded as potentially some kind of traitor who can undermine the loyalty of others. As an editorial in the *Irish Rosary* put it: 'We allow no claim to good will come from those brought up in the Catholic faith if they abandon it, but we can admire the good faith of those born outside the Church, even while we detest their errors'.

In 1985 the Catholic School Manager's Association issued guidelines concerning the appointment of teachers which required, *inter alia*, that appointees should be practicing Roman Catholics, and in the same year a judgement from the Irish High Court implied that a secondary school was justified in sacking a teacher whose private life did not conform to the norms and values promulgated by the Roman Catholic Church (Inglis, 1987, pp. 55, 58).

The vast array of buildings owned and controlled by the Church has to be maintained and serviced, and their inhabitants - and there were over 21,000 of them in 1982 - have to be fed and watered, meaning, of course, that the Church is a lucrative source of business for local contractors, suppliers and merchants of various sorts. Being a 'good Catholic' and on

214

'good terms' with the religious establishment is unlikely to be a hindrance to those who compete for the custom of the vast clerical organisation, while, judging from the tenor of the *Irish Rosary* editorial, open dissent from the Church could clearly be very costly in business terms. And this observation by no means applies only to business people in their dealings with clerical customers; it applies equally to their dealings with the Catholic laity.

The Church is, therefore, in a position of very great power in Irish society; as a moral entrepreneur its position is supreme; it is far and a way the most influential institution in Irish society, indeed, it would probably be true to say that no church anywhere in the world has a power, influence and institutional presence that is equal, let alone superior, to the power, influence and institutional presence of Irish Roman Catholicism. The Church, as we have seen, has a large and effective organisation. Its priests enjoy great prestige; they are involved and influential in all important departments of life and are in a strong position to morally supervise and control their flocks. The Church is in an overwhelmingly dominant position in education; it has the mind of almost every Irish Catholic child under its control and so has enormous influence over the secondary socialisation process. It has a large presence in health and welfare provision, which together with its control over education, and its organisational needs, give it extensive powers of patronage. It enjoys the support of governments and of a loyal people. This is crucial: Roman Catholicism does not have to impose itself on the majority of the Irish; it enjoys the loyalty and willing support of large numbers because, as we have seen, of the close identification of Catholicism with Irishness in the canon. Its greatest strength probably lies here; the Irish have never been troubled by anything in the nature of a serious anti-clericalism.

Prioritisation and regulation: final comments

Like all branches of the Christian Church, Roman Catholicism is concerned, first and above all, with the salvation of the soul. Believing Roman Catholics, therefore, have their minds fixed on this issue; it is instilled into their consciousness from the primary school onwards that the achievement of salvation must be their first and most fundamental objective, to which all else must be subordinated. From this it follows that the minds of believing Roman Catholics are fixed on the afterlife; for them the really crucial question is: what will be the destination of my soul after my death? According to Roman Catholic teaching three destinations are possible: heaven - in which the soul enjoys an eternity of bliss in the sight of God; hell - in which the soul is deprived of God and is subjected to an eternity of suffering as a result; and purgatory - an intermediate zone of purification. In the light of these considerations the crucial question now becomes: what determines the destination of the believer's soul after he or she dies?

To the Roman Catholic view a believer can attain to heaven provided he or she dies without mortal sin and with a sufficient amount of merit earned through the performance of good works performed in the faith, i.e.

in loyal obedience to the laws and teachings of the Church. To die in mortal sin and out of the faith, i.e. in a condition of rebellion against the laws and teachings of the Church, will result in the certain loss of heaven and thus an eternity of damnation in hell. Roman Catholicism, however, also recognises an intermediate state between the two extremes of heaven and hell. This is purgatory. As its name implies this is taken to be a place of purification; it receives the souls of Christians who die in a state of venial sin, i.e. sin which is not grave enough to justify damnation, but which needs to be purged in the intermediate state before the soul is spiritually clean enough to enter heaven. Purgatory is thus a zone of spiritual transition; those whose souls are confined there will be purged of guilt, and will, eventually, enjoy the bliss of heaven.

The Church, therefore, seeks to convince its children that their principle end in life must be the salvation of their souls. It also makes it clear to them that this end can only be achieved by loyalty to the Church and its teachings; outside the Church there is no salvation, and Roman Catholics must, in consequence, remain loyal to the Church and cultivate the good life as defined by the Church as the only legitimate interpreter of God's laws and commandments. Of course the Church recognises that human beings are frail creatures and that not all believers will be equally committed to, or capable of, living lives of ethical perfection as defined by Divine laws. The Church, however, holds itself to be more than just the supreme and authoritative interpreter of God's laws; it is also the dispenser of His grace and mercy. The Roman Catholic Church is, therefore, in every sense the mediator between the believer and his or her God; it is through the Church that believers learn what kind of life God requires them to lead; it is through the Church, and only through the Church, that they have access to God's grace and mercy.

Grace and mercy are controlled and mediated by the Church through the media of the sacraments and indulgences. Sacraments are institutional mechanisms through which some gift of God, which is held to be beneficial to his or her spiritual welfare, is communicated and given to the believer - in the sacrament of penance (confession), for example, believers' sins are forgiven and penances are imposed and discharged; in holy communion the believer is fed and strengthened by the body and blood of Christ. Indulgences are remissions of the punishment which is due to sin. As the imposition of penance after confession suggests, the forgiveness of sins does not imply that the believer will not suffer some punishment for his or her infractions of the moral code - believers cannot expect to get away 'scot free', as it were, if only because justice requires that some price must be paid for the sins committed, either in this life or in purgatory. Indulgences are remissions of some or all of this price. According to Roman Catholic teaching they are available to believers because exemplary Christians through the ages have, by the sheer ethical quality of their lives, earned more merit than they needed to enter heaven. This surplus merit is stored up in a sort of treasury which is at the disposal of the Church, which, through the mechanism of indulgences, can apply it to less worthy believers in order to give them some remission from the punishment due to their transgressions. Believers can obtain these indulgences by various means; they are attached, for example, to the saying of certain prayers and the performance of certain rites and ritual practices and to the wearing of holy medals and other emblems of the faith. The effect of indulgences is ultimately to shorten the time spent in purgatory by those who die in venial sin and/or with some punishment outstanding. This period can also be reduced through the agency of having Masses read for the souls of those who have died; it is quite a common thing for Roman Catholics to make bequests of sums of money to priests for the purposes of having Masses celebrated for the benefit of their souls; relatives of those who have have died also quite commonly have Masses said for the repose of the souls of the deceased persons.

Control over the Church's teaching and grace dispensing activities is a monopoly of its sacerdotal establishment; lay people play no significant part in the government of the Church and have no input into the formation of its teachings, doctrines and policies; the Church is not, and neither claims nor pretends to be a democracy, which derives its power and authority from its people, but is a hierarchical bureaucracy dominated by its clergy which rules the lives of its people on the basis of the claim that its authority derives from God. Roman Catholics do not, therefore, enjoy freedom of conscience, at least in any sense of that term as it might be understood by Protestants or secular-liberals. Inglis (1987, p. 39) is able to quote some episcopal authority on this point:

> The Church necessarily advocates a legalistic adherence to its rules and regulations. It discourages following one's own conscience because, as the Irish hierarchy put it, 'it can err, and in fact often does' [Irish Episcopal Conference, 1980]. Faithful Catholics are expected to accept all the Church's teachings. As Bishop Newman of Limerick put it, there are 'some Catholics [who] manage to persuade themselves that they are faithful to their Church even though they reject some points of its teaching' [quoted in *Irish Times*, 1981]. To make a moral decision, according to the Irish hierarchy, the individual conscience must not only be informed, it 'must be guided by Church authority'. In other words, it is permissible for a Catholic to follow his or her own conscience as long as it is guided by Church principles and does not contravene any specific regulation. As the Bishops' pastoral put it: 'It is for conscience to consider each new situation in the light of the overall command of love and the relevant moral values, and make the appropriate response. This response must always be in accordance with the specific commandments of God, as authoritatively interpreted by the Church, and must never violate the prohibitions contained in them [Irish Episcopal Conference, 1980].

From these statements it is clear that what the Irish Roman Catholic Church requires from its lay members is obedience; the good Catholic is one who receives the sacraments, keeps the Church's laws and cultivates the virtue of innocence in the 'simple faith' in which individuals do not question their religion or its sacerdotal representatives (Inglis, 1987, p. 2). Obviously this provides lay Roman Catholics with very little incentive to engage intellectually, let alone critically, with the tenets of their faith and with the sacerdotal establishment which is responsible for propagating it. While the Irish Roman Catholic Church has, therefore, succeeded in maintaining high levels of religious observance among the faithful, of which more anon, the associated patterns of religiosity have tended to be unreflectively legalistic, based on submission to Church law and authority rather than on ethical principles which are understood and adopted for their own sake (Inglis, 1987, pp. 24-26; O'Doherty, 1969, p. 588). Submission to priestly authority rather than individual conscience is the required norm for Irish Catholics.

The formalistic patterns of religiosity, the submission to priestly authority, and the omnipresence of the priest in so many walks of life, tend to support the claims made by McCarthy and Plunkett which we noted in Chapter 6 touching on the lack of independence from sacerdotalism that was characteristic of the Irish Catholic people. From where we stand, however, that is not the most important issue. This lies rather with the matters of prioritisation and regulation which we were discussing earlier.

From all that has been said thus far there can be no question that the believing Roman Catholic must make the salvation of the soul his or her number one priority. Salvation, therefore, becomes, for the Catholic, the ultimate rationalising term governing life and activity. By what means can salvation, or more properly the believers' subjective assurance of salvation, be achieved? Again the answers to this question are very clear: Loyalty to the Church; acceptance of its doctrines; obedience to its laws through the living of a life that is consistent with Catholic faith and morals in which believers do their duty. All these are merit-earning acts; works of devotion, piety and charity, the grounds on which believers can 'earn' the price of their passage to bliss in the future life. In addition believers are enjoined and encouraged in the regular use and reception of the Church's means of grace; these are important duties, and indeed vital helps to Heaven, since forgiveness, grace and remission of punishment due to ethical transgressions are imparted to sinners through the sacraments and indulgences.

According to the *Catechism of Catholic Doctrine* the commandments of the Church are as follows:

1. First: To hear Mass on Sundays and holydays of obligation.
2. Second: To fast and abstain on the days appointed.
3. Third: To confess our sins at least once a year.
4. Fourth: To receive worthily the Blessed Eucharist at Easter time.
5. Fifth: To contribute to the support of our pastors.
6. Sixth: To observe the marriage laws of the Church (quoted in Inglis, 1987, pp. 24-5).

The general purport of these precepts is, we think, clear enough; the first four are of a formal devotional character, the fifth has to do with the material maintenance of the sacerdotal establishment, and only one, the sixth, has any reference to what we might term worldly activity. Here the reference is to the marriage laws of the Church, laws which are directed towards upholding the Church's view of the sanctity of that estate, its sacramental character, its indissolubility, its procreative purpose and to the protection of the faith by the imposition of decrees requiring non-Roman Catholic partners in mixed marriages to bring their offspring up in the Catholic faith. These emphases are, of course, closely related to the Church's concern with the regulation of the body and of sexual activity in the interests of maintaining purity. The Irish Roman Catholic Church places great emphasis on sins against chastity and purity and tries to ensure public regulation of behaviour in accordance with the reference of the precepts. In contrast there is no reference at all to economic life or civic duties to be found in the precepts, though these are, of course, implied in the *Decalogue* with its proscriptions of stealing and lying and its requirement to neighbourly love, which the Church also upholds. Nevertheless, the truth is that the matters covered in the six precepts are also implied in the Ten Commandments - if we possibly except some of the specific references in Catholic marriage laws. Yet, and this is the significant point, the Church has clearly thought it expedient to set them forth expressly for the edification of its flock. This must indicate that it attaches a special importance to them and wants to elevate them, and fix them especially strongly in believers' minds.

We are not criticising the Roman catholic Church and its priorities; we are simply observing that it has those priorities and that its most cherished precepts have no reference to economic life and civic morals. Some readers may wish to chide us, at this point, for, by implication at any rate, expecting the Church to become involved in areas which, it could be argued, do not lie fully within its jurisdiction. Arguments of this kind can, indeed, be reasonable and there are circumstances in which we would certainly accept them and eschew any specific concern with the Church's role and influence on economic behaviour. The circumstances concerned are those which relate to situations in which the socialisation and education and training of the young are under secular control; circumstances in which Church activity is confined to catechising and in which all other responsibilities devolve on those who are outside of its control and supervision. As we know by now such a situation does not obtain in Ireland. There the Church has demanded, and been granted, effective control over the education system; it does not confine itself to a limited role of catechising and allow others to handle the remainder in conditions of independence from its control and influence. It insists that its influence shall be all-pervading; it requires that education shall be given in an atmosphere that is permeated by religion and it has achieved its objective. As a result its responsibilities go beyond catechising and extend to everything connected with the preparation of the young for their lives in this and in the next world. As we saw above, it has educated the Irish Catholic elite, and has done so with a clear idea of how important it is that their education should be, from its own point of view, a sound education. Since it has not, publicly at any rate, indulged in any paroxysms of self-criticism touching on the moral effectiveness of its superior education, we must conclude that it is content with the job that it is doing.

In Ireland, therefore, it is true to say that the legions of tax evaders, 'Phoenix syndrome' operators, fraudsters, smugglers and easy-going, ethically indifferent farmers and entrepreneurs, whose conduct has been described in these pages, together with those who are formally or informally in a position to regulate their activities, are, for the most part products of the Church thanks to its general influence and its control over secondary socialisation. Its influence on prioritisation and regulation is, therefore, quite crucial and, as we shall show, turns very much on the prioritisation expressed in the six precepts. These are singled out, given the highest priority and are subject to strong regulative review. Economic life, by comparison, is accorded little salience; it has no relation to religion or to any kind of duty, being, to remember, but a means to the end of maintaining life's comforts.

The six precepts outlined above are important in two senses: Firstly, because adherence to them provides believers with an assurance that they are on the right road to salvation. Secondly, because in a Roman Catholic country in which they have the sanction of public opinion, public adherence to them becomes essential to the maintenance of believers' good standing in their communities. The regulative emphasis on the terms of the precepts derives very strongly from the force of public opinion acting on the State and on individuals. In relevant areas, not least those having to do with Catholic marriage laws and sexual regulation, the State has taken a leading role. For the rest, individuals whose internal motives for compliance are weak or non-existent face the sanctions of public opinion.

We can begin to demonstrate the truth of these propositions from a brief review of the regulative activities of the independent Irish legislature. In independent Ireland publications and films were quickly brought under a censorship that was designed to exclude material that was offensive to Roman Catholic morality, especially sexual morality; divorce was proscribed and was ultimately made unconstitutional; contraception was outlawed; abortion was made, and remains, unconstitutional. All these regulative activities clearly reflect the matter of the sixth precept, having to do, for the most part, with the indissolubility and procreative purposes of the marriage bond and with the control of sexuality. These measures were not imposed upon a reluctant or indifferent public; they were overwhelmingly supported by the public, which often mobilised and agitated for them, and whose members were evidently ever-vigilant in defence of Irish culture against the vulgar and the profane. Although we could provide many, two examples from the late nineteen-fifties will demonstrate the strength of opinion point well enough. The first concerns a proposal by the Dublin Theatre Festival to stage a play by Sean O'Casey and a dramatic realisation of Joyce's *Bloomsday*. Brown (1985, p. 229) can be allowed to take up the story:

> When it became evident that the Archbishop of Dublin, John Charles McQuaid, was opposed to the production of the O'Casey play and of *Bloomsday* (he had been asked, unwisely, to open the Festival with a Votive Mass) and when powerful representatives of public opinion including Dublin trade unions supported his view, the organisers withdrew the play (they were bound by their constitution to avoid controversy) and eventually cancelled the festival for that year.

220

The second example concerns an attempt to stage a performance of Tennessee Williams's *The Rose Tattoo* by Alan Simpson. For his pains Simpson was arrested and charged with 'presenting for gain an indecent and profane performance'. As Brown (1985, pp. 239-40) tells us, Simpson:

> was charged on a summary warrant normally used only to arrest armed criminals and members of the IRA, refused to give an undertaking that he would withdraw the play and stood trial. Released on bail he decided that the play should continue and before the next performance the entire cast was advised by the police that by appearing in such a play they ran the risk of arrest.

Fortunately for him Simpson was acquitted at his subsequent trial.

Irish censorship is nothing like so draconian these days; the supporters of the Catholic-nationalist canon have had to make some concessions to a growing body of liberal opinion touching on regulation of the arts and the media. Nevertheless, the fact that, in the last decade or so, the upholders of the canon were able to mobilise opinion to an extent sufficient to have a prohibition against abortion built into the constitution, and to defeat an attempt to remove the constitutional prohibition on divorce, demonstrates that they are still a potent force - both achievements required majorities in referenda. The fact that the upholders of the canon instituted no similar mobilisation in the interests of dealing with tax evaders speaks eloquently to the point we are making: namely, that sexual morality, and thus its regulation, is seen as far more important than economic or civic morality.

The ability to control access to respectability is a useful regulative device, made more useful by reference to the fact that the Church, in many cases, controls access to employment - through its direct patronage in education and social services, its moral influence on medical and social ethics and the influence of the priestly reference on behalf of the hopeful job applicant. The regulative power results from, and is a result of, the Irish Church's phenomenal success in maintaining the loyalty of its flock; a comparative survey carried out in the nineteen-eighties found that eighty-two per cent of Irish Catholics attended weekly Mass, compared to only forty-one per cent in Spain and thirty-six per cent in Italy (Fogarty, Ryan and Lee, 1984, pp. 125-6). Visitors to Ireland will find, in addition, a formidable array of evidence confirming the strong attachment to the faith; shrines and grottoes abound; religious symbols are everywhere, in the home and in public places; pilgrimages and other devotional activities are popular; support for religious causes is widespread, including support for missionary endeavours and for the relief of suffering in the poorer countries, in the furtherance of which causes the Irish display a caritavistic devotion which is second to none. Opinion in Ireland is still, therefore, very much Catholic opinion; generous and open and loyal to the precepts of its Church.

It is from this loyalty, of course, that the weight of regulation ultimately derives and ensures that those who have 'lost the faith', or are lukewarm in their dispositions, remain outwardly conformist and do not, in public at any rate, criticise the Church and try to undermine its influence. The following case, reported by Paul Blanchard (1953, p. 186) illustrates the point nicely:

> Dr. X and his wife, both baptised Catholics, have long ceased to believe in the major Catholic doctrines. In private conversation they express strong criticism of priestly policy. When Dr. X started to drift away from the Church openly by failing to attend Mass, he was warned by the priest. Now he attends conspicuously with his wife 'I must live you know', he says, 'My practice would disappear if I were branded as a lapsed Catholic.

In the same vein Whyte (1984, P. 313) quotes the examples of two ex cabinet ministers who had ceased to believe, but who would not say so in public. He also provides us with the following amusing example, citing a letter written to a newspaper by a member of the Irish Parliament which was critical of a bishop. Part of the letter reads as follows:

> I, as a member of the Dail, neither now or at any other time in the future will accept dictation from the bishops, or from a bishop, on matters of a political nature; and, even if it meant retiring from public life as a result of making a stand on this question, I would gladly do so.

Alas, as Whyte (1984, p. 313) notes:

> these fighting words were belied by the end of the letter. He concluded: 'I am not signing my name to this letter, because I do not want to finish my political career before it starts ... I hate but one thing, hypocrisy! Yours, etc. "Quo Vadis"'.

In circumstances like these it is easy to appreciate the sentiments which a frightened dissenting Catholic expressed in 1983, when explaining his failure to speak out against the Church: 'you'd be destroyed - you'd be ostracised' for doing so (quoted in Inglis, 1987, p. 72). In the same vein booksellers, chemists and other traders, in some areas of the country, would not carry, at least openly, items that offended Catholic tastes and morals; to do so would provoke too many into withdrawing their custom (Inglis, 1987, p. 71).

The objects of the regulative activity we have described, once again, lie in the six precepts; predicated as it often is to the view that those who do not conform may undermine the faith and morals of others, it is directed towards securing outward loyalty to the Church in terms of obedience to the precepts. Any reference to economic activity under the rubric of faith and morals is, however, not in evidence, and the result is that Ireland presents a strange 'contrast of the moralities': high levels of religious observance in terms of the precepts of the Church coupled with low levels of economic and civic morality. It is very difficult to avoid the conclusion that this is, indeed, the result of the circumstances we have described: the low view of economic life expressed in the Catholic-nationalist canon, which, in stripping it of moral significance, also stripped the sins associated with it of moral significance. It is not the case that the Irish do not uphold morality, rather that morality as they conceive it touches economic activity with the lightest of hands. As a result:

> Irishmen see little wrong with living only for themselves. In Ireland the term vocation has only a religious connotation. In the secular field the Irish follow careers they find profitable, and not those for which they are naturally adapted. This is not seen as reflecting a professed obligation to develop their own talents and to give of their best to society. Archbishop Temple's view that to choose a career on selfish grounds is the 'greatest single sin an individual can commit' is incomprehensible to the Irish .... So profound, indeed, has been the social failure of Irish Catholicism that those who live outside convent or monastery are mostly in a moral wilderness (Sheehy, 1968, pp. 212-213).

For Sheehy the most striking feature of this 'moral wilderness' is tax evasion coupled with the 'remarkable fact' that:

> the Irish clergy connive at this fraud, treating infringements of the tax code as penal not moral. The argument of the clergy seems to be that since wholesale fraud exists, in fact, the individual is justified in treating the particular charge made on him as exorbitant; thus overlooking the consideration that, in exonerating the defaulters from blame, they help to perpetuate an unjust charge on [those who have to pay, because their incomes are taxed at source, or who choose to do so on grounds of civic morality] (Sheehy, 1968, p. 121 and see also Blanchard, 1954, pp. 178-9).

The clerical response which Sheehy describes does 'make sense' when viewed in a certain way. If a society fails to socialise the 'virtues' of 'honesty, integrity and hard and purposeful work' then it will inevitably create an environment in which the cultivation of these 'virtues' will simply not 'pay off'. The fact that a Parliamentary committee can report that 'Businesses which have tried to observe the law have been decimated' (*Oireachtas Eareann,* 1964, p. 16), suggests that Ireland is, indeed, such an environment. Orientation to traditionalistic values has, therefore, created a bahavioural environment which reinforces and thus perpetuates the values; those who try to break the pattern through the exercise of the 'virtues' of 'honesty, integrity and hard and purposeful work' in the interests of growing a business are confronted, on the one hand, by the resentment of those who wish to preserve the traditionalistic status order, and who, in Quinn's words, 'rip them to pieces', and, on the other, by pressure from operators whose disregard for the law and for the niceties of commercial and civic morality damage them through unfair competition and by alienating potential customers. We are not, to remember, arguing that there are not external obstacles lying in the path of Ireland's progress to development-achievement; we are not suggesting that Irish economic actors could make history just as they pleased. What will now be evident, however, is that there are also barriers within Ireland, internal obstacles lying in the value system from which the traditionalistic patterns of low prioritisation and weak regulation derive, find their sanction and their legitimacy, and in the behaviour patterns which result from, and reinforce, the orientations derived from the values. The result is a stultifying and self-reinforcing traditionalism which has hindered the achievement of effective economic development, and which continues to do so to this day.

Conclusion

It is now time to sum up, not only the chapter, but the book as a whole. Before we do so, however, it will do no harm to say a few words about the nature and purpose of the argument in the book. To begin with we are not arguing that the cultural values to which actors relate their economic interests are the only significant determinant of development; we do not wish to place a naive over-emphasis on culture and subjective factors, especially in terms of generalisation from the Irish case to other less developed countries which are not as fortunately placed with reference to objective facors, i.e. means and opportunities as Ireland is. This is a study of a particular economy and society, one that is predicated to the view that a detailed study of objective factors is necessary before any judgement concerning the impact of culture on economic development can be entered in respect of any society. We have tried to provide such a study, but one that is clearly delimited to the Irish case. It is not to be generalised beyond it.

Nor should our study be taken as claiming that culture is the only significant variable in the Irish case. We are not, in other words, trying to argue that objective factors are not of some significance and are such as to permit of Ireland becoming the economic equal of Germany or Japan. All we are suggesting is that Ireland had the potential - and still has - to develop more than she has, and we are arguing only that culture has militated against her achieving this, not that it has prevented her from becoming an economic superpower. That much will, we hope, be evident.

In introducing this book we went to some lengths to emphasise that we were not intending to make moral judgements about either the behaviour, or the cultural values, we were trying to describe and analyse. As far as we are concerned there are no objective grounds available to us, or to anyone else, on which to base value judgements on cultural values; different cultures are not superior or inferior, they are just different and that is all. Technical judgements are possible in terms that relate to specific purposes, but that is as far as it is possible, or indeed, necessary to go. Any judgements entered in this book are of this kind; the terms that we have employed have to do with the suitability of behaviours and values as means to the end of achieving economic development. We have tried to show that Irish orientations are not best suited and we have tried to set out the grounds on which we have arrived at this conclusion. In doing so we are not judging the behaviour as good or bad; we are not approving or disapproving.

We have, it is true, employed terms which have ethical connotations; we have described behaviour as ethically unregulated and characterised it as amoral, anti-social and greedy. We have used these terms with regret precisely because they are open to misunderstanding. We have used them only because they seemed necessary to the business of capturing the meanings of actions. We are creatures of our culture, we have learned its vocabulary, through which, of course, we have to interpret and express meaning. Although many of the terms we have used carry evaluative connotations, they are also descriptive terms in the vocabulary which our culture - Irish culture - has given us. As English speaking Irishmen we understand from our dictionaries that words like 'greed', 'selfishness', and 'amoral' and 'anti-social' can be applied to describe states of mind as expressed through peoples' activities and the observed consequences of those activities. 'Greed', for example, refers to appetite, desire for possession. 'Moral' has to do with questions of virtue, of right and wrong. The term 'selfish' also has a clear descriptive reference; we apply it to action which appears to be devoid of reference to others; to behaviour which is 'anti-social' in the sense that the actor performing an act is unconcerned with the objective consequences which the act entails for others. All the terms under discussion, and other morally-loaded terms used in this book, are used descriptively. When we characterise behaviour as 'selfish' and 'anti-social', we do so because these terms describe its objective consequences: namely, hurt and harm to others. Likewise when we employ the term 'amoral' we do so in order to describe behaviour which seems to have no roots in morality as our culture understands the term; the reference is not to some view of our own, but to the conventional view of morality holding in our culture, which, descriptively, still holds, for example, that it is formally wrong to steal. As citizens, of course, we uphold that value. As social analysts, however, we are morally blind. All we are doing is saying that a culture has a formal, conventional moral view, and that many in that society evidently disregard it and so engage in behaviour that is, in that society's terms, amoral, something that enables us to conclude that, since actors are allowed to persist in deviant behaviour, the moral order may, at points, be an empty formalism as opposed to a guide to peoples' actual behaviour. The framework is descriptive. Moral judgements, on our part, are neither called for nor entered.

Nor is it any part of our purpose here to argue that there is anything in Gaelic culture and the Irish language and traditions that is incompatible with modernisation; as the Japanese, Germans, Danes and many other peoples have demonstrated a distinctive culture and a national language, and a strong desire to protect both, are no barriers to the achievement of the highest levels of economic development. What applies to these countries applies equally to the case of Ireland. All we are saying here is that, at a crucial time in Ireland's economic and social development, the Catholic-nationalist identity was moulded by people whose concerns were far removed from those of modern industrial life; by people who despised industrial modernity and its spirit, who believed it to be inferior to what the Irish had and who sought, in consequence, to preserve and propagate an ethos of a restorationist kind. Parsons describes the consequences of

225

nationalism of the restorationist kind very well when he notes (1960, p. 121) that:

> nationalism and the search for a new independent status necessarily activates *conservative* elements in the indigenous social structure. Independence inevitably tends to be interpreted, to some extent, as 'restoration' of a pre-colonial system, with renewed freedom for the implementation of the *traditional* values of the society. Such restoration is, however, directly inimical to economic development.(emphasis in the original)

The reason for this is not far to seek. As Goldring (1987, p. 42) tells us:

> The colonizing power is usually a source of modernisation and the colony is a zone of archaism which provides primary materials. So modernisation acts from the 'outside' whilst what is inside comes from the past.

Restorationism thus involves a turning inwards and backwards; it is a reaction in favour of archaism and against the processes and values of modern industrial society. The result is a canonisation of tradition and a strongly negative characterisation of all that is seen to stand opposed to it. What counts as virtue in modernity can thus all too easily be counted as a vice in the traditionalist scheme of things; modernity's belief in the virtue of progress couched in terms of material prosperity can be designated a vice; its belief in the virtues of tolerance and pluralism, insofar as they indulge secularism, can be seen as a vice; its equation of virtue with the industrial character and the industrial spirit can likewise be interpreted as vicious and depraved; the modernist's positive value in occupational diligence and thrift can all too easily be characterised by the traditionalist as cunning and cupidity. All that we have tried to do is to show that the Irish, for what seemed to them to be good and sufficient reasons, took the anti-modernist option, and trace out the consequences of their having done so.

Our argument is, therefore, an argument about cultural choice. Nothing in these pages should be taken as suggesting in any degree that there is some inherent defect in the character of the Irish people - racist claptrap of that, or of any kind, is beyond the pale of this discourse. The Irish opted for what they took to be a defensible ideal of civilisation. If, for example, the Irish had a thrusting industrialising bourgeoisie - and as the nineteenth century experience of the Six Counties demonstrates, they might well have done so if their middle classes had not related to the cult of the aristocratic gentleman - and this bourgeoisie developed a love affair with a cultural nationalism then there is no reason why they, as opposed to any other group, could not have put their stamp on nationalism and made Ireland Gaelic and industrial; we know of no reason why Gaelic culture could not have been adapted to such a purpose, just as other cultures were. And the same thought, of course, applies to Roman Catholicism. Roman Catholic countries like Belgium achieved industrialisation and modernisation, so we cannot say that Roman Catholicism per se is inimical to industrial development. There are grounds for believing that it is less accommodating to certain aspects of bourgeois individualism than certain branches of Protestantism have been, but that is not to say that it is incapable of 'coming on board' in a modern industrial economy and society. Our remarks about Roman Catholicism must not, therefore, be carelessly generalised beyond the Irish case; the Church does not live in isolation from the material circumstances of its members, and, after all, draws its priests from the ranks of its members. It would be surprising if, in these circumstances, the Irish Church did not reflect and edify what it did reflect and edify; it drew its leaders from middle Ireland and so reflected its outlook and concerns. If it had drawn them from other strata, or from middle strata that were differently circumstanced, a different outcome might have ensued.

Nor should anything in this text be taken as suggesting that we hold the view that nationalism is bad for development. It is not nationalism, as such, but the character of nationalism that matters. Nationalism can act to inspire actors in the economic as much as in any other sphere. And with reference to Denmark, for example, there is evidence which suggests that nationalism did precisely this. For example,

> The idea of reclaiming the moors of Central and West Jutland was a century old but in the thirty years after 1850 half of it was accomplished. In part it was a patriotic response to the call for action after the loss of Schleswig Holstein. 'What we have lost without we will gain within.' Indeed much of Danish history in the middle and later nineteenth century was marked by this kind of emotion and in this instance the long run economic benefits were highly satisfactory, though not surprisingly the short run effect of reclamation was to reduce overall agricultural productivity quite markedly (Milward and Saul, 1973, pp. 502-3).

Danish nationalism, therefore, took an economistic turn and seems to have produced a people with an enthusiasm for new ideas, rather than an unbending traditionalism. The reason for this is not fully clear, though many writers trace the development to the influence of the Folk High Schools. These were the inspiration of the poet, historian and churchman Bishop Grundvig. Grundvig (1783-1872) was evidently a remarkable man; having experienced Denmark's humiliation in the Napoleonic wars, he came to share the widespread desire for Danish freedom and democracy and was also much influenced by the economic and social development of Britain. Grundvig founded the Folk High Schools with a definite view to securing democracy, fostering a sense of Danishness and building up the cultural and material standards of the people. The schools are widely credited with breaking down conservatism and hostility to new ideas and with stimulating 'a democratic approach to both political and economic problems' (Milward and Saul, 1973, p. 509). While the Folk High Schools cannot be seen in isolation - Denmark instituted compulsory education for children between seven and fourteen in 1814 and began to develop schools of agriculture from 1867 - they seem to have inculcated a high appreciation of Danish language and culture in combination with a strong taste for economic and material progress. Without this Milward and Saul argue that the cooperative movements would have been less vigorous if those who ran them had not received from the High Schools a strong 'incentive to personal effort for a common as well as for a private good'. As a former pupil put matters in the eighteen-seventies:

> We did not talk much of what we had heard but all the more of the great things which we would still have time to do in this life ... As those who had been to High School grew older, and got families of their own, it was from their homes that progress got into its stride. It was these families that set up co-operative societies, co-operative stores, dairies and bacon factories ... (quoted in Milward and Saul, 1973, p. 509).

We have seen just how much those cooperatives achieved and compared the Danish and Irish economic performances. The one sanctified tradition and stagnated, the other valued progress and achieved.

One last point remains to be made before we close the account. It has to do with capitalism and ethical behaviour. To put the matter simply, we are not so naive as to believe that unethical activity in economic life is a uniquely Irish phenomenon. Far from it. As Sidney Pollard (1992, p. 147) reminds us:

> There has indeed never been any doubt that even in the most progressive economies, businessmen, managers, and workers will include illicit and immoral action in their repertoire of maximizing their gains, if they think they can get away with them. 'Institutional' economics and economic history are based on this recognition, and have been concerned for many years with describing these methods of maximisation as well as counting the costs of contract enforcements.

What is problematic about the Irish case, therefore, is not the presence of dishonesty, but rather the lengths to which it is carried, the rather relaxed attitude that is taken towards regulating it, and, not least, the fact that it is combined with a disinterest in economic productivity. We know of no North-western European country, for example, in which the ranks of legitimate businesses have been decimated by the activities of illicit operators; we know of no North-western European economy in which the capacity of firms to operate on export markets has been damaged by the illicit activities of other units in their economy, or by their manifest failures to attend to marketing, product specifications that are appropriate to markets, consistency and reliability of supply and feedback from customers. Although we have no evidence that they do, we are quite ready to accept the possibility that, the Danes for example, might not be averse to illicit gain-seeking through tax evasion and other unethical expedients - is any people, in its entirety, so saintly as to eschew such temptations? Nevertheless, and this is the point, they have not carried this interest through to the extent of indulging in self-destructive orgies of short-term gain seeking by selling 'bad eggs and worse butter' into a valuable export market; they have not combined it with a disinterest in productive activity, with a stultifying traditionalism, that has left the industries concerned with the processing of the natural resources at low level of development in terms of the value-added and the range and quality of the products marketed. Just the opposite is the case. As we have seen they set their food processing industries on a progressive, upward development curve; they attended to quality; they made sure that their product specifications were appropriate to the markets into which they wished to sell; they sought feedback from customers; they listened, they learned and put effort into marketing; they increased the amount of value added and extended their product ranges, responding dynamically and flexibly to the challenges which confronted them in the struggle to achieve growth and prosperity. The contrast with Ireland has already been drawn out at some length and the details need not be repeated. All that we need to do is to remember that the contrast is a powerful one in all respects; Irish processing remains, by comparison, somewhat basic, and, consisting as they do in a narrow range of low value-added commodity products, the character of its exports testifies to this fact loudly, clearly and trenchantly.

The truth, therefore, seems to be unavoidable: namely, that the Irish combination of low prioritisation and weak regulation is, by North-west European standards, quite exceptional. It is that combination that we have tried to describe and explain in the book we are now concluding. As we have demonstrated it is not possible to explain this combination - and Ireland's consequent failure to develop - exclusively by reference to objective factors lying in the structure of means and opportunities which Irish economic actors have had to confront. We were thus driven back to subjective factors, and to the cultural values to which Irish economic actors related their economic activities and so rendered them meaningful. In building up our explanation we showed that those parts of Ireland that escaped the large-scale influence of ascetic Protestantism oriented, in the nineteenth century, to an essentially pre-commercial value system rooted in the cult of aristocracy and peasant spontaneity, tendencies towards which the religion of the great majority - Roman Catholicism - offered no resistance and to which, indeed, it came to offer a more than tacit approval. We also showed that at a crucial point in its development, i.e. that of its national reawakening, Ireland was provided with a canon of Irishness worked out by priests, poets, revolutionaries and aristocrats who were remote from industrial and commercial life and who detested it. The adoption of this canon inhibited any move towards a more commercially appropriate value system, especially given that the Irish were able to insulate themselves from the pressures of the market which might, in other circumstances, have forced them out of the 'lethargy'. In the absence of pressure from the milieu, and with a value system which hallowed and sanctified their tradition, the Irish were enabled to go their own way; they learned to read the texts of their economic lives from a book a book of values which indicated to them that their approach was the proper Irish approach, good, moral and superior, and so to be cultivated and defended. The result was the stultifying traditionalism which have described. The traditionalism which has inhibited the economic development and modernisation of Ireland.

Before we conclude one final point needs to be made. Cultures are not, as we took care to observe, immutable; they are created by human beings and human beings can recreate and transform them. The Irish are no less capable of transforming their culture than any other people and there is no reason to think that they will not, ultimately, do so, developing, in the process, a regulative order which will be less tolerant of unethical and imprudent dealings and a climate of public opinion which will be more strident in demanding that those who have the privilege of owning and controlling resources take a more responsible and development-appropriate attitude to their use and deployment. Much of the evidence used in this book has come from a crop of growth-oriented Irish entrepreneurs and their supporters; these have broken the mould and the evidence which their comments provide is evidence, not only of the strength of the traditionalism, but also of the fact that a number of Irish economic activists are frustrated by it and are eager for, and demanding, change. As the evidence presented, and indeed their own comments, shows, they have a battle on their hands. Nevertheless, the battle is being fought, the traditionalism is coming under increasing scrutiny and challenge.

This little book is, of course, a part of the scrutiny, and may even, if people choose so to use it, become part of the challenge. As social scientists, however, we would wish to preserve a certain value neutrality. Our desire here does not stem from a pious ritualism, but rather from the view that we have no right to proclaim ourselves as moral entrepreneurs who go about offering gratuitous advice to people. All we can do is observe what we have observed: namely, that from the late nineteen-fifties Irish governments, supported by public opinion, promulgated the objective of economic development and modernisation: they willed the end. In continuing to conduct their economic lives traditionalistically, however, the Irish clearly have not come to will the means. Those who will an end, but who do not will the means, will travel long, and, no doubt, will travel hopefully. They will not arrive; their destination will remain beyond their reach and their grasp. As the remarks of the successful Irish entrepreneurs, Fergal Quinn, demonstrate well enough, there is a growing awareness that something needs to be done about this imbalance. We have cited Quinn before and we are now going to leave the last words of this book with him. As reported by Kerr (1986) Quinn's reflections convinced him that unless Irish attitudes to economic activity changed fundamentally no purely policy measures of a purely economic kind would stand much chance of success. That is a truth that seems to us to stand in contempt of question. If the Irish wish to develop, therefore, they can listen to Quinn and to others like him. They have no need of any further advice, least of all from us.

230

Bibliography

Abbot, J. (1961), 'Visitations by priests in Irish rural parishes', *Irish Ecclesiastical Record,* vol. XCVI.

Barry, G. et al. (1989a), 'Where's the beef?', *Sunday Tribune*, 19 March, Dublin.

Barry, G. et al. (1989b), 'Company boss "doesn't know who owner is"', *Sunday Tribune*, 19 March, Dublin.

Beach, K. (1988), 'Irish smugglers in gun battle with customs', *Independent*, 14 July, London.

Bell, B. (1987), 'IDA switch R&D emphasis to new products', *Irish Press,* 27 November, Dublin.

Black, R.D.C. (1960), *Economic Thought and the Irish Question 1817-1870,* Cambridge University Press, Cambridge.

Blanchard, P. (1953), *The Irish and Catholic Power,* Beacon Press, Boston.

Bonn, M. (1906), *Modern Ireland*, Hodges and Figgis, Dublin.

Boyle, G. (1987), *How Technically Efficient is Irish Agriculture? An Foras Taluntis,* Dublin.

Bradley, D. (1983), 'The Irish office market', *The Irish Banking Review,* September.

Browne, T. (1985), *Ireland: A Social and Cultural History,* Fontana, London.

Brunt, B. (1988), *The Republic of Ireland,* Chapman Publishing, London.

Burke, R. (1987), 'Meat plants must accept seized cattle', *Irish Press,* 18 Februrary, Dublin.

Carr, M. (1987), 'Planning laws - a speculators' charter', *New Hibernia,* August, Dublin.

Clarke, D. (1984), *Church and State,* Cork University Press, Cork.

Colley, D. (1989), 'Smuggling ring is smashed' *Evening Echo,* 21 December, *Cork.*

Connell, K. (1950), *The Population of Ireland 1750-1845,* Clarendon Press, Oxford.

Connell, K. (1968), *Irish Peasant Society,* Clarendon Press, Oxford.

Connellan, L. (1986), Statement quoted in *Irish Independent,* 17 August, Dublin.

Connolly, S. (1983), 'Religion, Work-Discipline and Economic Attitudes: The Case of Ireland'in Devine, T. and Dickson, D. (eds.), *Ireland and Scotland 1600-1859,* John Donald, Edinburgh.

Coogan, T.P. (1987), *Disillusioned Decades: Ireland 1966-87,* Gill and Macmillan, Dublin.

Cooper, C. and Whelan, N. (1973), 'Science, technology and industry in Ireland', Report to the National Science Council, The Stationery Office, Dublin.

Cooper, M. (1992a), '"We don't want the crumbs, we want the whole bakery"', *Sunday Business Post,* 2 August, Dublin.

Cooper, M. (1992b), '£60,000 payment links Haughey to Freezone: Desmond gave loan for repair of Haughey Yacht', *Sunday Business Post,* 9 August, Dublin.

Cork Examiner, (1988a), 'Priest, Gardai dodged tax', *Cork Examiner,* 12 February, Cork.

Cork Examiner, (1988b), 'Water scam leaves pubs high and dry', *Cork Examiner,* 18 July, Cork.

Cork Examiner, (1992), 'MacSharry: Beef Inquiry "witch hunt"', *Cork Examiner,* 25 August, Cork.

Crotty, R. (1986), *Ireland in Crisis: A Study in Capitalist Colonial Undevelopment,* Brandon, Dingle.

Cullen, L. (1969), 'Irish Economic History: Fact and Myth' in Cullen, L. (ed.), *The Formation of the Irish Economy,* Mercier Press, Cork.

Cullen, L. (1987), *An Economic History of Ireland Since 1660,* Batsford, London.

Cullen, T. (1988), 'Better incomes must be sought', *Cork Examiner, Farm Exam,* 7 July, Cork.

Curtis, E. (1942), *A History of Ireland,* Methuen, London.

Department of Finance, (1958), *Economic Development,* The Stationery Office, Dublin.

Dillon, W. and McKenna, G. (1990), 'Euro expert blasts Irish bad record on bovine TB', *Irish Independent,* 2 March, Dublin.

Doheny, F. (1990), 'Clampdown planned on companies' register', *Irish Press,* 4 March, Dublin.

Donahue, M. (1986), 'Irishness bad for tourism says co-op boss', *Irish Press,* 28 November, Dublin.

Dooley, C. (1989), 'Storm over TB as vets blame ICOS', *Irish Press,* 5 September, Dublin.

Downes, M. (1991), 'Survey shows alarming lack of preparedness', *Sunday Business Post,* 13 January, Dublin.

Evening Herald, (1988), 'Customs clash', *Evening Herald,* 26 April, Dublin.

Flaherty, B. (1987), 'Farm drugs treason: vets', *Irish Independent*, 7 December, Dublin.

Fogarty, M. (1973), *Irish Entrepreneurs Speak for Themselves*, Economic and Social Research Institute, Dublin.

Fogarty, M., Ryan, L. and Lee, J. (1984), *Irish Values and Attitudes*, Dominican Publications, Dublin.

Foster, R. (1988), *Modern Ireland 1660-1972*, Allen Lane, London.

Frank, A. (1978), *Dependent Accumulation and Underdevelopment*, Macmillan, London.

Gallagher, J. (1991), 'High Court will examine £1m loan', *Irish Times*, 12 September, Dublin.

Gilmore, F. (1959), *A Survey of Agricultural Credit in Ireland*, The Stationery Office, Dublin.

Godson, R. (1989a), 'IFA accuses minister over Goodman probe', *Sunday Tribune*, 1 June, Dublin.

Godson, R. (1989b), 'Report may force O'Malley to clip Goodman's wings', *Sunday Tribune*, 17 December, Dublin.

Goldring, M. (1982), *Faith of our Fathers*, Repsol, Dublin.

Goldthorpe, J. (1975), *The Sociology of the Third World: Disparity and Development*, Cambridge University Press, Cambridge.

Gormon, L. and Molloy, E. (1972), *People, Jobs and Organisations*, Irish Management Institute, Dublin.

Granada, (1991), 'Money for nothing', World in Action broadcast, 13 May, Granada TV, Manchester.

Green, E. (1969), 'Industrial Decline in the Nineteenth Century' in Cullen, L. (ed.), *The Formation of the Irish Economy*, Mercier press, Cork.

Halligan, B, (1986) 'Speech to the Irish hotel and catering industry seminar', *Evening Herald*, 15 November, Dublin.

Harrison, D. (1988), *The Sociology of Modernisation and Development*, Unwin Hyman, London.

Holmes, G. (1949), *Report on the Present State and Method for Improvement of Irish Land*, The The Stationery Office, Dublin.

Hoppen, K.T. (1989), *Ireland Since 1800: Conflict & Conformity*, Longman, London and New York.

Howick, P. (1987), 'The black forest economy', *Evening Herald*, 5 January, Dublin.

Humphries, S. (1966), *The New Dubliners*, Routledge, London.

Hutchinson, B. (1970), 'On the study of non-economic factors in Irish economic development', *Economic and Social Review*, vol. 1.

ICTU (1986), *Public Enterprise: Everybody's Business*, Irish Congress of Trade Unions, Dublin.

IDA (1977), *Development Study of the Irish Beef Packing and Processing Industry*, Industrial Development Authority, Dublin.

IDA (1986), *Annual Report*, Industrial Development Authority, Dublin.

IFA, (1990), *Defending the Family Farm in the 1990s*, The Irish Farmers' Association, Dublin.

Inglis, T. (1987), *Moral Monopoly: The Catholic Church in Modern Irish Society*, Gill and Macmillan, Dublin.

Irish Press, (1987), 'Cash owed by farmers won't be collected', *Irish*

Press, 13 May, Dublin.

Irish Press, (1988), 'Crack tax collection team is disbanded', *Irish Press,* 15 January, Dublin.

ITOU, (1987), *The Sick Tax System,* Irish Tax Officials' Union, Dublin.

Jackson, T. (1973), *Ireland Her Own: An outline History of the Irish Struggle,* Lawrence and Wishart, London.

Johansen, H. (1987), *The Danish Economy in the Twentieth Century,* Croom Helm, London.

Jordan, P. (1988), 'Food industry needs action in '88', *Industry and Commerce,* March.

Joyce, J. and Murtagh, J. (1983), *The Boss,* Poolbeg, Dublin.

Keating, P. (1985), *Clerics and Capitalists: A Critique of the Weber Thesis,* Salford Papers in Sociology and Anthropology, 2, University of Salford, Salford.

Keats, J. (1899), *Complete Poetical Works and Letters,* Houghton Mifflin, Cambridge.

Kelly, J. (1987), 'Illicit booze reaps bonanza for customs', *Sunday Press,* 22 November, Dublin.

Kennedy, G. (1992), 'Inquiry into Telecom site purchase a factor in move against Haughey', *The Irish Times,* 1 August, Dublin.

Kennedy, K. Giblin, T. and McHugh, D. (1988), *The Economic Development of Ireland in the Twentieth Century,* Routledge, London.

Kennedy, L. (1978), 'The Roman Catholic Church and economic growth in nineteenth century Ireland', *Economic and Social review,* vol. X.

Kerr, M. (1986), '"Shut up and do it" entrepreneurs told', *Irish Independent,* 17 August, Dublin.

Kiberd, D. (1988), 'Group to fight "Phoenix" traders', *Sunday Tribune,* 11 September, Dublin.

Lattimore, J. (1987), 'Reynolds in new onslaught on "rogue" directors', *Evening Herald,* 5 May, Dublin.

Lattimore, J. (1989), 'Irish small firms lack skills and ambition', *Irish Press,* 6 April, Dublin.

Lecky, W. (1916), *A History of Ireland in the Eighteenth Century,* Longmans Green, London.

Lee, J. (1969),'Capital in the Irish Economy' in Cullen, L. (ed.) *The Formation of the Irish Economy,* Mercier Press, Cork.

Lee, J. (1973), *The Modernisation of Irish Society,* Gill and Macmillan, Dublin.

Lee, J. (1989), *Ireland 1912-1985: Politics and Society,* Cambridge University Press, Cambridge.

Leitch, T. (1987), Statement by Egg Producers Committee quoted in 'Firms demand clampdown on egg smugglers', *Irish Independent,* 27 January, Dublin.

Lyons, F. (1979), *Culture and Anarchy in Ireland,* Oxford University Press, Oxford.

Magee, J. (1988), 'Fraud: why the war is being lost, *Business and Finance,* 11 August, Dublin.

Maguire, C. (1979), *Research and Development in Ireland 1977,* National Board for Science and Technology, Dublin.

Maher, J. (1992), 'Paths in the money trail still to be explored', *Irish*

Times, 1 August.

Mansergh, N. (1965), *The Irish Question: 1849-1921,* Allen and Unwin, London.

Marshall, G. (1982), *In Search of the Spirit of Capitalism: An Essay on Max Weber's Protestant Ethic Thesis,* Hutchinson, London.

Marx, K. (1934), *The Eighteenth Brumaire of Louis Bonaparte,* Co-op Publishing Society (Marxist-Leninist Library), Moscow.

Marx, K. (1963), *Economic and Philosophical Manuscripts,* Lawrence and Wishart, London.

Maxwell, C. (1940), *Country and Town in Ireland Under the Georges,* Harrap, London.

McAlease, J. (1983), 'The black economy: how black is black?', *Business and Finance,* 27 October, Dublin.

McArdle, P. (1987), 'It's all out war say smugglers', *Sunday World,* 26 April, Dublin.

McCarthy, M. (1902), *Priests and People in Ireland,* Hodder and Stoughton, London.

McDonald, F. (1985), *The Destruction of Dublin,* Gill and Macmillan, Dublin.

McDonald, F. (1989), *Saving the City: How to halt the Destruction of Dublin,* Tomar, Dublin.

Mckinsey & Co. (1977), *A Marketing Opportunity for Agricultural Products - Beyond the Farm Gate,* McKinsey & Co, Inc., London.

McLoughlin, B. (1990), 'Tax officials lash 50 year tax check', *Irish Press,* 4 March, Dublin.

Meenan, J. (1970), *The Irish Economy since 1922,* Liverpool University Press, Liverpool.

Millotte, M. (1990a), 'The showdown at the Master Meats corral', *Sunday Tribune,* 15 April, Dublin.

Millotte, M. (1990b), 'Goodman cowed by £550m debts', *Sunday Tribune,* 26 August, Dublin.

Millotte, M. (1990c), 'Beef, banana skins and Baghdad: how Larry slipped up', *Sunday Tribune,* 26 August, Dublin.

Millotte, M. (1990d), 'Link found between Classic Meats and Goodman-owned firm', *Sunday Tribune,* 16 September, Dublin.

Millotte, M. (1990e), 'Stunned Goodman bankers demand details of hidden companies, *Sunday Tribune,* 16 September, Dublin.

Millotte, M. (1990f), 'MacSharry and Braks: both can't be right', *Sunday Tribune,* 30 September, Dublin.

Millotte, M. (1990g), 'Goodman Intnl 'misused' £12m', *Sunday Tribune,* 14 October, Dublin.

Millotte, M. (1990h), ''New row over green belt change', *Sunday Tribune,* 20 May, Dublin.

Millotte, M. (1991), 'Haughey and a Goodman fraud', *Sunday Tribune,* 15 December, Dublin.

Millotte, M. (1992a), 'Fraud let slip by defects in law', *Sunday Tribune,* 26 January, Dublin.

Millotte, M. (1992b), 'Former Goodman employee gives evidence of his own malpractice', *Sunday Tribune,* 2 February, Dublin.

Millotte, M. (1992c), 'Reynolds' failure to heed advice may cost the taxpayer £160m', *Sunday Tribune,* 29 March, Dublin.

Millotte, M. (1992d), 'Tribunal's get-tough option', *Sunday Tribune,* 14 June, Dublin.

Milward, A. and Saul, S. (1973), *The Economic Development of Continental Europe 1780-1870,* Allen and Unwin, London.

Moloney, E. (1988), Public statement by Irish Tax Officials Union quoted in 'Jail urged for tax dodge criminals', *Evening Herald,* 26 March, Dublin.

Morahan, J. (1992), 'Company never knew about policy of confining cover', *Cork Examiner,* 28 May, Cork.

Moran, D. (1905), *The Philosophy of Irish Ireland,* James Duffy and M.H. Gill, Dublin.

Mulligan, G. (1987), 'Many fail in quest for quality', *Irish Independent,* 16 July, Dublin.

Murphy, D. and Fitzgerald, M. (1973), *Research and Development in Ireland 1971,* The Stationery Office, Dublin.

Murphy, D. and O'Brolchain, D. (1971), *Research and Development in Ireland 1969,* The Stationery Office, Dublin.

Murphy, D. and O'Luanaigh, L. (1975), *Research and Development in Ireland 1974,* The Stationery Office, Dublin.

Murphy, J. (1965), 'The support of the Catholic clergy in Ireland, 1750-1850', *Historical Studies,* vol. V.

Nally, D. (1990), 'A Classic Meats case of mystery, mergers and money', *Sunday Tribune,* 15 April, Dublin.

Nally, D. (1992), 'Tax: pint of bitter for pubs', *Sunday Tribune,* 14 June, Dublin.

O'Brien, C.C. (1970), 'Introduction', in O'Brien, C.C. (ed.) *The Shaping of Modern Ireland,* Routledge and Kegan Paul, London.

O'Doherty, K. (1969), 'Where have all the faithful gone?', *The Furrow,* vol. XX.

O'Farrell, P. (1975), *England and Ireland Since 1800,* Oxford University Press, London.

O'Farrell, P. (1986), *Entrepreneurs and Industrial Change,* Irish Management Institute, Dublin.

O'Halloran, M., Kilfeather, F. and Newman, C. (1992), 'Evidence given on exports', *Irish Times,* 8 May, Dublin.

O Keeffe, S. (1990a), 'Further fraud claims against Ballybay', *Sunday Business Post,* 14 January, Dublin.

O'Keeffe, S. (1990b), 'Counting the cost of Ballybay', *Sunday Business Post,* 21 January, Dublin.

O'Loughlin, E. (1990), 'FF accused of ignoring advice from planners', *Sunday Tribune,* 15 April, Dublin.

O'Mahony, B. (1990), 'Goodman crisis may push bank rates up', *Cork Examiner,* 30 August, Cork.

O'Malley, E. (1985), 'The Performance of Irish Indigenous Industry: Lessons for the 1980s', in Fitzpatrick, J. and Kelly, J.(eds), *Perspectives on Irish Industry,* Irish Management Institute, Dublin.

O'Morain, P. (1987), 'Brennan warns firms may be struck off register', *Irish Times,* 6 April, Dublin.

O'Reilly, M. (1865), *Progress of Catholicity in Ireland in the Nineteenth*

Century, Kelly, Dublin.

O'Riordan, M. (1906), *Catholicity and Progress in Ireland,* Kegan Paul, London.

O'Toole, A. (1987), 'Can management be pulled from the rut?', *Business and Finance,* 11 June, Dublin.

O'Toole, A. (1990), 'Ineffectiveness of fraud detection highlighted by Gallagher case', *Sunday Business Post,* 23 September, Dublin.

O'Toole, F. (1992), 'Heated exchange between Hamilton and state marks first birthday', *Irish Times,* 30 May, Dublin.

Oireachtas Eareann (1984), *Second Report of the Joint Committee on Small Businesses,* Government Publication Office, Dublin.

Parsons, T. (1960), *Structure and Process in Modern Societies,* The Free Press, Glencoe.

Plunkett, H. (1904), *Ireland in the New century,* John Murray, London.

Pollard, S. (1992), 'Cultural Influences on Economic Action' in Melling, J. and Barry, J. (eds), *Culture in History,* Exeter University Press, Exeter.

Reynolds, A. (1987), Speech at the presentation of the Irish National Insurance quality awards, *Irish Press,* 4 November, Dublin.

Riegel, R. (1992), 'Greencore in crisis: chronology', *Cork Examiner,* 4 March, Cork.

Robinson, L. (1951), *Ireland's Abbey Theatre,* Sedgwick and Jackson, London.

Roche, M. (1989), *Irish Food and Agribusiness: An AIS Perspective,* Allied Irish Securities, Dublin.

Rostow, W. (1960), *The Stages of Economic Growth: A Non-Communist Manifesto,* Cambridge University Press, London.

Roxborough, I. (1979), *Theories of Underdevelopment,* Macmillan, London.

RTE (1991a), 'Ballybay Meats', Today-Tonight broadcast, 18 April, RTE TV, Dublin.

RTE (1991b), 'Ballybay Meats', Today-Tonight broadcast, 30 April, RTE TV, Dublin.

Rush, F. (1970), *Denmark Farms On,* Danish Agricultural Producers, London.

Ryan, T. (1988a), 'Hormones "rackets by truckers"', *Irish Press,* 29 March, Dublin.

Ryan, T. (1988b), 'French pan Irish lamb quality', *Irish Press,* 19 July, Dublin.

Schumpeter, J. (1934), *The Theory of Economic Development,* Harvard University Press, Cambridge, Mass.

Seekamp, G. (1992), 'MP calls on government to 'come clean' on bank collapse', *Sunday Business Post,* 30 August, Dublin.

Sheehy, M. (1968), *Is Ireland Dying?* Hollis and Carter, London.

Sheehy, S. (1978), *Address to the Commerce and Economics Society,* Commerce and Economics Society, University College Cork, Cork.

Spain, K. (1987), 'Smuggling of grain causes major problem', *Irish Press,* 24 February, Dublin.

Stanley, J. (1990), 'Bankers considering legal action over Goodman examiner', *Irish Times,* 14 September, Dublin.

Sunday Business Post, (1992), 'MacSharry makes sense', *Sunday Business Post,* 30 August, Dublin.

Sunday Tribune, (1992), 'Creating Jobs at £750,000 a head', *Sunday Tribune,* 29 March, Dublin.

Titley, E.B. (1983), *Church, State and the Controlling of Schooling in Ireland 1900-1944,* Gill and Macmillan, Dublin.

Wall, M. (1958), 'The rise of the Catholic middle class in eighteenth century Ireland', *Irish Historical Studies,* vol. XI.

Wall, M. (1969), 'Catholics in economic life' in Cullen, L. (ed.), *The Formation of the Irish Economy,* Mercier Press, Cork.

Wallerstein, I. (1979), *The Capitalist World Economy,* Cambridge University Press, Cambridge.

Weber, M. (1930a), 'Introduction to the Collected Writings on the Sociology of religion' in *The Protestant Ethic and the Spirit of Capitalism,* Allen and Unwin, London.

Weber, M. (1930b), *The Protestant Ethic and the Spirit of Capitalism,* Allen and Unwin, London.

Weber, M. (1950), *General Economic History,* The Free Press, Glencoe.

Worsley, P. (1984), *The Three Worlds: Culture and World Development,* Weidenfield and Nicholson, London.

Whyte, J. (1984), *Church and State in Modern Ireland 1923-1979,* Gill and Macmillan, Dublin.

Yeats, W.B. (1970a), *Reveries over Childhood and Youth,* Macmillan, London.

Yeats, W.B. (1970b), *Mythologies,* Macmillan, London.